The Essential Guide to Business for Artists and Designers

The Essential Guide to Business for Artists and Designers

An enterprise manual for visual artists and creative professionals

Alison Branagan

A & C Black • London

First published in Great Britain in 2011
A & C Black Publishers Limited
36 Soho Square
London W1D 3QY
www.acblack.com

ISBN 978-14081-19037

A CIP catalogue record for this book is available
from the British Library

Details for the tax rates and allowances included
in this publication are subject to change. Neither
the author nor the publishers can take any
responsibility for alterations to tax rates, or for
contact details for the various businesses and
organisations contained herein; all details were
correct at the time of going to press. If alterations
or corrections are found to be necessary, please
contact the publishers who will endeavor to
correct any errors or omissions on reprinting.

Design: Susan McIntyre
Cover design: Sutchinda Thompson
Commissioning editor: Linda Lambert

Illustrations © Tim Bradford 2011
www.timbradford.com

With special thanks to photographer Karl Grupe
© 2009 www.karlgrupe.com

Typeset in 9.5 on 14pt FS Me Regular
Printed and bound by Star Standard Pte Ltd,
Singapore

This book is produced using paper that is made
from wood grown in managed, sustainable forests.
It is natural, renewable and recyclable. The logging
and manufacturing processes conform to the
environmental regulations of the country of origin.

Contents

Foreword

In 1966 I started at at the Royal College of Art, London. At that point my ambition was to become an artist. By my second year of study I had gravitated towards industrial design, and by the third I was developing a landing craft for Rotork, an engineering company.

Since then I've worked as engineer, making things that solve problems. Although I'm not a businessman, I've had to learn the skills to run a company by necessity.

Today I have an expert team to look after the business, so I can get on with the engineering. But when I first started out with the Ballbarrow, and then the vacuum cleaner, I didn't have the luxury of such support. I learned by doing, whether that was developing an idea through an iterative process, tying my hand at sales, or working out how to fund the manufacture of my machines.

I made mistakes – many of them. Some were necessary: my approach to invention for example, where every failure teaches you something about your idea. Others were calculated risks that didn't pay off (sometimes for the best); some were born of inexperience, like losing the patent rights to the Ballbarrow, my own invention.

Despite the years of uncertainty and financial worries, going it alone was the right thing to do. I'd encourage anyone with a good idea to do the same. It will be hard, but just knowing where to start helps: whether it's securing a loan, promoting a show, or filing a patent. This book cuts through the clatter and jargon of business, giving clear, simple advice about how to succeed.

Sir James Dyson

Acknowledgements

Firstly I wish to acknowledge the pioneering work of David Butler and the Artists Information Company in raising awareness of business skills within the visual arts sector.

I would like to thank my commissioning editor Linda Lambert for commissioning this book and also to give credit to the photographer Karl Grupe for his huge contribution to this project. Special thanks go to consultants Jenny Bloy, Alison Britton, Trevor Burgess, Karl Grupe, John Foster, Alana Pryce, Inspired Software UK Ltd, Tony Laws, MediVisas UK LLP, Harley Miller, Davida Saunders, Dean Shepherd from Tax by Design Ltd, Silverman Sherliker LLP, David Stubbs, Peter Town and Virtuallee Ltd.

Further, most valued contributions came from Caterina Izzo, June Chanpoomidole, Edd China of Cummfy Banana Ltd, and Richard Whitehead.

Further acknowledgement must go to Kensington and Chelsea College, City University, Central Saint Martins College of Art and Design and the Association of Illustrators, for giving me the opportunity to teach creative business and enterprise courses.

Finally, I am indebted to John Naylor for his advice and consistent support.

Introduction

'After Beyond the Fringe had been on Broadway my father asked
if I knew what I really wanted to do...In a sense I still don't.'
Dr Jonathan Miller (1934–), artist, writer and director

The Essential Guide to Business for Artists and Designers aims to
help any artist or designer set themselves up in business, either
as self-employed, as a partnership or a company. This guide
covers a number of important topics, essential knowledge areas
and enterprise skills. Certain chapters concerning tax and legal
matters are written specifically for UK readers. However, creatives
based around the globe will find this guide extremely useful. This
is especially true for those who wish to visit, trade with, showcase
or set up a business in the UK.

Earning a living from art and design activities can be an
uncertain prospect. The commissioning of this book is a response
to the many difficulties recent arts graduates and those who
graduated several years ago may encounter. I hope that the
readers who have recently started a business, or have been trading
for a number of years, will find the practical advice outlined in this
book helpful.

It's worth bearing in mind this is only a business start-up book.
To gain more in-depth knowledge about a particular industry
sector, readers should explore the recommended texts and links.

Business beginnings

If you are currently a student, you may not be aware that art
and design graduates are three to four times more likely to set
up in business or register as self-employed than anyone else. It's
possible that you haven't received much guidance about how

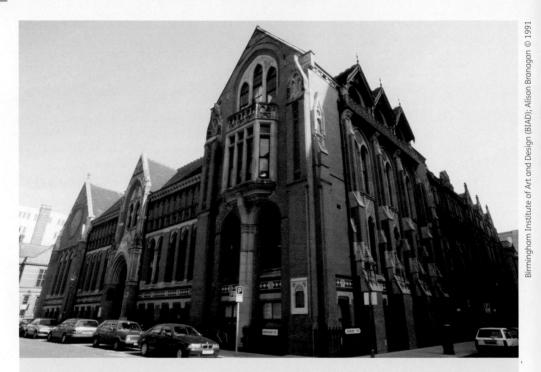

Institutions of the imagination.
At art school we all dream of success, but how do we make it
a reality?

to earn a living after graduation. I know from my own painful experience of being a naïve novice starting out in the marketplace that without good advice artists and designers can struggle to generate sufficient income, and can be easily ripped off by unscrupulous opportunists.

The intention of this book is to help you make informed decisions about your business, avoid elementary mistakes, and earn a decent living from your creativity.

Useful information for the reader

This book is designed for a broad readership. Therefore, please spend a few moments reading explanations of key phrases and terms.

Key phrases

The most common phrase in this book is '**artists and designers**'. This is a general description referring to any artist, designer, designer-maker, architect, inventor, illustrator, animator, image-maker, film-maker or photographer.

When my comments apply specifically to a particular discipline, I'll use, for example, 'sculptor', 'furniture designer' or 'documentary photographer'.

For the contemporary crafts sector – which includes jewellery, silversmithing, metalwork, letter cutting, glass, ceramics, textiles, furniture, woodwork, automata, toys and musical instruments – I use the appellations '**applied arts**' and '**designer-makers**'.

Most designer-makers will generally fall within the general category of 'designer'. It's worth bearing in mind that the term is broad enough to include, among others, interior designers, industrial and product designers, fashion illustrators and architects.

Business terms

I refer to '**arts or artists**' as opposed to '**commercial arts/artists or creatives**', the reason being that certain sectors of the visual arts are less commercially oriented then others. There are some creatives, such as fine artists, who are more focused upon their own personal practice and are thereby disconnected to some extent from the marketplace. They may supplement their profits from commissions and sales to collectors with additional income from part-time employment. I use the term '**arts practitioner**' to refer to such visual and applied artists who prefer not to use the term 'business' when describing their activities.

Alternatively, when I employ the phrase '**creative businesses**' I mean artists or designers who are more comfortable with the idea that they are running a business, whether as self-employed/freelance (a sole-trader), together with others (in a partnership), or as a director of their own company (private limited company). Commercial creatives, such as illustrators and graphic designers, usually work to a brief. They may embark on their own occasional 'authorial projects', but mainly generate income from meeting the demands of clients.

It's worth noting that, although you might think of yourself as a non-commercial arts practitioner, if you occasionally sell work or undertake other freelance work such as facilitating children's art workshops then you should have some formal 'trading status' such as being registered as self-employed with HM Revenue and Customs (HMRC; formerly known as the Inland Revenue).

Creative products and services

Due to the vast creative output of the different sectors, I refer to physical artwork or objects (e.g. paintings, furniture, prototypes, textiles, photographs) mainly as the '**product**'. Although this strips the work of its philosophical, academic, innovative or even emotional associations, for which I apologise in advance, it was a necessary step to avoid the text becoming too cumbersome to read. Equally, in describing different practical skills such as mould-making, animation for leisure software or teaching private art classes, I use the term '**service**'. So please apply your own definitions to the phrase '**creative products and services**'.

I hope that the reader will be able to find their own method in using this book, while accepting that it's attempting to embrace a broad spectrum of creative people and practices.

As certain words may warrant further explanation there is a selective **glossary** of business, financial and legal jargon. Readers will also find a list of useful British, American, Canadian and Australian organisations located towards the end of this book. 'Resources', such as important websites and recommended reading, are listed at the end of each chapter.

Featured UK artists and designers

This book includes seven featured artists and designers representing different disciplines. Making the choice of who to include was extremely difficult. A mere seven visual artists cannot possibly represent all the diverse interests of the visual arts. However, I hope the profiles provide some typical examples of how many creative practitioners earn their living. The featured creatives represent a cross section of commercial, traditional, contemporary, market-led, experimental, innovative and poetical enterprises.

In all but one case, each of the contributors has run their business for ten years or more, the one exception being the view from a recent start-up. Many of them have studied at regional art and design colleges. One previously completed his art studies in his country of origin. Others have not even undertaken art degrees, yet they are highly successful in their fields. This demonstrates that attending a British, European, American, Canadian or Australian art college, though helpful, is not a prerequisite to success in particular areas of trade. It's possible to prosper in certain sectors of the visual arts with no academic qualifications at all.

In summary

Every reader's business will be unique. Earning a living from any enterprise requires a great deal of effort and understanding of how your particular industry works. This guide is only an overview of how to start a creative business. Although there are diagnostic tools and mind maps, it's still necessary for readers to attend talks and courses, and to seek further advice concerning their own venture.

1

Making Creativity Pay

'Irrespective of talent, chances among those who choose to become artists are unequally distributed. The myth that talent is all that counts prevents the gathering of accurate information about what is required in this profession in order to stand a chance.'

Hans Abbing (1944–), artist and economist

There has been much analysis in the last ten years of the relationship between creativity and economics, together with studies exploring fees, pricing and market demand for products and services across all spectrums of the visual arts. Research includes surveys of daily rates charged by freelance commercial artists and designers, as well as comparative studies of salaries. If you are interested in reading these reports, please see some of the key papers listed at the end of this chapter.

We'll look further into the detail of professional fees in Chapter 4, Money Management. However, before rushing ahead, let's analyse some of the current difficulties that many arts practitioners or creative businesses face.

Why can creatives become poor?

'I have no money at all: I live, or am supposed to live, on a few francs a day...Like dear St Francis of Assisi I am wedded to Poverty: but in my case the marriage is not a success.'

Oscar Wilde (1854–1900), playwright and wit, letter, 1899

Firstly, there are particular sectors of the arts that have a greater commercial advantage than other others. These include publishing, television, music, commercial photography, and illustration, all of which have traditionally been far better rights-managed than the fine and applied-arts sectors.

By 'rights-managed' I mean stipulated payments in the shape of licensing copyright and the payment of royalties to authors and creators. These are fully established within those industries.

By contrast, the majority of fine artists, sculptors and other designer-makers are more reliant on selling 'objects' or working for a 'daily rate' than being able to generate wealth by licensing reproduction of artwork or products through printing, replication or manufacture.

Secondly, in the commercial domain there are many well-paid jobs or freelance opportunities for animators and architects, as well as graphic and product designers. Yet it's extremely rare to find any full-time vacancies for illustrators, film-makers, photographers, and fine or applied artists. Rates of pay for employed and freelance work within the arts and public sectors are poor in comparison with the commercial sector.

I recall an established figure in the arts declaring that low pay within the arts was not a problem, and there were other rewards to be had in working for arts organisations. It's easy to make such a comment, but the truth is that long-term experience of being overworked and underpaid creates a poverty trap. Being poor isn't some romantic idyll. It's stressful, and means living in substandard housing, relying on public transport, counting every penny, and having no safety net if things should go wrong.

Poverty is a real issue amongst arts practitioners who fail to realise that we live in an economy based upon market demand. Visual artists must continually generate earnings so that a decent level of income can be achieved; there is only a small, if significant, minority of creatives who have the benefit of wealth inherited through family, spouse or a previous career.

Making creativity pay

Whilst there are those who derive a financially viable and sustainable income from their creativity, there are also many talented and hardworking artists and designers who live well below the poverty line. There's a combination of reasons for this, among which are: a lack of business awareness, money-management problems and insufficient demand for their products or services.

The crux of the problem with many arts practitioners lies in an idealised notion of what being a professional artist or designer is. They can often fail simply from not being given specific financial and legal advice at key stages in their early careers.

My own experience in my mid-twenties affected me financially as I didn't understand how to agree royalty payments or negotiate commercial contracts. In another instance I spent months on an illustration, only to have it rejected on delivery. Had I known of the Association of Illustrators (AOI) terms and conditions, the client would still have been legally obliged to pay me 50% of the fee.

Artists and commercial creatives who haven't learned how to approach and work with clients, or don't understand about contract law or what to charge, can be repeatedly taken advantage of, and will not be properly paid for years.

Another factor that can damage a creative businesses is being uninformed about risk. A client of mine failed to secure proper 'goods in transit' insurance for a large object. The van crashed, leaving him liable for £20,000. It took him five years to pay off a bank loan on top of his other business overheads for this costly mistake.

Important opportunities do not turn up every day. It's vital to execute large commissions properly, minimising your personal liability while maximising income. More examples of other types of errors that can easily be avoided are mentioned in further chapters.

What history tells us

Since the 19th century there have been dramatic changes in attitudes to the arts. One effect is the division of the arts into separate disciplines, which caused a shift from cultivating 'artisanship' to focusing more on distinct forms of practice. Art-school education has changed dramatically from the late 19th century to the present day.

There has been a deliberate move away from the idea of 'art and crafts' as being 'trades' represented by guilds, towards them becoming 'professions' represented by professional bodies. Yet the arts and commercial arts today are closer to the 19th-century idea of trades, nearer to the original 'artisan' approach, than is generally acknowledged.

Hans Abbing, in his groundbreaking book *Why Are Artists Poor? The Exceptional Economy of the Arts*, delved deep into the history of the 'arts and crafts' movement. He takes the reader on a journey through various arguments concerning artists in the present day and the complex environment in which they have to operate.

Artists' London: Holbein to Hirst, by Kit Wedd, Lucy Peltz and Cathy Ross, provides us with a rare insight into how artists in different eras ran their businesses, travelling back even further to mid-16th-century London. Portrait painting in the 18th century is described as a collaborative affair, which included the commissioned artist and a cast of assistants, with walk-on roles from artisans painting background scenery, drapery, lace and hands (always a problem) and the participation of other extras in the form of models, framers and gilders. The artisan knew that if he was to turn a profit, he had to subcontract work to other tradesmen and not try to do everything himself.

Today's issues

The vast majority of art-history books give us a narrow view of economic situations, preferring to focus on the art rather than on how the artist earned a living. But it's impossible to live on fresh air. There has to be money coming from somewhere for you to have a reasonable standard of living. You may be fortunate and have an income or allowance coming in, but if not you need to figure out how you can make enough to sustain yourself.

Let's take a quick snapshot of the financial situation of artists and designers both past and present:

- Dutch post-impressionist painter Vincent Van Gogh lived upon an allowance from his younger brother Theo, who incidentally was an art dealer, yet could not sell his older brother's work!
- Filippo Tommaso Marinetti, the famous Italian futurist, inherited a vast fortune from his father, which enabled him to pursue a bohemian adventure as a poet and agent provocateur.
- Barbara Hepworth, the British abstract sculptor, was an extremely talented student and won a number of scholarships and awards which helped her to study, work and travel abroad.

- Yves Klein, the French conceptual artist, taught karate as his main source of income virtually right up to his death.
- Joseph Beuys, the German conceptual artist, was originally an air pilot in the Second World War and later supported himself by becoming a lecturer.
- René Magritte, the Belgian surrealist painter, designed wallpaper before his paintings began to sell.
- Vivienne Westwood, the British fashion designer, spent many years working as a primary school teacher before setting up in business with the late Malcolm McLaren.
- James Rosenquist, the American pop artist, worked as a commercial artist painting billboards before achieving gallery sales.
- Beryl Cook, the British 'populist' painter, ran a pub and a theatrical boarding house before gaining gallery representation later in life.
- Wayne Hemingway, the British designer, spent several years selling second-hand clothes on a stall in Camden Market in London before having enough money to set up his first boutique.
- Jeff Koons, the American conceptual artist, worked and earned a great deal of money as a commodities trader in Wall Street before pursuing his venture as a controversial artist.
- Tracey Emin, the British biographical artist, worked (rather less glamorously) as a youth tutor for Southwark Council before courting the attention of the art world.

Where's the money?

There are many different types of creative businesses. Some will sell their creative products online, through chain stores or design boutiques. Others make a very good living from taking on contract work from other businesses, such as advertising agencies, fashion houses or corporate firms. Many arts practitioners earn money by selling artworks at exhibitions and pitching for public and private commissions. A large proportion of artists find they can generate regular income from running workshops and demonstrating art materials at Expos while retaining a part-time job.

Innovation *vs* market demand

Art education develops creativity, problem-solving skills and the ability to conceptualise. It gives students the freedom to experiment and learn new skills. By contrast the marketplace, for a number of commercial artists, art practitioners and designers, can be more like a straitjacket. For instance, if you secure a dealer or an agent, they will expect your style and subject matter to be consistent for many years, as it takes time to build a market for your work. I've met several fine artists who've had to cease painting for a year or so in order to break free of contracts with dealers. Designer-makers and craftspeople can also be easily overwhelmed by the amount of repetitive tasks required to continually supply stockists.

Such a situation can be easily avoided if you are prepared for the cold realities of business.

If you wish to manufacture and sell your own products and services, then you'll have to undergo a change of mindset and embrace learning more about how your industry works. For the majority of artists and designers who wish to practise or trade there are few options. It's highly unlikely that some mystical person will suddenly knock on your door and offer to organise your life and provide introductions to hordes of eager clients.

Debunking the discovery myth

> 'Business Art is the step that comes after Art.'
> *Andy Warhol (Andrew Warhola; 1928–1987), artist*

Unfortunately, there's still a prevailing myth among arts graduates that, during degree shows, fairs and exhibitions, employers, buyers or agents will magically appear in a puff of sparkly stardust and sign them up. Students can thus be disappointed with their experience of degree shows and industry showcasing events.

It's vital to prepare for major showcasing opportunities by inviting buyers and attracting press attention. Before exhibiting professionally, make sure designs or patents have been filed with the Intellectual Property Office (IPO), and have good-quality marketing materials prepared.

I would encourage any student to consider it a lottery win if they are talent-spotted at an event. Certainly, if you studied at one of the London art colleges it's more likely that buyers, collectors, critics, stylists, agents and dealers will have been invited by the institution from their event mailing list. These longstanding relationships with key players and contacts in the art world and design sector will improve the likelihood of students making sales, gaining commissions or even being offered a show or representation.

As you will see later in Chapter 6, in the Building Networks mind map, there are obvious and sometimes invisible forces at work regarding certain individuals' journeys to recognition. There are many routes to financial success in this life, but making it to the top in any industry is dependent on a mixture of factors, including the essential ingredient of good luck!

Don't forget your major cities

If you've attended a regional art and design college it could be in your best interests to persuade fellow students or the head of department to showcase degree-show work in London. If not, it could be advantageous to come to London either for further study on a diploma or MA course, or at least for regular visits. No capital city or major art centre can be ignored in any artist's or designer's life plan, as this is where the majority of agents, dealers, critics, stylists, galleries, fashion houses, boutiques, publishers, advertising agencies, art schools, arts and design bodies and public museums are based.

It's worth considering that the richest portion of the UK population, who have the funds to commission and collect artefacts from artists and designers, have homes in London, or to the immediate west and south of the capital.

The importance of planning and preparation

If you are currently studying at college either in your second or third year, it's advisable to plan your own marketing campaign. If you are in the third year, start a promotional campaign, if possible, in the November before your summer degree show. It's best to start at least eight months before any kind of showcasing event, whether a degree show or other exhibition in a gallery or design fair.

The earlier you start contacting the media, clients or potential employers the better. It's still possible to do a reasonable amount of promotion two to three months before a show, but it's unlikely

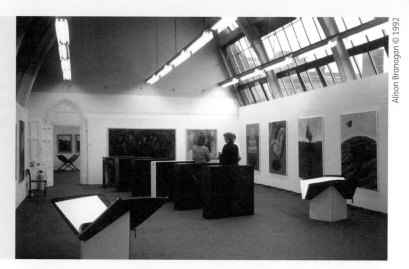

Alison Branagan © 1992

A degree show

you will gain any magazine features in the large-circulation style monthlies or design periodicals within such a short timeframe. For example a June issue is most likely being printed in the first week of April or even earlier.

Invite industry contacts

A mini-marketing plan and tips appear in Chapter 7, Self-promotion. Please don't just rely on others to do the marketing for you. No one but yourself will have your best interests in mind.

It's likely they may already be going. If not, they may still be delighted to see your show. Always be prepared to arrange to meet potential employers, agents, buyers or clients at other times than during the event. Remember that key players in the visual arts are inundated by these types of requests, especially coming up to major fairs and degree shows.

Try not to be too disappointed if particular contacts don't show on the night. Always ring up the next day and see if they'd still like to visit the show later in the week. If they're still too busy, perhaps ask if you can visit them after the show has ended. This will give you an opportunity to present your portfolio or sample products and cultivate sales or commissions. Even in this email age, there is nothing like making a bit of effort and going to talk to people. Degree shows, gallery exhibitions and design fairs are crucial showcasing events. Make the most of them.

Developing an entrepreneurial outlook

'Live out your imagination not your history.'
Stephen Covey (1932–), business guru

If you're fortunate enough to find an enjoyable well-paid job, then stick with it. It's possible, especially in the design field, to have a fulfilling and eventful career, with progression from junior to senior positions.

However, many artists and commercial creatives are unable to obtain the luxury of a tailor-made professional career within one company or institution. As mentioned earlier, many sectors within the creative industries do not provide opportunities for full-time employment. Nevertheless, you should expect, with a little perseverance, to find creative part-time employment relevant to your discipline. A part-time job is essential, as it acts as a regular income stream to fall back on if earnings from the early days of self-employment are unreliable.

If you wish to develop your own creative products and services, or pursue an artistic practice, then the world of full-time employment won't be for you, though bear in mind that having some previous industry experience can be usefully applied to your own business.

The differences between 'market-led' and 'innovative' enterprises

Most businesses in the world are market-led; they supply a demand. On the other hand, most emerging artists and designers are more innovative in their ambitions. So in order to make money they have to adopt an entrepreneurial outlook.

The word 'entrepreneur' derives from the French word *entreprendre*, meaning to set about something. Modern dictionaries define the word in two ways – firstly as a person whose venture carries some degree of risk, and secondly as a 'go-between or intermediary', such as an agent or dealer who acts as a link between the artist and the marketplace.

All creative people are really entrepreneurs. They develop new ideas, artwork, products or services and then try to cultivate interest or develop a market.

The importance of research

A common mistake of many artists and designers is the failure to undertake sufficient market research. The most successful entrepreneurs in business undertake research and don't simply rely on gut instinct.

I've met postgraduate students, often on MA courses, who have spent long periods developing a product without checking the patent or registered design lists published on the Intellectual Property Office's website (www.ipo.gov.uk). I remember in particular one student, who had spent a year developing a product. In a chance conversation I asked him if he had done basic checks before proceeding. He had not. On checking the patent register, he discovered that a UK company had filed the invention several years earlier. They had trademarked the product and it was on sale.

This demonstrates how a lack of research can mean a great deal of time, energy and money is wasted simply through not undertaking simple checks.

Cultivating entrepreneurial skills

An entrepreneurial model of enterprise is the hardest type of business to get off the ground. The reason is that entrepreneurs require not only hard cash for investment in the business but also buyers. Dogged persistence in pursuit of goals is nothing new to the artist or designer. Artists, like entrepreneurs, are willing to sacrifice creature comforts, their time, social life and sleep in order to bring ideas to a market which often is not ready to accept or buy in to the creative vision. (Does any of this sound familiar?)

To be entrepreneurial, you don't just need generic business skills and a detailed understanding of legal matters but a whole gamut of qualities, attributes, behaviours and skills. In the visual arts, you have to go out and find or make your own opportunities. This is why developing contacts and having the confidence to approach agents or pitch proposals to buyers are essential skills.

Other entrepreneurial qualities

Another facet of developing an entrepreneurial outlook is flexibility and responsiveness to change. While UK art schools foster creativity, it's often with a 'mono focus'. By this I mean that many arts graduates find it difficult to explore other possibilities outside their discipline. In other countries, the visual-arts culture is much broader than our own, with artists and designers working across several disciplines, comfortably mixing private with public, and commercial with non-commercial projects.

It is my belief that if you are a creative person then in order to thrive and prosper it is essential to acquire the ability to change direction. There could be many reasons why you should change discipline and find a different route. For instance, it could be that the market for your business is too small, that there's insufficient demand, that you can't earn decent fees or that technological advancement is making your skills obsolete.

Be free of restriction

Entrepreneurs are great believers in trusting their instincts, so if you feel drawn in another direction, then explore it. Remember that Francis Bacon, the British painter, originally trained in furniture design. The British designer–maker Andrew Logan spent many years studying architecture, before realising that the profession was not for him. The American film-maker and writer Rebecca Miller had earlier trained as a painter. Various British musicians and singer-songwriters studied first at art school, including, Freddie Mercury, Ian Dury, David Bowie, Jarvis Cocker and M.I.A. (Mathangi 'Maya' Arulpragasam).

So be bold. If you feel it's right, just throw those paintbrushes away! If unhappy with the discipline you have trained in, don't be frightened or worried about what others may think if you want to change. You haven't failed or given up. All you are doing is just undertaking something new.

Therefore let go of any idealised vision of working in a garret, living on Smarties and mugs of herbal tea. Forget the notion of being discovered. But most importantly of all, if you desire to earn your living outside the confines of secure employment, then acquiring practical enterprise skills is the only realistic alternative.

The Photographer

Karl Grupe

Karl Grupe is a Canadian-born photographer and a lecturer at Central Saint Martins College of Art and Design.

Though he originally studied architecture at the University of Manitoba, he has established himself in the photography industry. He and his partner Julia Massey-Stewart have a studio, The Mango Lab, in London, where they host exhibitions, run workshops and a mentoring programme.

His own stock photography is represented by the Getty Images library, which has been licensed for a range of purposes from book covers to billboards. His client list includes *The Times*, AXA Insurance, Microsoft, *Town and Country* and *Table Magazine*. After nine years living in London he's moved to the Chilterns, where he feeds the cows, drives a Harley Davidson and trains for triathlons.

Karl's portfolio and blog can be viewed at www.karlgrupe.com/blog

To view forthcoming events at his studio visit www.themangolab.co.uk

His five essential tips are:

1. Me Inc.! (aka Ltd)

The great part of working for yourself is the feeling that it's about you, though it takes courage to put yourself out in the open and search for opportunities. Find people who will be supportive and champion your ambition.

2. Find ways to discipline yourself

Creatives that succeed more quickly than others maintain a disciplined approach. Find ways to calculate how much time is spent on your business per week. Examine

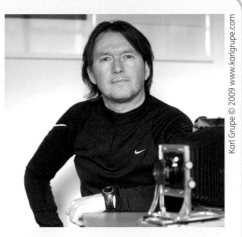

Karl Grupe © 2009 www.karlgrupe.com

which activities actually lead to making money, either directly or indirectly.

3. Get 'it' out there

Interesting ideas sitting on a hard drive or stuffed in filing cabinets have no potential to grow. It is like keeping a dormant seed in its packet. Getting 'it' out there will increase the likelihood of growth and attract new opportunities.

4. Shake life up and be flexible

I began with dreams of being a world-renowned photographer. As the journey progressed the realisation struck that I would be lucky even to make a living in the industry. Leaving your home or native country isn't easy. However, to make progress, be prepared to take a few risks.

5. Futureshop

It's important to review business and personal goals regularly, to check you're travelling in the right direction. Take stock and think about what's to be done next. Play – push the boat out a bit and see what happens. Always recognise the positive, though also be prepared to pull the plug on a venture when it feels like a dead end.

RESOURCES

Research and Downloads

Artists' Fees and Payments (series): *Good practice in paying artists* (2002); *Establishing a charge rate for a working artist* (2006); *Good exhibition practice* (2005). All published by The Artists Information Company. Also see *a-n Magazine*, www.a-n.co.uk/research (subscription service/ many useful articles available without needing to subscribe)

Artquest, money section, www.artquest.org.uk

Do It Yourself: Cultural and creative self-employment for hard times, edited by Martin Bright and Barbara Gunnell (July 2009). www.artscouncil.org.uk

Taste Buds: How to cultivate the art market, by Morris Hargreaves McIntyre (October 2004). www.artscouncil.org.uk

Market Matters: The dynamics of the contemporary art market, by Louisa Buck (October 2004). www.artscouncil.org.uk

Illustration Fees and Standards of Pricing 2007 (AOI Report), www.theaoi.com

Freelance Fees Guide, www.londonfreelance.org (part of the NUJ website)

MAD Freelance and Interim Salary & Benefit Survey July 2007, www.mad.co.uk (subscription service)

Creative Review magazine, www.creativereview.co.uk

Design Week Salary Survey March 2008, 2009 & 2010, plus other articles in Design Week, www.designweek.co.uk

The Craft Blueprint: A workforce development plan for craft in the UK (June 2009); *The Visual Arts Blueprint: Towards a better-valued sector* (November 2009). www.ccskills.org.uk

Making it in the 21st Century (2003), www.craftscouncil.org.uk

Books

Artists' London: Holbein to Hirst, Kit Wedd, Lucy Peltz, & Cathy Ross (London: Merrell Publishers)

Why are Artists Poor? The Exceptional Economy of the Arts, Hans Abbing (Amsterdam University Press)

Children's Writers' and Artists' Yearbook, Francesca Simon (London: A & C Black)

Writers' and Artists' Yearbook, Jo Herbert (London: A & C Black)

The Artists' Yearbook, Ossian Ward (London: Thames and Hudson)

2

How to Make a Living

> 'To become skilled requires, personally, that one be obedient.'
> *Richard Sennett (1943–), author and professor of sociology*

Art schools encourage students to focus on developing a practice, a recognisable style, and an interest in particular themes or subject matter. Conceptual thinking is nurtured across many disciplines. Once the brain has been stimulated in this manner, it can become more difficult to concentrate on one activity at a time.

No artist or designer has ever managed to execute all their ideas during their lifetimes. To attempt numerous projects at any one time can result in frustration and slow progress. Success can only be achieved by being selective and gaining a clear focus.

This chapter is about helping you to achieve focus and become more aware about how to make a living.

Gaining focus

> 'My success, if any, has come incrementally. It's not an overnight thing. I'm very glad of that because it's all very digestible. You have the confidence to say I want to work at my own pace, pick and choose the things I want to do, and screen the things coming in which could be a diversion.'
> *Cornelia Parker (1956–), artist*

Many artists and designers have other factors that affect their perception of time in relation to money, such as emotional involvement with the work or the equally mixed blessing of obsessive perfectionism. It's best to learn, sooner rather than later, that these qualities have to be reined in when running a creative business.

Learning to make professional judgements

As mentioned in the previous chapter, the 18th- and 19th-century artisan understood the relation between learning a skill and its practical application in terms of earning a living.

From my early interviews with artists and commercial creatives who were making large sums of money from their businesses, I observed how they had developed a professional detachment from commissions and projects and simply viewed them as jobs, to be managed efficiently, priced accurately, and done well.

Developing focus

Some artists and designers have huge ambitions, which demand exceptional focus and energy. To achieve progress it is best to concentrate on only one or two activities at a time.

If you tend to take too much on, here are some suggestions for reining yourself in:

- Take on a part-time job, and on free days prepare work for a show and organise a small marketing campaign.
- Secure a paid contract to run regular art or craft workshops, while undertaking commissions.
- Rent a market stall two days a week, and spend the rest of the week making stock and supplying products to other retail outlets.
- Set up a full-time business, manufacturing and establishing a market for a small range of two to three products.

Nothing is worth bankruptcy

The artist Delacroix once said that artists who seek for perfection in everything achieve it in nothing. Perfectionism can contribute to a permanent state of financial embarrassment. Creatives commonly stay up all night working on portfolio images or other projects in search of perfection. Attention to detail and aspiring to do the best you can are necessary, but must be balanced within the scope and resources of the project. Otherwise you can end up working for less than nothing. This preoccupation with detail has much to do with the perception of the maker.

It pays to be selective

There will always be opportunities and shows in which you can participate. Art and design magazines and news loops list numerous unpaid exhibitions, some of which may not generate any sales or press attention at all. These types of opportunities can simply sap your time and resources and may not be worth the effort involved. So it pays to be selective.

Before investing any time and money in any group show, decide whether it's worth the risk. I would suggest checking back catalogues and contacting previous exhibitors. Phone them up and ask them if they made any money or gained any orders from the event in previous years before committing yourself.

In your early years after leaving college, it's wise to gain some experience of showcasing and other arts-related opportunities, such as working as an artist's assistant or in the community. If a project is unpaid, then unless it will be good for your CV, helps you to acquire new skills, or brings you into contact with your favourite artist or designer, then it could simply be an unnecessary distraction.

Avoid working on art projects for free (if you can)

If offered 'no fee' project work, there is an excellent response you can fall back on which may help to improve the offer. It goes something along the lines of, 'Yes I am very interested in the project. However, I'm unable to take part without some form of remuneration (or assistance with expenses). So please do come back to me if you manage to get a bit more funding.'

You may find some time later that if the interested parties really do desire your involvement then they will offer to pay a fee, or at least provide you with basic costs. If they don't, then it's likely they will simply contact another applicant. Most arts or design organisations will take anyone on if they offer their time for free. If there's nothing in the opportunity which is of significant value to your career, such as raising your profile, gaining vital contacts or simply a reference for a future job, then don't do it.

However, it has to be said that many visual-arts graduates spend years working hard for free. There is a volunteer culture within the arts, due to an oversupply of graduates keen to gain experience.

Difficult choices

It's therefore essential to gather your thoughts and prioritise activities. This can be difficult when it means you can't do everything you wish to do. Many artists and designers find this extremely painful, which is why they often continue to make slow progress as they spread themselves too thinly. Another problem is the failure to devote a realistic amount of time to activities or projects.

Learning how to focus requires obedience and self-discipline. It helps if your environment is ordered and tidy. Confusion in your home or personal life can affect your ability to formulate decisions. There will always be distractions that might knock you off course, but try not to be distracted by small irritations and concentrate on making the most of valuable opportunities.

Self-employment and paid employment

'To be a teacher is my greatest work of art.'

Joseph Beuys (1921–1986), conceptual artist

It's possible to be employed and self-employed at the same time. However, if you are an employee of a large firm and have specialist skills – say, in software design – it's worth checking your employment contract. Most firms, especially those working in areas of design such as those specialising in architecture, for instance, do not approve of employees running any kind of business outside their employment, especially if it's similar in nature to, and therefore in direct competition with, the job you do for them.

In the vast majority of cases, it's quite acceptable to have a part- or full-time job and run your own business on days when you're not working for your employer. In a sector where there is a plethora of well-paid work opportunities, more options will then be open to you. You could either work full-time and build a professional career within the industry, or set up in business.

If you are one of the many who finds difficulty in securing well-paid part- or full-time employment, then you'll have to set up a business, either 'freelancing' (taking on contract work) or a 'business' (selling products and services), either on a part- or full-time basis.

Pay gaps

In addition to the well-publicised pay gap between men and women generally, there are, as mentioned previously, large differences between the arts and commercial arts and the public and private sectors. Recently, in the *Guardian* newspaper, a full-time administrative post in an arts organisation was advertised at £18,000 per annum. The same page showed an advert for a similar post within a design agency at £30,000–£35,000 per annum plus benefits.

Why work part-time?

So should you get a job or not? If you intend to be self-employed or to set up a company, unless you have generous benefactors you need a regular income source during the first few months at least. So it may be beneficial to you in the long run to find a part-time job, especially if it's related to your field.

Is teaching in art schools the answer?

A huge number of art and design graduates wish to enter into part-time lecturing at art and design colleges. This is a highly competitive marketplace with few fractional posts available. The University of the Arts in London, for example, has about 300 applications for any job which is advertised.

It's also worth realising that people who secure lecturing jobs at art colleges usually gain posts by word-of-mouth recommendation. You have to be proactive to obtain teaching work, and you have to really want to do it. If you are a graduate, to increase your chances keep on good terms with your lecturers and consider sending tutors an occasion letter every six months or so informing them about interesting developments. Your practice and experience of running a creative business will inform your teaching. Achieving recognition in the outside world is vital to securing any teaching work.

It's worth knowing that it's quite possible to gain work from heads of departments and short-course managers by 'proposing' ideas to them.

Gaining adult teaching qualifications

A further consideration is that new graduates to the lecturing profession are now required to obtain adult teacher-training qualifications either before or after they join the academic staff. However, if you're only undertaking occasional 'visiting tutor' work, then gaining a qualification probably won't be necessary. If you want to lecture regularly at universities or teach short courses at adult or further education colleges, on the other hand, you'll find that most UK institutions now require basic adult teaching qualifications. It's likely that under new employment contracts you will be required to continue your professional development, which may include gaining a higher level of teaching qualification while in the post.

The regulations governing teaching in higher, further and adult-education institutions in the UK vary widely. I would advise you to contact the Human Resources Department of the particular college you wish to work at and ask them directly what qualifications are desirable and whether they provide further training when in post.

Positions are usually advertised in the *Times Higher Education Supplement*, the *Guardian* or 'job alerts' sent by email, or appear on the college's website. Before rushing to apply, check the job specification.

Lecturing at AE (adult education), FE (further education) or HE (higher education) level is a relatively poorly paid profession in comparison with the private sector. The hourly rate ignores the fact that a high level of administration and preparation may be required. After tax it's unlikely you will be working for much more than £15 per hour.

Internships

Work experience in art and design organisations or businesses can be an essential stepping stone to greater things. However, many interns can be exploited, working long hours for nothing more than travel expenses. To avoid turning into an unpaid employee, I would suggest that the length of your internship is fixed. Towards the end of the period, request a reference to use in gaining further employment. Then, if the organisation can't offer you any paid work, gracefully exit at the end of your agreed term.

If you do stay on for a while, seek a reference in any case, especially if you've bonded well with your current manager, as people in the visual arts move around a good deal.

Gaining self-employment status can be useful during this time. If you have been a successful intern and your employers know you intend to gain trading status, they may be willing to offer the occasional paid day or even a freelance contract.

Try not to end up in a cycle of endless internships. You must use them as part of your professional development and work experience. Continue to apply for paid positions whilst you are an intern, as having a current role – even an unpaid one – can significantly improve your chances of gaining a job.

Importance of business and enterprise skills

'One of the big failings of art schools is that students aren't given any teaching on how to survive as a one-person business, which is what it is.'

Stuart Pearson Wright (1975–), portrait painter

There is an enormous amount to learn about setting up and running a successful business. There are four key areas which I would recommend investigating. This can be achieved by attending courses and workshops, and seeking out professional (visual arts/creative industry) advisers.

Professional development
- Managing an exhibition
- Planning a marketing campaign
- Arts and studio administration
- Working in teams
- How to undertake a commission
- Applying for funding and sponsorship
- Philosophy and art/design theory
- Teacher training
- Health and Safety
- Basic introduction to self-employment

Business theory and knowledge
- Introduction to business start-up
- Basic marketing materials
- Professional bodies and networks
- Market research
- Unique selling point
- Intellectual property, contracts and insurances
- Business planning
- Money management
- Financial planning and cash flow
- Tax, NI and bookkeeping

Practical enterprise and interpersonal skills

- Vision generation
- Networking
- Working in teams and leadership
- Presentation skills
- How to sell
- Self-promotion
- Negotiation tactics
- Creative thinking (problem solving)
- Risk assessment
- Innovation and technology

Big business

- Advanced business and financial planning
- Applying for loans or pitching for investment
- Taking on premises
- Intellectual property, branding and trademarks
- Contract law, terms and conditions, insurances, and Health and Safety
- Company formation and regulations
- Import/export, e-commerce and distance-selling regulations
- Manufacturing and licensing
- Employing people and setting up a payroll system
- Tax, National Insurance, VAT, and accounting software

Professional development – the basics

Professional development is something all artists and designers should understand. A number of elements described here are being injected into many undergraduate programmes.

Artists and designers really have to master most of the professional development menu before going on to start their own business. This will be far harder to achieve when there is little or no provision for professional development within your degree syllabus or post-graduation. I hope this book will assist you by filling in some of these knowledge gaps.

Business theory and knowledge

Business skills are acquired by learning essential knowledge areas and basic business theory. Many business start-up courses are quite generic and not particularly suitable for creative people. Try to find courses that are aimed towards the visual arts or creative industries.

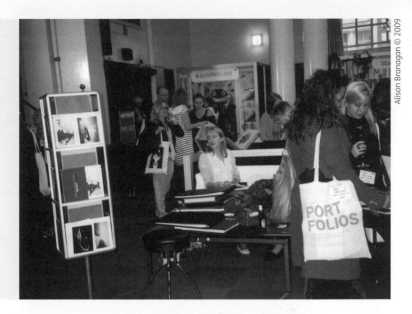

Alison Branagan © 2009

A portfolio fair

Practical enterprise and interpersonal skills

Enterprise, interpersonal skills and entrepreneurship are more about being confident, being able to judge and take risks and being able to practically apply business know-how.

Big business

Big business is for people who have the desire to grow a large enterprise. The scale of growth involved in this level of enterprise makes it suitable only for creatives who really enjoy the business side of creativity and have a commercial product which either has a lucrative niche or mass-market appeal.

These four key areas are not universally agreed art-business rules. They are simply my view about which topics are vital to any growing enterprise. These skills and knowledge areas can be acquired in different ways, not just through attending courses. You may pick up valuable experience from an internship, reading books and periodicals, and in real life by trial and error.

As your business expands you might hire in expertise from web designers, accountants, business advisers, solicitors and marketing consultants. If your business is growing into a larger enterprise you may choose to team up with people with complementary skills or, when you can afford to, simply employ them.

35

Agents and dealers

Many artists and designers seek representation from galleries, dealers or agents. This is an extremely competitive market. A top illustration agent has told me he has about 20 enquiries every week via email (over 1,000 a year!). This is similar to the number of enquiries that established London galleries receive.

It's still traditional for fine artists, sculptors and designer-makers to send out information packs as well as contacting galleries via phone and email. Unfortunately, only a minority of UK artists and designers obtain professional representation. Some commercial creatives, such as illustrators, have several different agents, one representing their advertising interests, another for editorial commissions. Agents and dealers also work not only in specific sectors but also by limits of territory – for instance, representing the artist's interests in the UK only, or the US only, Japan only, worldwide, etc.

Being unrepresented

Try not to be disheartened if you fail to attract interest from an agent or dealer. Even if you have representation, it's not guaranteed they will be able to provide you with a constant flow of sales or commissions. Many artists and designers who have agents still work part-time, create their own products and self-generate commissions. Moreover, sometimes the working relationship with an agent isn't an easy one. There are also some pretty unscrupulous people out there masquerading as agents when they are simply crooks.

Attracting interest

Approaching agents and dealers is fine, but don't be too disappointed if they are not interested. What can help impress them is if you have won awards for your artwork or products, or have succeeded in building up a number of clients or opportunities yourself.

If you do manage to secure a big opportunity such as a lucrative advertising contract, then it is worth contacting appropriate agents to see if they would be willing to represent you on a one-off basis. They will then undertake all the negotiation for you but will take a commission of up to 30–40% (percentage only appropriate for large-scale deals such as advertising and for work outside the UK) for their time and business acumen in closing the deal. Paying a commission to an agent is worth it if the opportunity brings in many tens of thousands of pounds.

Remember, if you come to public attention, from being featured in industry periodicals, hosting a stand at art or design fairs or winning or being shortlisted for prizes, then agents will come to you. If you've been turned down by agents in the past, don't give up hope. Keep trying to find new ones and making fresh approaches.

HERE ARE A FEW TIPS TO KEEP YOU OUT OF TROUBLE:

- Always check with professional bodies or other advisers before signing any kind of contract agreement.
- If approached by an unknown agent or dealer, don't just blindly accept their offer of representation. There may be other more established agents in the field who are also be interested in your artwork and products.
- Should you have several people representing you, or different ways of making money from your creative business then any conflicts of interest have to be thought through. For instance, if you are e-trading online and selling products in shops or galleries, the retail price should not be more than your own internet or website pricing.

For more information on agents and dealers see Chapter 10, Confidence and Negotiation Tactics (pages 177–80), and a list of professional associations in the Useful Organisations section at the end of this book.

In summary

To be successful in the visual arts and creative industries requires a great deal of physical and mental energy. Adopting a more flexible approach to work opportunities is essential if you wish to earn a living. In the visual arts there are openings everywhere, but you may not recognise them as such. This can be due to what you perceive as the 'right' type of project. In the commercial arts and design worlds there are many avenues you can explore, and to succeed you might have to be more open-minded.

Gaining a part-time job while you start a creative business can be helpful. Understanding more about business and exploiting intellectual rights is vital. Securing representation is not essential, though it can make life a great deal easier.

RESOURCES

The Artists Information Company, *a-n Magazine*, www.a-n.co.uk

Artquest, www.artquest.org.uk (useful articles about self-employment and business start-up)

Lecturing

Adult teacher-training qualifications:

City and Guilds, www.cityandguilds.com

University and College Union, www.ucu.org.uk

Check with the AE, FE or HE institution concerned before applying to any course about what type of qualification you require.

Internships

These are a number of web-based e-news services where internships and other voluntary opportunities are advertised. A (free) subscription is required:

www.artscouncil.org.uk

www.artsadmin.co.uk

www.creative-capital.org.uk

www.arts-consultants.org.uk

www.fashioncapital.co.uk.

www.talentcircle.co.uk

www.mandy.com

www.gumtree.com

www.craigslist.org

www.enternships.com

Research about careers

Emerging workers: A fair future for entering the creative industries, by Kit Friend (April 2010), www.artsgroup.org.uk

www.prospects.ac.uk

The People Theme, Nadine Andrews and Roanne Dods (May 2010), www.missionmodelsmoney.org.uk

Creative Graduates, Creative Futures, by L. Ball, E. Pollard, N. Stanley (January 2010), www.employment-studies.co.uk

www.yourcreativefuture.org

Also, contact your university careers service.

Creative economy

www.creativeconomy.org.uk

Agents and dealers

www.illustratorsagents.co.uk

www.theaoi.com

www.greetingcardassociation.org.uk

www.slad.org.uk

www.vaga.co.uk

www.artquest.org.uk/showing-and-selling/agents.htm

http://home.the-aop.org/AOP_Agents

Books

Please also refer to the books listed in Chapter 1.

The Craftsman, Richard Sennett (London: Penguin)

Master Key to Riches, Napoleon Hill (London: Vermilion)

The Power of Impossible Thinking, Yoram Jerry Wind, Colin Crook and Robert Gunther (New Jersey: Wharton School Publishing)

Making Sense of Business: A no-nonsense guide to business skills for managers and entrepreneurs, Alison Branagan (London: Kogan Page)

3

Overview of Business Start-up

> 'I didn't spend three years doing a photography degree to bloody end up answering somebody else's telephone all day.'
>
> *Gulnur Mustafa Nafi (1979–), photographer*

The comment above from a recent graduate brings home the fact that learning about business should be embraced rather than ignored.

If a suitable job doesn't materialise after you choose to become a professional creative then the prospect of setting up in business has to be seriously considered. Self-employment isn't for everyone, but unfortunately you might not have any choice. Most film-makers, photographers, illustrators, and fine and applied artists have to be self-employed, otherwise they can't earn any income from their creative products and skills.

Why set up in business?

> 'Artists live in an imperfect world where affairs of the heart must sometimes be compromised with business.'
>
> *Sara Genn (1972–), artist and songwriter*

Many arts practitioners and other professionals within the arts and design spectrum come to an uneasy acceptance that to earn a living you must trade.

If you don't have any contacts in the art and design sectors, then things will not simply just happen for you. Learning about business is only one piece of the 'what-you-have-to-know' cake. To earn a living in the visual arts a change of mindset has to be realised. Wishful thinking or a passion for art isn't enough to put food on the table. In fact that's why the artist William Blake's wife Catherine would place an empty plate on the dining table, to remind her husband to earn some money from engraving and printing business flyers.

Moving into the professional world

In the commercial world, artists and designers have to learn about self-management. Over the last ten years I've given hundreds of lectures in art schools and very rarely did they start on time. In the outside world, any lateness of employees or freelancers is not tolerated for long.

But why should I register as self-employed or set up a limited company?

The reason is that if you're selling products, supplying services, undertaking commissions or working as a freelancer for the odd few days, then you are indeed trading and should register as self-employed. There is no *de minimis* amount for registering as self-employed. You still have to register, even if you are making a loss.

What is PAYE?

If you've been officially taken on as a casual, part-time or full-time employee, then your income tax and national insurance is deducted at source, using the system known as PAYE – Pay As You Earn.

What's not PAYE?

Anything else outside official employment that results in money in your pocket in the form of cash, cheque or digital payments into your bank account is a taxable source of income. If you don't register as self-employed and continue to put money in your pocket or stuff it in a savings account, that constitutes tax evasion, which is a criminal offence. If (or more likely when) the Revenue discover you are trading without being registered you're likely to be fined and to receive a demand for backdated income-tax payments.

If the HMRC discover that you are working for an organisation or business as a freelancer without registering as self-employed, then it's not just you who will be liable for missed income-tax and National Insurance contributions. It's likely the organisation concerned can be fined. Depending on the length of tax avoidance the business may be liable for National Insurance contributions on your earnings.

Important information

It's unlikely you will get into trouble if you have just been a bit naïve and have only received payments for the odd thing. However, if you are starting to sweat a bit while reading this, seek advice from an accountant or business adviser with creative-industry experience. If you're trading and not registered, then it is possible to backdate a start date for self-employment to within three calendar months. (This can be done when completing the registration form CWFI.) If you have been selling work or undertaking other freelance activities for a year or so, again you should contact an accountant. It is likely you will be fined £100 by the Revenue, and you'll have to go back in time and unearth what has been earned and also what relevant expenses may be claimed.

Should you be in a bit of a mess, I would always advise paying a professional to help with any communications with HMRC. If you do find yourself in this situation, don't worry about it. Accountants are quite accustomed to solving this kind of problem. See 'step seven' in the next section and read Chapter 11, Records, Tax and Basic Bookkeeping.

It really isn't worth trading without registering. You're a professional person and therefore, like everyone else who wishes to earn their own living, you need to comply with the law. Register yourself as a business (e.g. as self-employed/sole trader) and get yourself out of the black market.

Seven steps to self-employment

'If you are to succeed, then you have to accept that you will be working in a competitive market where, only the most dedicated and responsible artists will come out well.'
Harley Miller (1934–), entrepreneurial artist

The 'Seven steps to self-employment' is a short overview to help you understand the process of setting up as self-employed.

Step one – research

Everybody who sets up a business has to undertake research in their own way.

It's beneficial to develop a commercial mindset, even if you are a fine-art graduate and your work is quite ephemeral or poetic. You have to find some kind of market demand for your creative products and services, or adapt them to activities that will generate income. Art practitioners whose work is conceptual or philosophical in nature may find that they could be more suited to working in advertising, or alternatively in the community – in arts organisations and schools. Other creatives such as illustrators or designers may prefer to firmly root themselves within a market, and to develop a recognisable style, collection or range of products.

Approaches to research can be wide-ranging. Here is a useful list:

- Attend business start-up courses, workshops or other talks.
- Find out what help is available from local arts and design organisations, enterprise agencies, innovation hubs or support networks.
- Join art/design/business networks and professional bodies.
- Subscribe to industry periodicals to assist in your search for opportunities.
- Do your best to make friends in the industry.
- Read articles or books about how other artists and designers succeeded in business.
- Find established artists or designers who might be willing to offer you some feedback on your portfolio and future ambitions.
- Collect examples of creative businesses' marketing materials.
- Find out about agents, dealers, boutique owners, art and product buyers.
- Make up samples of your products and see if owners or buyers from stores would be interested. Conduct some research by asking a few buyers what sort of products and goods they are looking for.
- Investigate industry-sector art books, catalogues, awards, prizes and scholarships.
- Visit art and design fairs.
- If appropriate try to test the market by selling your products

on a market stall or through 'sale and return' with retailers.
* Explore the possibility of undertaking further training and learning new skills.

Step two – unemployment (not mandatory!)

If you can't find any suitable employment or find it too difficult to earn any money from business activities then you can sign on and claim state benefits. If you're claiming state benefits such as income support or Jobseeker's Allowance, it's still possible to register as self-employed, but only if you're trading for under 16 hours a week.

Remember that unemployment-related benefits are to do with finding and being available for employment, not exploring business opportunities. The rules have tightened up, so it's likely in order to be eligible that you will have to demonstrate that no money has come in from self-employment (if registered) or that you have no full-time job. If you state, for example, 15 hours a week, because this is 'freelance time' – say, preparing work for an exhibition or product development – they may just simply cut about 50% of your money, so beware!

You must search for PAYE work and provide evidence to continue claiming Jobseeker's Allowance. If you end up claiming these benefits it may be worth asking the Job Centre advisers about any 'New Deal'-type self-employment programmes in your local area. Usually these schemes last for the best part of a year, with 'trainees' writing a business plan and then legally 'trading', with no interruption to their benefits, for six months.

Who can claim unemployment or other state benefits in the UK?
If you're a UK national (have gained British citizenship), have 'indefinite leave to remain', or you're a European Union citizen (i.e. a citizen of one of the EU member countries), you can claim benefits, if you have also been allocated a National Insurance number. In most cases, for EU citizens to be eligible for benefits it's usual to have been previously employed in the UK for 12 months.

If you are 'non-EU' then it's likely you can't claim any state funds. If unsure, check your visa status with the Job Centre, talk to the Tax Credit Helpline, or if necessary contact the Home Office.

Step three – seeking advice and writing a business plan

As you can see from the simple mind map on pages 82–3, business planning for most self-employed people does not need to be complicated. The plan outline in Chapter 5, Business Planning, is a useful tool to help you plan your business. Some kind of plan is crucial to understanding what you're doing and how much it will cost. Business plans are essential, allowing business advisers to quickly see what research has been undertaken and whether you're ready to start.

Equally, if you plan to work as a partnership or form a company, you and your partner should have an agreed vision for the business and share the responsibility of putting the plan into practice. Finally, if you require grant funding (rarely available now) or are applying for a bank loan, the bank's business manager will want to read your plan. A useful tip: when applying for a bank loan it's advisable to use the bank's own software rather than the template provided with this book.

Step four – gaining funding

You may be fortunate to have some savings, or generous friends and family who will either give you some money or lend you sufficient funds to purchase or hire the resources you require. If friends and family are unable to help, or you simply wish to be independent, then in the absence of grants you'll have to apply for a loan.

After setting up your business bank account (see next step), you can apply for a loan from your bank. The business plan usually indicates that you'll be investing in the venture yourself. Therefore, if you require £3,000 you would ideally be able to put in £1,000. If turned down by the bank, then I would advise contacting your local enterprise agency for further information about other government-supported lending schemes. For more information about loans please read Chapter 8, Funding and Sponsorship.

Step five – opening a business bank account

In the UK, a business bank account isn't required if you're registered as self-employed and only earning small sums. However, as soon as money starts to come in, pop down to your local branch and collect the business bank-account packs. Look through them all and decide which one is best for you. During the first 12–24 months they usually offer free banking, i.e. no bank charges. They may also offer other deals, such as free software, business start-up books and access to free advice.

Opening a business account is part of running a professional business – trading from a personal account is at best amateurish. New rules have been brought in by HMRC, which mean they have more powers to look into your affairs and spot-check your records. If you have a business bank account, it becomes that much more difficult for HMRC to investigate your personal current account.

Before you contact the bank, either in person or online, it's a good idea to be registered on the electoral roll. The bank will credit-check you and may ask for some proof of trading, such as a few pages of accounts or a business card. If you're not on the electoral roll or have a poor credit rating this could be a barrier to you opening a business account.

If you're suffering from credit problems, you may still find that there are some accounts suitable for you; in the UK, try the Royal Bank of Scotland or the Foundation Current Account with NatWest. At the time of writing, due to the crisis in the economy most banks require £100 to be deposited in the account; it used to be £50, and of course it may return to this more reasonable sum in the future. For more on business bank accounts check with the bank directly and read Chapter 11, Records, Tax and Basic Bookkeeping.

Step six – seeing an accountant and bookkeeping

Most artists and designers dislike the tedium of keeping records – but it has to be done. It's best to learn at the outset about keeping accounts and tax regulations. Most accountants offer an initial free consultation. Maintaining regular records of income and expenses is a legal requirement. In the early years, doing your own bookkeeping will give you more understanding of your financial affairs.

In the future, when you're earning a decent amount of money, hire an accountant or local bookkeeper to do your accounts. This will free up personal creative time, albeit at some cost. For more information about bookkeeping please read Chapter 11, Records, Tax and Basic Bookkeeping.

Step seven – registering with the HMRC

When you're ready, it is important to register with HMRC, and gain a self-employment number, also known as a self-assessment number or UTR (unique taxpayer reference). In the UK it's free to register as self-employed. The process is simple, but the forms are not very well designed and can be confusing.

To register as self-employed in the UK you can either phone 08459 15 45 15 or download the registration form 'CWF1' as a PDF from www.hmrc.gov.uk. To download this form, type 'CWF1 registration PDF' into the 'search' box on the HMRC website. Print out the form, fill it in and post it back. I would advise printing the form from the website rather than phoning to register. Always remember to photocopy the form and keep it with your records.

Class 2 National Insurance

It's helpful, before you start trading, if you can predict your profit or loss for the year ahead. Estimate your business income and deduct your business expenses. If you are only likely to make a few thousand pounds or less, you may opt to apply for a Certificate of Small Earnings Exception and gain exemption from paying Class 2 NI contributions. This exception form is coded as 'CF10'.

However, if more money is likely to roll in then you'll need to set up a direct debit for Class 2 NI contributions from your personal current account. Class 2 NI is a personal tax on being self-employed just as Class 1 is for employees. The code for the form to set up the direct debit is 'CA5601'. All these forms can be downloaded from the HMRC website.

Sometimes HMRC will send you the form 'CA5601' automatically even after you have posted back the 'CF10' form. Just ignore it – a Certificate of Small Earnings Exception should arrive shortly thereafter. For more information about NI, tax and submitting tax returns please read Chapter 11, Records, Tax and Basic Bookkeeping.

Informing the local or borough council

If you register your home as a business address then you do not need to inform the council unless:

- You plan to convert part of your home, e.g. build an extension or convert a garage into a studio, workshop, office or gallery exclusively for business use.
- You desire to attach or paint a sign on your home advertising your business.
- You wish to have a separate entrance to the area that is exclusively for business use.
- You plan to have people, e.g. clients or customers, coming to your house for business purposes.

Other questions of entitlement

If I'm from outside the European Union, can I set up in business in the UK?

If you are a non-EU citizen, it is increasingly difficult, though still possible, to come and set up as self-employed or form a company in the UK.

Overseas (non-EU) students

If you're 'non-EU' and here on a student visa, you can only work as an employee and have no rights to set up a business.

Gaining British citizenship

After ten consecutive years of legal stay in the UK on a student visa you can apply for settled status and residency, also known as 'indefinite leave to remain', though there is no guarantee that this will be automatically granted. Once you have settled status you can then go on to apply for British citizenship.

British citizenship can also be gained through marriage. Once married, you can set up a business in the UK. Please note, however, that it is illegal to marry a British subject simply to gain citizenship. Marriages and civil partnerships to those from outside the EU are monitored by immigration officers.

Other visas

It's possible as a 'Tier 1 skilled migrant' with sufficient points under the current immigration 'points system' to set up as self-employed on securing entry to the UK.

You can also switch your visa status to a 'Tier 1 Entrepreneur visa', obtainable from the UK Home Office. However, at the time of writing you'll normally require a substantial sum of your own money to invest in establishing a business in the UK. This is currently set at £200,000.

It's becoming more difficult for UK-based arts organisations to invite non-EU artists to Britain for short periods to collaborate or make artwork. UK organisations have to 'sponsor a migrant', which is costly and bureaucratic for both parties.

However, if you're a non-EU resident and wish to visit the UK from time to time, for business meetings and attending trade fairs, you might consider going into business in your own country and applying for a 'business visitor's visa'. Make contact with the British Embassy in your own country to find out more.

You should not be too concerned if you are currently studying in the UK but find that you can't trade in the UK after graduation. Much business is conducted via the internet these days, and you can still visit Britain regularly if you hold a business visitor's visa.

Please note that regulations frequently change, so you'd be well advised to obtain further information from a UK immigration solicitor or the Home Office.

Other business structures

'Artists are often excellent businessmen. They have to be. Otherwise they do not remain artists.'
Alexander Young Jackson (1882–1974), painter

This section provides a brief outline of various types of legal statuses open to UK-based businesses. Most of the provisions concerning self-employment are described in this book.

Have a go at walking first
I would strongly urge readers of this book, unless taking on high levels of financial risk, to start out as self-employed, i.e. being a sole trader. In the future, as the business grows, you could set up a private company. It's common for creatives to retain their self-

employment status and set up in business with others, such as forming a limited company or partnership.

Never rush into trading formally with others. It's wise to trial working as a team enterprise for a few months before making any long-term commitments. Before forming any partnership or company, even if it's just an experiment, seek the advice of a solicitor and have a working agreement drawn up. Should you wish to establish a more advanced form of business such as a partnership or company then seek advice from an accountant, solicitor or business adviser.

In sectors such as television, music, events and media, it is more appropriate for individuals to set up private companies. Other types of enterprises that have an educational, cultural or environmental purpose are usually set up by artists or performers, who tender for funding to run community projects from local authorities and other charitable sources. These are usually termed 'social enterprises' or 'not-for-profit' companies, as the main motivation in setting up this form of business is providing a social service rather than pursuing personal financial gain.

Working for yourself

When you work for yourself you have immense freedom. It can be lonely, though. If in the future you decide to work with others, it's essential to realise that you won't be able to get your own way all the time.

Sole trader (self-employed)

Registering as a sole trader is relatively straightforward. A drawback is that the self-employed are exposed to more liabilities and have no asset protection. One advantage is the simple registration system with HMRC.

Working with others

Finding other artists and designers to team up with is a good idea. In the early days you may encounter some problems, but don't let this put you off from working with others.

It is wise in any joint venture that rights should be clearly established in legal agreements drawn up by a solicitor. Don't attempt to make your own. The ownership and control of future intellectual property rights has to be agreed. In the absence of such an agreement, difficulties will arise should there be any falling out between parties. Remember, Sir James Dyson lost his rights to the Barrow Ball, as he signed his patent over to the company rather than retaining it under his own name.

Collective

Collectives can be informal associations between other self-employed creatives, in which members pool their resources and talent for projects, commercial ventures and exhibitions. Successful collectives tend to develop into registered private companies, with the option of using model rules developed by Co-operatives UK or by local Co-operative Development Agencies (CDAs). Other structures and options are available.

Partnership

It's essential to have a 'deed of partnership' drawn up by a solicitor when planning to go into business with others. As with being self-employed, partners are personally and in this case jointly liable for any debts owed by the business and other partners. Partnerships have to be registered with HMRC.

Limited partnership; limited liability partnership

These structures are similar to, but with significantly more advantages than, a partnership, such as limited personal liability. They are slightly more complex, with more rules concerning internal administration and organisation. Such types of partnerships must register their details at Companies House.

Private limited company

When you set up a company as either a sole director or with others, it is advisable to engage the services of an accountant. A 'shareholders' agreement' should be drawn up by a solicitor, agreeing roles and responsibilities. Limited companies are registered with Companies House. There is much to learn when setting up this form of business, as they are heavily regulated.

Forming a not-for-profit organisation

There are many different routes to forming a cultural or social enterprise. Many businesses with these types of structures will be eligible for grants from regional development agencies, local councils, arts bodies and trusts.

Voluntary organisation (unincorporated organisation)

With a voluntary organisation there is no need to register anywhere, though a constitution does have to be drawn up by a solicitor. Unincorporated organisations or 'community groups' are independent and self-governing. Committee members work on behalf of the community and not for financial gain. Again, funding may be obtainable from local sources.

Company limited by guarantee; community-interest company

These are two different structures that are useful for cultural, social and educational purposes. Community Interest Companies (CICs) have strong social aims, though are more about 'trade' than providing beneficial educational community projects. Both these types of businesses can apply for grants and funding. All not-for-profit companies have to register with Companies House.

Business start-up checklist

This diagnostic tool (overleaf) will help you to professionally research and plan your business.

Don't give up...

If you find that you can't answer many of these questions, or you simply give up, then you must undertake some serious investigation of these topics, especially if you have started trading. This book will help with most of the answers. By the time the final chapter is read you'll be able to fill in this diagnostic tool much more confidently.

If you've lots of comments in answers to the questions, then you are doing extremely well. Even most people who have been in business for several years can't answer all of these important questions.

BUSINESS START-UP CHECKLIST

1. Of which professional bodies, clubs, unions, or societies are you a member? e.g. college alumni, Chartered Institute of Designers, BECTU, etc.

2. Are you a member of any business or legal-protection organisation? e.g. Federation of Small Businesses, chamber of commerce, local enterprise club, an magazine subscriber, ACID, Design Protect, etc.

3. Do you have a business adviser?

4. Do you have an accountant?

5. Do you have a solicitor or access to legal advice through your membership of another organisation?

6. Do you subscribe to any key periodicals? e.g. *Design Week, Crafts, Creative Review, a-n Magazine, Varoom, The Goldsmith Magazine*, etc.

7. Are you a member of any online news loops and networks? e.g. Arts News, Arts Jobs, Creative Capital, Arts Digest, Creative People, Facebook, Artquest, MAD, Own-it, etc.

8. Do you have your own website?

9. Do you showcase your work or CV/portfolio on any other website? e.g. local Arts Council website portal, Axis web, AOI portfolios, iSpot, D&AD Talent pool, Midwest, Saatchi, Hidden Art, Coroflot, Aquent, Talent Circle, Handbag, etc.

10. What promotional materials do you have? Do you have: professional-quality images of your artwork/products? professionally printed business cards and stationery? brochures, catalogues, leaflets or flyers? with a guide pricelist? PDF brochures on a download link?

11. If you are already starting to freelance, work to commission or sell products, have you registered as self-employed (with HMRC) or set up a company (with Companies House)?

12. Have you set up a business bank account?

13. Do you have public liability insurance? If you have, does your public liability insurance cover all of your activities? Have you thoroughly read the policy? Do you require other insurances such as product, equipment, professional indemnity, legal expenses insurance or 'all risks' insurance?

14. Have you set up your own bookkeeping system, in a cash ledger in hardcopy or using software such as Excel spreadsheets?

15. Do you know when the tax year ends? When does income tax and national insurance have to be paid? Can you fill in a self-assessment form (also known as a tax return)?

16. Have you undertaken any kind of business start-up course, marketing course, enterprise skills course or financial planning (money management) training?

17. Can you list three to five other practitioners or creative businesses similar to your own in the borough or region? If so, how do they differ from your own? What is special or unique about your art practice or creative business?

18. Have you written a business plan, marketing plan or action plan for the next 12 months?

19. Have you identified who your customers, clients or collectors will be? If so, who are they, where are they and how will you communicate with them?

20. Have you undertaken any kind of risk assessment to do with your future business ideas?

21. Do you understand the intellectual property rules to do with business or brand names?

22. Are you familiar with the basics of relevant intellectual property rules such as copyright, design right, trademarks and patents?

23. Are you familiar with other relevant key laws? e.g. general contract law, licensing, Health and Safety, COSHH, environment legislation, packaging regulations, CE marking, fibre-content labelling or distance-selling regulations?

24. Do you have a good understanding of professional fees, commercial rates and what the market can stand regarding costing and pricing?

25. Regarding vision, what kind of 'event' or 'lucky break' do you need to take your business onto the next level?

The surface and fabric designer

Annette Taylor-Anderson

Annette Taylor-Anderson is a British surface designer. She studied Textile Design and Surface Decoration at the University of East London. She completed her degree in 2005, and set up her business, ATA Designs (Annette Taylor-Anderson Designs), in 2006.

That same year she was selected to exhibit her wall hangings at New Designers One Year On and also at 100% East. Annette's collections have been featured in *Elle Decoration* and the *World of Interiors* magazines.

To view Annette's products visit www.atadesigns.com.

Her five essential tips are:

1. Seek expert advice

You may find starting a business isn't as easy as first anticipated, especially if you've little business or industry knowledge. Joining professional bodies and business support networks can be helpful. I'm a member of London-based organisations Craft Central and Hidden Arts. Furthermore, I found advice given by friends already established in business very useful.

2. The importance of networking

In the early years, it's essential to network as much as possible through social and business events. View networking as an opportunity to promote yourself and make new connections within your sector. Meeting new contacts can spark unexpected opportunities.

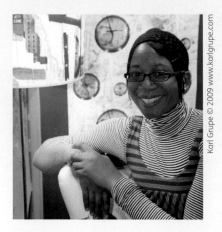

Karl Grupe © 2009 www.karlgrupe.com

3. Staying focused

It's very easy to jump from one idea to another – staying focused is the key. As creative people, it's likely you'll have numerous design ideas. Keep a note or sketch book to record them for possible future projects. It's impossible to explore all concepts fully and make progress, so be sensible and concentrate on one or two goals.

4. Selecting manufacturers

Undertake research to find the best manufacturer. Make the effort to visit them to find out how they work and what services they offer. It's essential to develop relationships with manufacturers so that they can fully understand your requirements. It's worth spending time prototyping or making samples before committing yourself to large-scale production.

5. Understanding your market

Test-marketing sample products at trade shows will help you ascertain market demand. This gives you the opportunity to make design refinements and adjustments to pricing.

RESOURCES

Government organisations

Department for Work and Pensions (DWP)
Contact your local Job Centre Plus office for information about entitlement to benefits and rules plus a link through to the New Deal scheme. UK Benefit Enquiry Line,
Tel: 0800 882 200. www.jobcentreplus.gov.uk
www.dwp.gov.uk

HM Revenue and Customs (HMRC)
This is where you register as self-employed or as a partnership. They also publish a number of small guides and leaflets.
Registration Line tel: 08459 15 45 15
www.hmrc.gov.uk

UK Home Office
For advice about 'business visas' for people on temporary visas and for general immigration enquiries about work permits.
Tel: 020 7035 4848
Text phone: 020 7035 4742
www.homeoffice.gov.uk
www.ukvisas.gov.uk (for UK visas)

MediVisas LLP. UK Visa and Immigration Specialists. www.medivisas.com

Research

Market Research Society, www.mrs.org.uk

www.cobwebinfo.com (useful condensed fact sheets)

www.startquest.net (free mini business course)

Enterprise agencies

Find your local enterprise and creative/cultural agencies.
www.nfea.com (find your local enterprise agency)

Business Link
A UK-wide organisation which can signpost you to local business support and offers useful free publications.
Tel: 0845 600 9006, www.businesslink.gov.uk

Enterprise Insight
Works with young people up to the age of 30.
www.starttalkingideas.org

Enterprise UK
www.enterpriseuk.org

Northern Ireland, Scotland and Wales have similar resources:

Northern Ireland Business
Tel: 0800 027 0639
www.nibusinessinfo.co.uk, www.detini.gov.uk

Business Gateway (Scotland)
Tel: 0845 609 6611
www.bgateway.com

Cultural Enterprise Office (Scotland)
www.culturalenterpriseoffice.co.uk
www.scottish-enterprise.com

Business Eye (Wales)
Tel: 0845 600 9006
www.businesseye.org.uk

The Prince's Initiative for Mature Enterprise (Prime)
An organisation which supports people over the age of 50, or who have a disability, who wish to set up in business.
www.primeinitiative.org.uk
www.primebusinessclub.co.uk
www.prime-cymru.co.uk (Wales)

Striding Out
Business support project for young people between the ages of 18 and 30.
www.stridingout.com

Business and disability

www.dada-south.org.uk/bookfactsheets.php

www.shapearts.org.uk

www.direct.gov.uk

www.princes-trust.org.uk

Royal National Institute for the Blind (RNIB) has a long list on their website of business support agencies that offer support.
Helpline tel: 0845 766 9999, www.rnib.org.uk

Sources of information about forming UK-based companies and co-ops

Companies House
This is where you register your business as a company, whether a 'private limited' company or one 'limited by guarantee'.
For England, Northern Ireland and Wales,
tel: 0303 1234 500

RESOURCES

For Scotland, tel: 0870 333 3636
Text phone: 02920 381245
www.companieshouse.gov.uk

Industrial Common Ownership Movement
Tel: 0161 246 2954
icom@icom.org.uk
www.icof.co.uk (main site is for finance)

National Council
www.ncvo-vol.org.uk

Social Enterprise

Useful websites and organisations that help not-for-profit businesses to become established.

www.can-online.org.uk

www.sel.org.uk (for London)

Community Interest Companies
www.cicregulator.gov.uk

www.smartresources.org

www.socialenterprise.org.uk

Books

The Architect in Practice, David Chappell and Andrew Willis (9th edn) (Oxford: Blackwell Publishing)

Business Start-up Guide for Designers and Makers, Rachel Moses (ed.) (London: Design Nation); see www.thedesigntrust.co.uk for a free download

Second Steps, Caroline Mornement (Yeovil, Somerset: BCF Books)

Graphic Design: A user's manual, Adrian Shaughnessy (London: Laurence King)

A Proper Living from Your Art: How to make your painting pay, Harley & Cally Miller; see www.harleymiller.com for a free download

Beyond The Lens, Gwen Thomas and Janet Ibbotson (eds) (London: The AOP)

The Pocket Business Guide for Artists and Designers, Alison Branagan (London: A&C Black)

4

Money Management

> 'This is a credit crisis, not a creative crisis.'
>
> *John Galliano (1960–), fashion designer*

It's possible the effects of the global financial crisis that began in 2008 will reverberate for some years. Many readers may have suffered financially through a reduced number of opportunities.

History shows that hardship doesn't prevent artists and designers from having ideas. However, insufficient income will eventually frustrate any ambition. A total deficiency of funds makes it impossible to do anything properly. A decent level of income is required for a reasonable quality of life, which is vital for physical and psychological well-being.

I'm afraid I can only give a brief introduction to the subject in this chapter, which is about managing your money and costing products. I advise readers to develop their knowledge further by reading the recommended texts included at the end of this chapter. There is no quick fix where pricing is concerned. Most creative businesses are in niche markets. Calculations can be extremely complicated – especially for commercial creatives when quoting for licensing rights or 'reuse' fees – but I hope this chapter will give you a starting point.

Basic calculations

> 'Your pictures would have been finished a long time ago if I were not forced every day to do something to earn money.'
>
> *Edgar Degas (1834–1917), artist*

Many artists have a distant relationship with the concept of making money. They're uncomfortable with the idea of pricing and selling work they may still be emotionally attached to. Unfortunately, artists and designers do operate in a highly competitive field. If you're keen to learn more about what to charge, then it's advisable to seek advice and study the pricing guides mentioned at the end of Chapter 1.

To be in with a chance, unless you're established in your field, your products and services have to be priced in relation to what the market can stand. There is a huge difference between 'costing and pricing' time and 'market rates'. Artists and commercial creatives must grasp several concepts before beginning to cost their time, materials and other expenses.

Key money-management areas
- Understanding the value of time
- Calculating a personal survival budget
- Working out realistic business start-up costs
- Keeping track of ongoing expenses (cash flow/accounts)
- Constructing a budget and working within it
- Finding out about trade and retail pricing
- How to quote commercial fees for commissions/projects
- Being able to draft out a basic cash-flow projection
- Profit forecasts and sales forecasts (if appropriate)
- Running a business account properly.

What happens if I don't make much money from my business?
In the UK, and in many parts of the world, if earnings from being self-employed or a company director are low, you can claim help with housing costs and other benefits. Many artists and designers have claimed state aid, though most gloss over the fact. It's refreshing when established creatives talk openly about difficult periods in their lives. (For more information please turn to Chapter 8, Funding and Sponsorship.)

A FEW TIPS TO KEEP YOU OUT OF TROUBLE

- It's essential to manage your financial dealings professionally.
- You must clearly understand what your earnings are.

- If you're hazy about recollecting what income and expenses are, you will not be able to plan the future properly or claim benefits.

- When registering as self-employed, remember the date, as this is when official records and accounts start.
- Make sure bookkeeping is done regularly.
- Avoid leaving completing tax returns until just before the final HMRC deadline. The consequence of procrastination is being unprepared for sudden tax demands.
- If money is managed properly you won't get behind with tax payments.
- Have a contingency fund for tax payments to avoid getting into debt.
- Avoid taking out loans to pay any tax owed.
- Open a business account. Then business and personal finances can be better organised.

Most of these money-management and 'keeping out of trouble' tips are covered in this and other chapters.

Don't become a mug

Being unprofessional, such as accepting cash payments without issuing an invoice and recording income in your accounts can expose you to what at best can be described as uncomfortable arrangements with dubious 'clients'. Once you start entering the 'for cash' economy it will be difficult in the future to charge market rates if you don't invoice clients professionally.

Where to begin?

To start with, calculate a Personal Survival Budget. The 'PSB' is an estimate of what your personal outgoings are for a year. This can be difficult to do, and first drafts of Personal Survival Budgets can be a bit vague. All financial planning in the beginning of any venture is a combination of research, gaining feedback and guesswork. In the first two years in business you will need to revisit some of the exercises covered in this chapter and the next.

An example of a Personal Survival Budget

To begin with, add up all your personal expenses over the year. This can be difficult. Remember, there are 52 weeks in the year, 12 calendar months, but 13 x 28-day periods. We include Class 2 National Insurance in the PSB, as this is a personal tax for being self-employed.

PERSONAL SURVIVAL BUDGET

EXPENDITURE	Annually £	Quarterly £	Monthly £	4 Weekly £	Weekly £	Total £
Amount payable and frequency of payment						
Mortgage or rent			600			7,200
Council tax and water rates	1,000					1,000
Gas and electricity			30			360
Personal and property insurances	200					200
Food and housekeeping					30	1,560
Clothing			50			600
Telephones			50			600
TV licence	140					140
Entertainment					10	520
Newspapers, magazines, clubs etc			10			120
Car – tax						–
Car – Insurance						
Car – Service and maintenance						–
Car – Fuel, oil, parking etc						–
Children (presents, maintenance etc)	135					135
Savings plans			20			240
Debt repayments (credit cards, agreements)						
Travel card/Oyster			100			1,200
Class 2 National Insurance contributions					2.40	125
Other						–
Other						–
TOTAL EXPENDITURE						14,000
ESTIMATED INCOME (NON-BUSINESS)						
Income from family/partner						–
Income from part time job						
Other						–
TOTAL INCOME (NON-BUSINESS)						–
ANNUAL SURVIVAL INCOME REQUIRED						**14,000**

Example of a Personal Survival Budget (PSB). Available on request from www.taxbydesign.com

At the bottom of the spreadsheet there is room for 'other non-business income'. This could be a salary from a part-time job, income from a spouse, or perhaps rent collected from a lodger. If money is coming in from sources unrelated to your business, then subtract it from your total personal expenditure.

For example, if you're in full-time work, your salary should be covering all your basic personal outgoings. So enter your total salary (after tax) in the 'non-business income' at the bottom of the PSB table, and then deduct this amount from your personal expenses total. You should find your earnings from the job can cancel out the calculation. This means you won't need to 'draw' money from your business in the beginning, if you're starting off as self-employed in your spare time. 'Drawings' are monies taken from your business to live on.

If you find that your personal expenses are not completely covered by your salary, and you have a 'minus' figure, then if your calculations are accurate you must have credit-card debts or you are living in overdraft!

Eventually, if you reduce your hours and work part-time you will have to 'draw' money out of the business to live on. If, for instance, you have a part-time job and are also self-employed, then it may end up as a 50/50 situation: half your livelihood is subsidised from wages and the other half from self-employment.

Don't be daunted by the figures. Remember, as mentioned earlier, if you're self-employed or you have a mix of employed and self-employed work, and you're on a low income, there may be subsidy in the form of benefits either from HMRC (tax credits) or your local council (Housing Benefit).

This exercise is the first step in understanding money management.

Start-up costs, ongoing or reinvestment costs

If you're about to set up your business, then undertake thorough research into what has to be spent. You might have a number of items such as basic tools, mobile phone, laptop, and software already. If this is the case then start-up costs will be very low, especially if neither premises nor vehicle are required.

For readers who are already trading, there will always be ongoing costs and periods of reinvestment in the business, e.g. for re-branding, a new website, updating software, registering designs or a trademark, extra training and so on. Therefore, instead of thinking about start-up costs, consider whether your business requires a revamp.

Failure to regularly inject money into a business will gradually slow it down over time, Outdated branding, a 'clunky' website, outmoded software packages, old equipment, a lack of investment in updating your own skills – each and any of these factors can have an impact.

Under-investing or spending money on the wrong things can destroy a business before it even gets started. Marketing, branding and legal matters are key areas where it's easy to make big and costly mistakes.

So don't rush in to setting up until you have enough money to cover the basic costs such as insurance, marketing materials, prototyping (if appropriate), professional photography, and legal or business advice.

Filling in your business start-up costs

Don't be afraid of adding up all the figures – you need to know what your outlay is. A sensible way to cut down on start-up costs is to start trading from home. Think about what's essential and what isn't.

SOME QUESTIONS YOU CAN ASK IF FACED WITH ENORMOUS START-UP COSTS

- Do you really need a studio or workshop?
- If you're desperate for a studio could you share the cost, or hire space for short periods of time?
- Is there a local innovation hub, university or business-incubation centre you could use at low cost, or where you could gain access to free hot-desking facilities?
- If you're dreaming of owning a shop, could this be a longer-term goal? Wouldn't it be better to start trading from market stalls, at local fairs and festivals?

- Is buying all that expensive equipment necessary at the outset?
- Is there a local creative organisation or university with specialised machines that can be accessed for a small fee instead?
- Equally, could equipment be hired or shared if you only need it occasionally?
- Is it worth buying a vehicle? Would it be less expensive to hire a van or employ specialist art handlers for occasional fairs or exhibitions?

Keeping overheads low

Studios, workshops or offices can be expensive places to rent on a regular basis. Sometimes, if the studio complex is well organised it can enhance the development of any creative practitioner or business. A well-organised studio has regular well-attended shows, events and business support. Avoid studios or other serviced office spaces which appear to be a ghost town. Always visit a studio complex first during the week, and be sure to attend

START-UP COSTS		
ANTICIPATED EXPENDITURE		£
Premises:	Lease premium	
	Rent	
	Rates	
	Fitting out	
	Legal fees	
Subtotal – Premises		
Fixed assets:	Motor vehicles	
	Equipment	1,000
Subtotal – Fixed assets		1,000
Telecoms:	Telephones	100
	Internet	70
	Network	
	Website	900
Subtotal – Telecoms		1,070
Other costs:	Stock	
	Marketing	1,000
	Stationery	250
	Public liability insurance	150
	Software/various	1,030
	Other	
Subtotal – Other costs		2,430
TOTAL START-UP COSTS		4,500
LESS: AVAILABLE FUNDS		
ADDITIONAL FINANCE REQUIRED		4,500

Example of Business Start-up Costs.

open-studio events, before making any commitment. It may be worth noting that most of the artists and designers profiled in this book work from home.

Valuing time

> 'I recently turned sixty. Practically a third of my life is over.'
> *Woody Allen (1935–), actor and film director*

Managing and valuing time is an underrated skill. It's important to be able to predict how long projects will take to complete, if profits are to be generated.

63

Failure to grasp the importance of the value of time, and how to make best use of it are key factors in the success of any enterprise, especially a creative one. John J. Kao in his book *Entrepreneurship , Creativity and Organisation* describes at great length the problem of the relationship between time, economics and creativity. It's not easy to make creativity profitable. If it were there would be no need for this book.

The art student's 'mindset' may not be used to the idea of deadlines, budgets and resource efficiency. However, to get any creative product to market some economic compromises have to occur. These include outsourcing parts of the manufacture to others – for example, buying pre-prepared canvas, getting reproductions, or moulds made, outsourcing printing or other technical services.

Make detailed records

If you're currently studying at college or in the early days of starting your creative enterprise I suggest you keep a notebook to record how long is spent creating an artwork or product design. Keep detailed records from the first sketch to the finished product. Alongside these observations of time, record all expenses – direct and indirect – and all materials, no matter how minuscule. These observations will help you to figure out ways of being more efficient and make it easier to cost future commissions and projects.

Don't let time drain away

Time is something to be understood, so try not to waste it. By productivity I mean concentrating on business development, networking, researching, and finding customers. To be successful, every minute must be valued. On the other hand, I don't advise being a workaholic – you must take breaks and rest properly. Burnout can easily happen when you're overworked.

The charts on pages 66–8 demonstrate the basis of costing and pricing your time.

Not all business time is money-making time. To understand the notion of costing time and products, you must work out how much physical time, in the form of days and hours, you have per week, month and year to dedicate to your business. Failure to think about time in this way can result in living and working in chaos. No artist or designer who is disorganised or unreliable can make a living from their work.

The trick with understanding time is to realise there will be never enough time for any given task. There is insufficient time in meetings, for instance, to discuss everything: the debate has to fit the time we make for meetings. Deadlines will always be pressing upon the creative. This is why self-management is vital. Whatever amount of time you mentally assign to a task, I always advise at least tripling the figure. If you think something will take a day to do, it usually takes three days or even several weeks!

Things to think about when costing time
- Research and preparation
- Travelling to and from studios, meetings, etc.
- Buying materials in shops or from suppliers
- Allowing for illness or tiredness
- Losing things
- Making mistakes
- Wasting time by sorting out your own and other people's errors
- Equipment failure
- Being let down by others, strikes, etc.
- Business administration, planning, emails, updating websites, etc.

No event or project is completed successfully without having to take all these matters and more into consideration. As you become more experienced at creating products and delivering services, you will develop short cuts and better systems so that output becomes more cost-effective.

Business time cake theory
These time cakes (see overleaf) demonstrate what business, leisure and money-making time there is. It is unlikely you will be working and generating income 365 days a year. After making deductions for weekends, holidays and illness, it's likely over the course of a year you will probably have about 220 days available for business activities.

How much business time is there in a year?

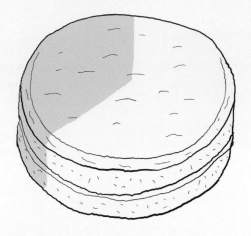

As you can see from this chart, after adding up all the days off you have about 220 days of business time. By 'days off' I mean the days you spend on other activities on such as having a rest or doing household chores, looking after children, going to the gym and other leisure activities such as going on holiday and visiting friends.

How much time will I have if I work in my job one day a week?

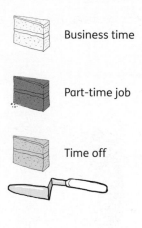

Business time

Part-time job

Time off

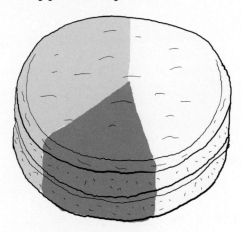

Even if you have a part-time job for one day a week it can significantly reduce the proportion of time you can dedicate to your practice or creative business.

If I have 220 days of business time, how is it spent?

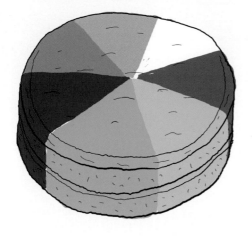

As you can observe in this chart, there are several areas of activity required to start a business and keep it going. Notice the segment for selling products and services is money-making time and the segment for creativity and manufacturing. If you don't have money pressures then you can afford to spend more time experimenting and making your creative products. This is great if you wish to establish an art practice with poetic ambitions or a creative business as a lifestyle or hobby business.

In the beginning, how will I use my time?

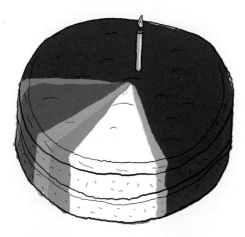

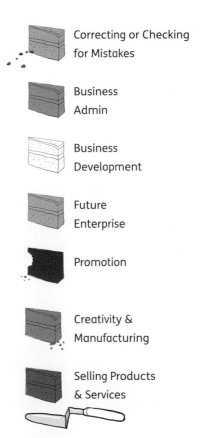

Correcting or Checking for Mistakes

Business Admin

Business Development

Future Enterprise

Promotion

Creativity & Manufacturing

Selling Products & Services

As you can see from this chart, if you would like to earn money from being an artist or designer in the early months and years of a business you will have to dedicate a large amount of time to promotion, networking and marketing if you are going to attract clients, customers or collectors.

On how many of these days should I be aiming to make money?

If you do wish to earn a living or grow a profitable business then a large proportion of the 220 days of business time will have to be spent generating money. As you earn money it's worth reinvesting it in the business to outsource any tasks such as bookkeeping or taking on an assistant. This will free up more time for creative and money-making time.

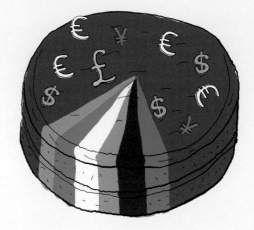

 Correcting or checking for mistakes

 Business Admin

 Business Development

 Future Enterprise

 Promotion

 Creativity & Manufacturing

 Selling Products & Services

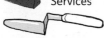

Days spent working for a daily rate could be reduced if you manage to create high demand or an exclusive niche market for your creative products or services. This will mean you can charge more substantial fees. Alternatively, being able to receive regular royalty payments from licensing your copyright, designs, patents and in the future even your trademark to other businesses is another way to generate income. If you can break into licensing your rights it can provide a labour-free source of income.

There is often an argument put forward that you should not think about time when setting prices, as it is about 'what' you do rather than how long it takes. I accept part of the argument, especially if you have an exceptional product or talent. However, no business can ignore the finite amount of business time and resources available, and the question of whether there is any market demand.

As you can see from these diagrams you might have less time than you think. A common problem which most artists and designers have is spending far too many days dedicated to the creativity segment. Creativity is the verve of any visual artist, but you must keep one eye on the bank balance and make sure that money is being generated on a regular basis.

Professional fees and pricing

> "'And what do I owe you?' she asked. "Five thousand francs," he answered. "But it only took you three minutes," she politely reminded him. "No," Picasso said. "It took me all my life."'
>
> *Anecdote from* Selling the Invisible
> *by Harry Beckwith (1949–), marketing guru*

Costing and pricing is not simply about time. The art of making money is also related to other factors. The Costing and Pricing quiz on page 74, at the end of this chapter, gives an insight into different approaches to pricing across the arts and commercial arts.

There are a few examples below to help you gain a sense of how rates and fees can be worked out. For more guidance please refer to the resources listed at the end of Chapter 1 and this chapter.

SOME THOUGHTS ON COSTING AND PRICING

- Market demand: if everyone wants your product, put your prices up – but do it slowly.
- For a specialised skill, services can be charged at a premium rate.
- The same is true for exclusive, niche, rare, unique, bespoke, limited edition or handmade products or artworks.
- Large-scale manufacture and buying materials in bulk can minimise costs and maximise profit margins.
- Particular styles, unless they are classic styles, go in and out of fashion.
- Changing fashions and trends mean that picking the right moment to enter the market is crucial.
- Don't be afraid of making a quick buck, tailoring products to tie in with seasons and events, e.g. Christmas, Valentine's Day, Mother's Day, local festivals, the Olympics, etc.
- Protect your intellectual property by asserting rights and licensing copyright, and registering designs, trademarks and inventions.
- Endorsement is a great boon to your business. This can come from a variety of sources: a prestigious art school, gallery, sponsor, stockist, client list, networks, critic or celebrity.
- Taking a risk with product development, innovation, research and experimentation, requires both time and money to undertake. Making new work or products can pay off in the long term.

Creative services

Fees for provision of design services are charged by an hourly and daily rate – for example, £180 per day, £250 per day, etc. Most freelancers rarely generate income on more than 150 days per year. The example may at first be complicated, and is explained further in Chapter 11, Records, Tax and Basic Bookkeeping.

A simple example 1: A self-employed graphic designer

£200 x 150 days = £30,000

£30,000 minus annual business expenses of £10,000 leaves £20,000 (net profit)

£20,000 minus £14,000 PSB (drawings of £14,000)
    = £6,000 surplus

For readers ready to understand how this is taxed:

Profits of £14,000 drawings plus the £6,000 surplus = £20,000 (net profit)

First £7,475 of profits is income-tax-free (this is your Personal Tax Allowance, PTA).

£20,000 minus £7,475 = £12,525

Income tax at 20% of £12,525 is £2,505

Class 2 National Insurance (NI) £124.80 (£2.40 per week x 52)

Class 4 NI £1,285.65 (9% of profits over £5,715)

(Class 4 NI is worked out by £20,000 minus £5,715 = £14,285.80 9% of £14,285.80 is £1,285.65)

The **total tax liability** on **net profits** of £20,000 is £2,505 (income tax) + £124.80 (C2 NI) + £1,285.65 (C4NI)
    = £3,915.45

This means you will have been able to live on £14,000, and after the income tax is paid you'll have a surplus of £2,084.55. This may be put into a savings account, blown on a few treats, or reinvested in the business.

Creative products

When trying to cost products that you make yourself, you have to take into account there is a limit to how many can be produced in a day, week, month, etc. As well as working out a 'Personal Survival

Budget', materials, labour and other costs have to be factored in. Then you have to think about the price to the customer. Retail pricing can be marked up between 100 and 300% on the trade price. Remember, your profit has to be included in the trade price when taking orders from stores.

The example below is simplified so that you can get the gist of working out very basic costing and pricing.

A simple example 2: A self-employed product maker

100 days a year are spent making products.

On each day five products are made

(it takes over an hour to make each product)

100 days x 5 products = 500 products per year.

The maker's Personal Survival Budget is £14,000 per year.

There are also a number of expenses, materials, electric power, etc.

£14,000 divided by 500 products = £28 each (as a proportion of the PSB)

For each product there is £10 of material/other costs, overheads, etc. (This equates to £5,000 of direct and indirect business costs per year.)

Then we add £12 as a bit of profit factored into the trade price, and to allow for tax payments and other investment, as outlined in the previous example.

Therefore the product's trade price is £50.

It's likely a retailer would sell this product at between £100 and £200.

That means the price on the product maker's website has to be the same as in the shops, if they have stockists.

If the product maker sells all 500 products made in a year, 500 x £50 = £25,000 per year will be generated.

This £25,000 they will use to pay themselves £14,000 (PSB), to cover business expenses of £5,000 spent through the year and tax payments totalling £3,915.45.

(Remember, **total tax liability** on **net profits** of £20,000 is £2,505 + £124.80 + £1,285.65 = £3,915.45)

This is a simplified example to help you understand some elementary principles. It's worth getting used to thinking backwards in pricing. If you only rely on costing products without concern as to what customers are willing to pay, then it doesn't matter how brilliant your product is: if it's unrealistically priced, very few people will buy it.

In the beginning you won't be able to compete on price with established design brands, but to build any manufacturing business it's essential to consider how to make your products within a realistic time and budget.

When you're starting to develop a range of products or a collection it's likely material and other costs will be more expensive than first anticipated. Many designers wish to keep manufacture within the UK. If you are one of them, it can be difficult to fulfil and make profits on substantial orders. If you discover that your products are attracting more interest and have to fulfil larger orders, then outsourcing services or taking on staff is the only option. Otherwise you will continue to run an unprofitable business and struggle with completing orders on time.

However, it is worth mentioning that there are design companies, such as Mathmos®, the lamp-makers, who continue to manufacture in Britain. They brand their boxes with the Union Jack and are very proud of their UK factory. They even have a picture of it on their packaging!

Licensing copyright, design right, trademarks and patents

Detailed guidance about licensing can be gleaned from patent/IP solicitors, industry reports, research published by professional bodies, and online. I highly recommend Simon Stern's book *The Illustrator's Guide to Law and Business Practice* (see Resources at the end of this chapter), which is the best introduction to licensing copyright and contract law for UK creatives that has ever been written. Although his book is designed for illustrators, it's suitable for most artists and designers.

For further information about licensing rights please read Chapter 9, Creative Crimes, and Chapter 10, Confidence and Negotiation Tactics.

The illustrator and cooker of fish fingers

Tim Bradford

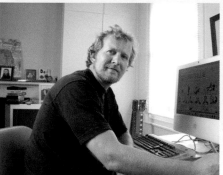

Tim Bradford is a British author and editorial illustrator. He studied English and Film at the University of East Anglia. After graduating he worked in various jobs including copywriting, surveying and as a picture librarian.

Tim's freelance career took off when he started contributing words and pictures to *When Saturday Comes* magazine. He also worked as a technical writer for *Amateur Photographer* magazine.

Over the last 15 years he's published several books and had cartoons commissioned by the *Observer* and *Guardian* newspapers. Now married with three children, he juggles his work with childcare duties.

You can view Tim's trajectory at www.timbradford.com

His five essential tips are:

1. Go for one big goal at a time

Avoid the mistake of trying to do too much in a day. This can leave you feeling that you haven't achieved enough. Decide what each day will be about, and then throw yourself into that job.

2. Plan ahead

If time is tight you need to take a long-term approach to personal projects if they're ever to come to fruition. The Japanese idea of *kaizen* – daily actions allowing an incremental movement towards the completion of each project – can be a valuable tool.

3. Seek down time

As effectively a part-time worker I sometimes feel that I should be working every spare minute of the day. This is wrong. It's necessary once in a while to leave your desk and get out – to a gallery or a café or just for a long walk. It will clear your head, slow down your perception of time, and help you achieve a better work/life balance.

4. Just say yes

I don't have much spare time for voluntary work. Therefore my approach is to help out good causes by illustrating posters and leaflets. Doing a couple of hours a month for other people is a chance to experiment and hone skills.

5. Get over your hatred of networking

Some illustrators dread the thought of hanging out with a load of media types in trendy bars. Luckily the reality is more enjoyable – a chance to discuss each other's work and throw ideas around.

And finally, don't burn the fish fingers! Put them in the middle of the grill so they don't cook too quickly. Kids hate fish fingers if they're too hard and crispy. Always have a guitar handy as a way of defusing disputes!

A COSTING AND PRICING QUIZ!

1. What is an acceptable daily rate for artists?

2. For designer-makers, what is the most popular price range for their products?

3. What is a freelance photographer's daily rate working for a national magazine?

4. What is the national average daily rate paid to creative freelancers in the UK?

5. What is the average salary for a junior designer in London and what is it outside London?

6. What is the hourly freelance rate charged by a senior artworker inside London and what is it outside London?

7. What do freelance illustrators charge for a book jacket for a mass-market fiction paperback, commissioned by a major UK publisher?

8. What's the recommended hourly rate for a freelance graphic designer?

9. What are the hourly PAYE rates for lecturers working in adult, further and higher education?

10. What is the UK national minimum hourly wage if you are 22 years of age or over?

RESOURCES

For information about fees please view industry reports listed at the end of Chapter 1 and contact your professional body.

National Union of Students
If you are a student or subscribe to an industry periodical, make the most of the discounts open to you.
www.nus.org.uk

Money management

The Financial Services Authority (FSA)
Free money management online calculators and advice
www.moneymadeclear.org.uk

Other useful money advice websites:
www.bbc.co.uk/moneybox
www.guardian.co.uk/money

Budget and savings advice

www.confused.com
www.gocompare.com
www.moneysavingexpert.com
www.moneysupermarket.com

Pricing and fees

Artnet, www.artnet.com (prices and art auction news)

Art Monthly (periodical), www.artmonthly.co.uk (regular features about art auctions; salerooms)

There are many online blogs, noticeboards and forums where artists and designers discuss what to charge.
www.a-n.co.uk
www.theaoi.com
www.creativereview.co.uk/cr-blog

www.graphicdesignforums.co.uk
www.skillset.org
www.videoforums.co.uk

Pensions

www.thepensionservice.gov.uk

Debt

Consumer Credit Counselling Service, Tel: 0800 1381111

National Debt Line, Tel: 0808 808 4000, www.nationaldebtline.co.uk

Manufacture

www.alibaba.com

Manufacturing Advisory Service, www.mas.bis.gov.uk

Mike Smith Studio, www.mikesmithstudio.com (design and fabrication service)

Books

Finance on a Beermat, Stephen King, Jeff Macklin and Chris West (London: Random House)

The Illustrator's Guide to Law and Business Practice, Simon Stern (London: The AOI)

Making it, Chris Lefteri (London: Laurence King)

Manufacturing Processes for Design Professionals, Rob Thompson (London: Thames and Hudson)

Entrepreneurship, Creativity and Organisation: Text, Cases and Readings, John K. Kao (New Jersey: Prentice Hall)

Please note that details of tax rates and allowances given in this chapter are subject to change. Please visit www.taxbydesign.com for the latest rates.

5

Business Planning

> 'I had reservations about making art a business, but I got over it.'
>
> *Mary Boone (1951–), New York art dealer*

Before starting a business it's advisable to think carefully about what you wish to achieve – as you can see from 'A simple plan for self-employment' (see pages 82–3), mind mapping is a useful tool to aid memory and clarify your thoughts. This mind map divides research activities into four themes; exploring market demand, self-promotion, money management, and legal issues.

The importance of business names

> 'It's worth remembering that you will have to live with your chosen name for a long time. Also, in years to come you might change the nature of your business so you don't want to be saddled with a name that is inappropriate.'
>
> *Adrian Shaughnessy (1953–), designer and writer*

Before picking up a pen, an important decision to make is whether to trade under your 'own name' or a 'business name'. The regulations concerning business, company names and trademarks are complicated and often misunderstood.

If you're trading under your 'own name' – for example, Alison Branagan – that's usually fine. However, if you wished to trade and happened to be called Damien Hirst, Vivienne Westwood or Pablo Picasso, I would consult with an intellectual property solicitor.

A 'business name' is anything else, e.g. Alison Branagan Studio, Branagan Design, Super Pink Fashions, Big Elephant Productions,

Blanks Gallery, etc. If you are thinking up your business name, I would suggest viewing the www.start.biz website. Start.biz is an easy-to-use business name search engine.

Maker's mark

Before we go on, let's discuss the important matter of the maker's mark.

Artists, designers and craftspeople have always marked their work with a signature, monogram or symbol, whether by a paintbrush, pen, pencil, stitch, ceramic transfer, engraving tool, punch or stamp. Film-makers' names are usually included in credits at the beginning and end of a film, while present-day commercial creatives often encrypt their artwork with a digital signature.

Your signature is an asset. If the auction house can't tell who made the work, then the artists, printmakers and sculptors concerned won't benefit from resale rights.

Orphan works

At the time of writing, newly proposed legislation by the US Copyright Office would make it possible for any US citizen to reproduce artworks by living artists, photographers and illustrators who can't be identified or traced. This is known as the 'Orphan Works Bill/Act'. If this legislation is passed by the US Senate then creators from around the world could find their copyrighted works being commercially exploited without their permission.

At the time of writing in the UK you can't just go about copying artists' work, as permission has to be sought from the copyright holder, who is usually still the author or creator provided they haven't assigned their rights to others.

It's vital to make sure artworks, photographs and illustrations are attributed to the artist, possibly dated and including a signature, initials or monogram on the front or back of the physical work. Sometimes painters sign the stretcher but not the canvas. It's worth considering the possibility that, after being sold, canvases or even framed prints are often re-mounted.

Illustrators should always request a credit next to any reproduced work. It's also advisable to include a statement on any website along the lines of 'All artwork is copyright of the artist and may not be reproduced without permission.'

Maker's mark and hallmarks

UK jewellers and silversmiths must register at an assay office and purchase a maker's mark in the form of a steel punch (or software for applying marks with a laser). The Assay Office has branches in London, Birmingham, Sheffield and Edinburgh.

A hallmark is a combination of the maker's mark, a metal fineness number and an Assay Office mark. Other optional marks include the traditional fineness symbol and date mark. Unless specifically exempted, all gold, silver and platinum articles offered for sale in the UK must be hallmarked.

Growth of the trademark

Artists' and designers' names and their signatures can be trademarks. Damien Hirst has registered a trademark of his name in a zillion categories. Picasso's name and signature is also registered. If you're a fashion designer, it is fundamental that you trademark your own name, signature or business name (as it appears on the label!). Stella McCartney has a trademark of her name as a graphic interpretation, whereas Zandra Rhodes has a register of her signature.

It's worth noting that you can only fully protect a business, company or domain name by registering the business name, signature, logo or image with the Intellectual Property Office as a trademark.

Domain names

Before deciding on and buying a web domain name such as .co.uk, .com or .net, it's a good idea to check that the name is not already a registered company or trademark by consulting www.start.biz or www.uktrademarkregistration.com

The selection of an easy-to-remember domain name, business name and eye-catching branding are important matters to get right. If you decide to trademark your own name or business name, understanding the following is crucial.

Before registering a UK-based business with HMRC, make some checks

When registering as self-employed or as a partnership with HM Revenue and Customs (HMRC), it's worth understanding that they don't check your business-name registration with Companies House or the trademark register. It's vital when you research a business name that it is not already trading as a business, whether locally or elsewhere in the UK, or registered as a limited company.

What's the big deal about using a name already in use?

It would be foolhardy to trade under the same business name as a local or well-established art or design business. It will cause confusion in the marketplace. The other trader may sue you under copyright law for 'passing off' your business as theirs. The date that you register a business name with HMRC is the date it is officially in use.

Registering as self-employed with the same business name as a currently registered limited company could similarly be a disaster. A company name is a separate right, though a registered company can sue a sole trader with the same business name if the company has registered their name with Companies House even if the sole trader has registered as self-employed with HMRC. The company will have a right to sue if there is any risk of confusion between the recently established business's name and their own. A risk simply not worth taking.

Additional checks must be made with the trademark register to determine that your business name is not already registered in exactly the same categories of goods and services as that of another business – for example, don't set up a fashion label with the name 'Gap'!

UK company names registered with Companies House

If you're planning to use your business name as part of the name of a limited company, you should be aware that Companies House do not make any checks to see if a proposed name is already a registered trademark. It's especially important that you avoid setting up a company with the same name as a currently registered trademark. Trademark owners, if they spot a company registered with the same name, can within one year after the date of a company registration, via Companies House, request the company changes their name. Refusal will result in legal action being brought against the new company. Even after that date they still have a right to challenge your use of the name.

Registered trademarks with the UK Intellectual Property Office

Nowadays it's advisable for artists and designers who wish to trade either under their 'own name' or a 'business name' to try to gain registration of the name and any branding, text stylisation or logo associated with it at the earliest possible date.

I have met many commercial creatives, designers and designer-makers who decided to put off protecting their business identity because of the expense. In this world it is far better to struggle to pay for a business or brand name to be protected by a trademark early on, rather than lose your rights to protect and exploit a name. A trademark is king – that's all you have to remember.

If trademark registration fails, which can happen for all kinds of reasons, it's likely you can continue to trade using ™ (trademark). Most businesses use ™ whilst waiting for registration to come through, or if the name has been rejected for registration, or use ™ if they can't be bothered to register their name. Only when you have registered a trademark can you legally use the ® and then stop using ™.

More about registering a trademark is covered in Chapter 9, Creative Crimes.

Why do I need a business plan?

'Having a business plan is essential when applying for loans or funding. It's also an invaluable tool for focusing your mind on important issues before plunging in.'

Barclay Price (1945–), author and Director of Arts & Business Scotland

It's foolish for anyone to start a business without first learning how their ideas can be turned into a profitable enterprise. Many artists and designers have never written a formal business plan.

It's worth considering that without an understanding of the basics of money management, legal matters and marketing, you will falter at some point. Many creatives would actually be financially better off if they were able to analyse and map their progress.

A business plan demonstrates to yourself and to others both market demand and financial viability. Writing a plan will help you understand what you are doing, and it is helpful when seeking advice to have a document which summarises your intentions. But if writing a formal plan doesn't appeal to you, then start by sketching a mind map to help you make an action plan.

Starting any type of business is a risk and it may not succeed. To minimise the chances of failure it is essential to undertake business planning and gain feedback on your proposals.

The first thing when developing any kind of project or venture is to invest in an A1 year planner. This will help in organising and prioritising tasks.

Overview of how to write a business plan

'My father's business expanded more quickly than his working capital. One Christmas Eve, as I was told, certain payments due did not mature, and he found himself unable to pay his men's wages.'

From The Village Carpenter (1937) by Walter Rose (1871–1960)

This quotation underlines the problems that can occur in business. Business planning and regularly reviewing a cash-flow forecast can help raise your awareness of risk. Reflecting on your plans will help you prepare for such difficulties through the devising of a contingency plan. This chapter provides you with a template to help you structure a business plan. Many creative people find it difficult to put things into words. This must be overcome if progress is to be made.

Remember, businesses can focus upon selling a range of products and services, or have a number of income streams from several activities, e.g. commercial design projects, commissions, royalties, licensing rights, teaching, private tuition, residencies, project management, consultancy, etc.

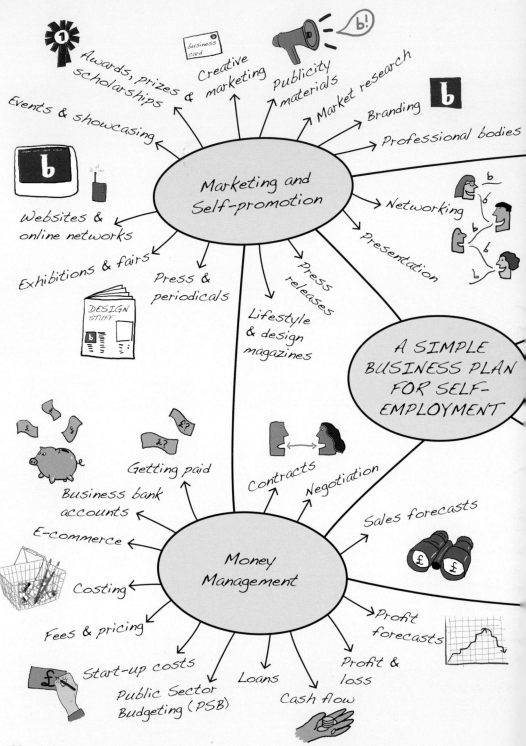

Awards, prizes & scholarships

Creative marketing

Publicity materials

Market research

Branding

Professional bodies

Events & showcasing

Networking

Presentation

Websites & online networks

Exhibitions & fairs

DESIGN STUFF

Press & periodicals

Press releases

Lifestyle & design magazines

Marketing and Self-promotion

A SIMPLE BUSINESS PLAN FOR SELF-EMPLOYMENT

Getting paid

Business bank accounts

E-commerce

Costing

Fees & pricing

Start-up costs

Public Sector Budgeting (PSB)

Contracts

Negotiation

Sales forecasts

Profit forecasts

Loans

Profit & loss

Cash flow

Money Management

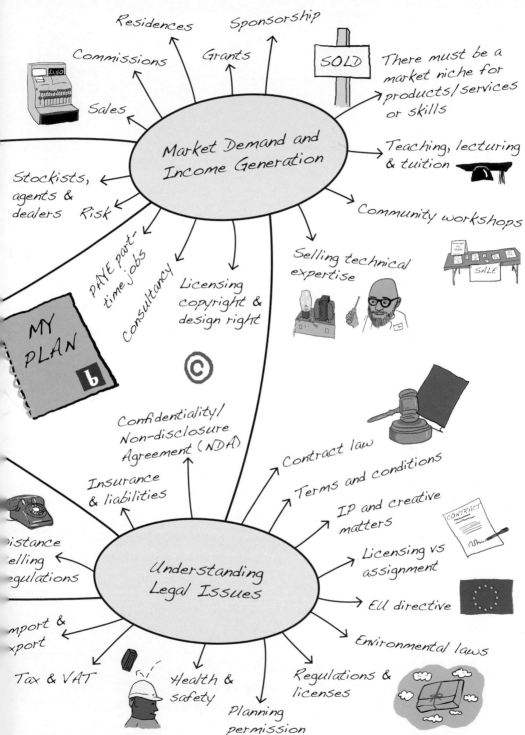

Market Demand and Income Generation

Residences

Sponsorship

Commissions

Grants

Sales

SOLD

There must be a market niche for products/services or skills

Stockists, agents & dealers

Risk

Teaching, lecturing & tuition

Community workshops

PAYE part-time jobs

Consultancy

Licensing copyright & design right

Selling technical expertise

MY PLAN

Understanding Legal Issues

Confidentiality/ Non-disclosure Agreement (NDA)

Insurance & liabilities

Contract law

Terms and conditions

IP and creative matters

Licensing vs assignment

EU directive

Environmental laws

Distance selling regulations

Import & export

Tax & VAT

Health & safety

Regulations & licenses

Planning permission

83

Business structure/name/description

The plan should state:

- Your own name or a business name
- Whether you are a sole trader, a partnership or a company
- What you are, e.g. artist, animator, fashion designer, etc.

Address

Write down your business address, which you plan to, or have already, registered with HMRC or Companies House. This could be your home, shop, office, studio or workshop.

Summary

Outline the proposed venture, how much finance has to be raised and how you propose to do this. Though this appears as the first heading in the plan, it's actually the last to be written – after the whole plan has been thought through. It's at this point that you should mention any major risks and how they can be minimised.

Aims and objectives

These will depend on what the venture is, but, for example, for self-employment as a 'sole trader' you will need to outline short-term (first few months), medium-term (next few years) and long-term (five–ten years) objectives. Set realistic targets. Many business training courses follow the SMART formula – specific, measurable, achievable, realistic, timed/targeted – when setting goals.

Full description of products and services

List the creative products to be sold and the services provided. Write a simple overview. Avoid too much detail; including photographs or images could be useful.

Product and service development plans

Summarise development plans for your business or project. These could include:

- How products will be sold and distributed
- Any plans you have to set up an e-commerce website
- Outlining further skills or training that may be necessary

- Describing any courses that could be completed before the business is set up
- Any planned expansion of the business premises or product range, etc.

People
Write a few sentences about who is involved in the project and what roles they play.

Legal matters and regulations
Outline the key legal matters concerning your business. These could include:
- Health and Safety at Work Act 1974 and revisions
- Terms and conditions
- Contracts, order forms, licensing agreements, etc.
- Copyright and design right, trademarks, patents
- Fibre-content labelling
- Distance-selling regulations
- Product and public-liability insurances, professional indemnity, etc.

SWOT box
Take stock of your strengths, weaknesses, opportunities and threats. (Remember, the person who reads your plan may be unfamiliar with the context of your business idea.) Develop an action plan showing how you intend to build on strengths and opportunities by combating threats and weaknesses.

Timescale
Explain how long the project will take. You may wish to make a plan showing, for example, what is happening, as well as when and where.

Premises
A short description is required about where the business is located and in what type of venue, e.g. business-incubation centre, office, studio, retail unit, home, etc. You may wish to rent business premises. If so, outline the pros and cons of doing so.

Resources and equipment

Outline the resources and equipment you have, then list what has to be rented, borrowed or purchased.

Market

Provide a brief overview of your industry sector. Include various market segments within the industry, with a particular focus on how they could impact on your business. Be sure to include any new products or other developments that could benefit or damage your business prospects.

Identify the competition. Indicate how your unique selling point (USP) will differentiate you from them. Define who your customers are – there may be several categories: individuals, buyers, audiences, readership, clients, collectors, agencies and other businesses.

Here are a few pointers:

- Location/occupation – outlining where customers and clients live or work
- Income – how much they are likely to spend – as well as their age, gender, lifestyle and interests
- Other creative businesses you could supply
- Arts organisations, schools and colleges that might require your services.

Trends and fashions

Write a few lines about any research supporting your plan, such as information about colours, textures, materials, shapes, technology and innovation.

Marketing plan

Describe your marketing and self-promotion strategies. Outline what is special about your enterprise by comparison with others. Include the following, if appropriate:

- Image, styling and brand identity
- Website, business cards and stationery
- Brochures, flyers or catalogues
- Databases
- Mail-outs, leaflet drops, posters, etc.
- Private views or trade fairs

- Publicity stunts
- Advertising
- Presentation packs
- Networking.

Costing and pricing

Outline how costs, fees, quotes, prices and profit margins will be calculated.

Finance

State in the plan how much money you have to invest in the business and where the rest is coming from. Any calculations must show whether borrowing money is required and how it will be paid back.

Other financial information

- Application for grants
- Offers of sponsorship
- Personal survival budget/drawings
- Start-up costs
- Cash-flow and profit forecasts for the first year
- Sales forecasts
- Profit and loss forecasts for the first year
- Other sources of income, e.g. part-time job, bank of mum and dad, tax credits, etc.

Confidentiality

If your business plan contains commercially sensitive ideas or other information relating to patents or design-right issues, ask readers to sign a confidentiality agreement.

For more information about business planning, see the resources at the end of this chapter or pick up a business planning guide from any high-street bank.

Cash flow

As this book is an introduction to business start-up we will only focus on the basics of financial planning, in the form of cash flow. A cash-flow forecast is based on a mix of research and guesswork.

A Beginner's CASH-FLOW FORECAST

	Pre Start £	April £	May £	June £	July £	August £	September £	October £	November £	December £	January £	February £	March £	Total £
OPENING CASH BALANCE		1,240	1,080	1,370	1,660	2,750	3,590	3,530	2,550	3,220	2,590	1,970	2,650	
CASH IN														
Sales		200	400	400	600	800			1,400	400	900	800	600	6,500
Workshops		200		200	400	1,000	400		400	200		400	400	3,600
Other project work/commissions					800		1,000	600		300		1,000	2,000	5,700
Owner's capital	2,500								500					3,000
Bank loan	2,500													2,500
Grant	500													500
Other														
TOTAL CASH IN	5,500	400	400	600	1,800	1,800	1,400	600	2,300	900	900	2,200	3,000	21,800
CASH OUT														
Purchases/materials		50	50	50	50	100	100	150	200	100	100	100	100	1,150
Premises (rent, rates, light, heat)														–
Telephone	100	50	50	50	50	50	50	50	50	50	40	40	1	631
Insurance	150													150
Equipment	1,000													1,000
Professional bodies/business advice		200				100	100						250	650
Stationery		250												250
Website, internet & general marketing	1,970													1,970
Software	1,030													1,030
Art & design periodicals	10	10	10	10	10	10	10	10	10	10	10	10	10	130
Other –														–
Other –														–
OPERATING EXPENSES SUBTOTAL	4,260	560	110	110	110	260	260	210	260	160	150	150	361	6,961
Equipment & other capital expenditure														–
Loan & financing repayments				200	200	200	200	200	200	200	200	200	200	2,000
Owner's drawings					400	500	1,000	1,170	1,170	1,170	1,170	1,170	1,170	8,920
TOTAL CASH OUT	4,260	560	110	310	710	960	1,460	1,580	1,630	1,530	1,520	1,520	1,731	17,881
NET CASH FLOW FOR PERIOD	1,240	(160)	290	290	1,090	840	(60)	(980)	670	(630)	(620)	680	1,270	3,920
CLOSING CASH BALANCE	1,240	1,080	1,370	1,660	2,750	3,590	2,550	2,550	3,220	2,590	1,970	2,650	3,920	3,920

Example of a cash-flow forecast. Available on request from www.taxbydesign.com

It's a method of predicting when money is due to flow into your business account and out again.

Cash out

To start with, draft out start-up and ongoing expenses for the year ahead. This can be difficult but you must try. From your research you know roughly what your start-up costs will be. You can estimate on a monthly basis what you'll need to 'draw' from the business to live on. Other 'cash out' expenses such as travel and mobile-phone usage can also be entered across the year.

A beginner's cash-flow forecast, for example, shows that in the first few months she's still in full-time work and is running the business in her spare time. You can see her 'drawings' gradually increase as the year goes by after she switches to part-time work.

Cash in

After drafting a guesstimate of expenses, you'll find the software will add up the figures and show you monthly and annual running costs. Then turn your attention to income, i.e. 'cash in'. Enter any grants, loans or savings coming into your business account. Consider how much monthly income has to be generated to cover monthly outgoings. Set yourself some targets. This may appear complicated at first, but you have to give it a go!

Why is cash flow important?

All financial plans start with a bit of guesswork. It's a matter of regularly revisiting your cash-flow forecasts – especially in the first two years of trading – making revisions and calculating more accurate forecasts. Failure to master the art of managing cash flow can lead to financial problems similar to those of Walter Rose's father, who found he was unable to pay his suppliers and himself.

Big payments in six months' time are meaningless if you don't have enough cash coming in to keep going. Imagine money is fuel. You need fuel to keep your business operating – without regular supplies, at some point it will simply conk out. Keeping an eye on your cash flow will help you foresee such problems, giving you time to take preventative steps such as staggering large payments, giving yourself a temporary pay cut, or asking for more money up front.

Cash-flow software can be downloaded from the internet for free, and can also be provided by an accountant or bank. I would advise before starting your business that you attend an introductory workshop on financial planning at a local college or enterprise agency.

RESOURCES

Please note previous organisations and websites listed. For more industry information contact your professional body. Many art and design associations offer publications and workshops that are available to non-members. Please check the Useful Organisations section at the end of this book.

Lawyers for your business

A scheme to give businesses a free half-hour with a solicitor.
www.lawsociety.org.uk

Hallmarking

Birmingham/London/Sheffield Assay Office, www.theassayoffice.co.uk

British Hallmarking Council, www.britishhallmarkingcouncil.gov.uk

Edinburgh Assay Office, www.assayofficescotland.com

The Goldsmith's Company, www.thegoldsmiths.co.uk

UK Guidance leaflets

Company Names GBF/2
Business Names GBF/3
www.companieshouse.gov.uk

Trademarks

Intellectual Property Office, www.ipo.gov.uk (free trademark search but complicated)

National Business Register, www.start.biz (easy-to-use search engine)

UK Trade Mark Registration, www.uktrademarkregistration.com (free trademark search engine)

Advice

For free business events visit: www.bstartup.com

Sources of professional advice:

Federation of Small Businesses, www.fsb.org.uk (membership organisation providing legal and tax advice)

British Library, www.bl.uk. Most towns and cities have a local or regional business library; contact your local authority for details.

Chartered Institute of Marketing, www.cim.co.uk

Chartered Institute of Public Relations, www.cipr.co.uk

Institute of Practitioners in Advertising, www.ipa.co.uk (for agencies only, not individuals)

Institute of Business Consultants, www.ibconsulting.org.uk

National Federation of Artists' Studio Providers, www.nfasp.org.uk

Royal Institute of Chartered Surveyors, www.rics.org (provides useful information online about taking on commercial property)

Books

Intellectual Property Law (Law Masters Series), Tina Hart, Linda Fazzini and Simon Clark (Hampshire: Palgrave Macmillan)

The Mind Map Book, Tony Buzan and Barry Buzan (Essex: BBC Active)

Starting a Business from Home: Choosing a Business, Getting Online, Reaching Your Market and Making a Profit, Colin Barrow (London: Kogan Page)

The Financial Times Guide to Business Start Up 2011, Sara Williams (Harlow: Prentice Hall)

6

Building Networks

> 'If I myself and several friends didn't starve to death in London, it was thanks to Daubigny.'
>
> *Claude Monet (1840–1926), artist*

This is Monet's acknowledgement of the help that artist Charles-François Daubigny gave him, for it was he who had helpfully introduced Monet and Pissarro to his art dealer Paul Durand-Ruel, thus rescuing them from destitution.

Networking isn't the modern activity we think it is. It's vital for emerging artists and designers to step out of their comfort zone, for example, if you're currently a second or even third-year student, I would urge you to make contact with local artists, designers, other creative businesses and more established figures within the arts. The earlier relationships are formed within your industry, the better.

The artist-entrepreneur Damien Hirst spent several years single-mindedly going to London parties and private views. Of course, this approach to profile-raising may not suit everyone, but there's a lot of truth in the art director Paul Arden's assertion that 'It's not what you know, it's who you know'. I've had students walk out of my lectures in the past, believing that it's their creative talent alone that will bring them fame and fortune. It isn't. Success is achieved by meeting the right people at the right time, and being championed by particular people of influence. Your own talent and ability are only part of the equation.

This chapter covers how to start making paper business plans a reality, by actually going out and meeting potential collectors, clients and customers.

The importance of networking

> 'Eight percent of success is turning up.'
> *Woody Allen (1935–), comedian, actor, writer, film director*

If you are a student, after degree shows have been taken down, it can be an extremely strange time. What will you do next?

- Do you stay in the city where you trained?
- Return home?
- Go to live in London, New York, Paris or another major international city?
- Try to find work?

Most people who study in a major cultural centre like London usually stay there. It's often said that over 50% of all UK artists and designers live in London or the South-east of England. In a recent national UK survey of fees and salaries by *Creative Review*, over 80% of the respondents lived in London.

It's difficult to move to a new town or city, especially if you don't have any relatives based there. It's easy to become isolated without friends or contacts. This is why it's vital to maintain some form of relationship with your current friends. If you're taking the bold step of moving to a new town, then make new friends by attending evening courses, or joining local business or art clubs.

Networking

Wherever you decide to live, the capital city can't be ignored. With the advancement of email and e-networks it's possible to maintain and develop relationships with people from around the world without much effort. However, the virtual world will never replace the benefits to be gained in the physical one.

There are relatively few occasions when the opportunity arises to meet established artists and designers. There may be only an odd moment to catch a potential contact's attention. Therefore be prepared before visiting any fair, expo, private view or conference.

SOME TIPS

Don't...

- ignore people at any social, educational or business function. Try to pluck up the courage to start a conversation.
- get drunk at your degree show or other business networking opportunities.
- turn up drunk either.
- bring strange acquaintances to prestigious events. They may become a distraction.
- cling to walls hoping people will make their way over.
- stuff your business cards in purses or wallets. Dog-eared, bent cards will do you no favours.
- waffle on and on about yourself.
- hog people for ages and ages.

Do...

- make an attempt during and after graduation to attend events.
- go to events and meet new people regularly.
- get your hair done, brush your teeth and take mints to keep your breath fresh.
- smile and ask people about themselves.
- have business cards, in a metal or plastic card holder.
- have images of artwork and products stored in your phone, iPod or in a pocket-sized A5 portfolio in your bag.
- move on tactfully from one person or group to another.
- write notes on people's business cards as an aide-memoire.
- follow up important offers with an email.
- if someone expresses the desire to see more of your work, phone them up after a day or so to arrange an appointment. You may have the opportunity to invite them to your forthcoming exhibition or studio event. But avoid phoning on Monday mornings and Friday afternoons.

How to navigate networks

'He didn't get in with the right people. He missed the wave.'
Billy Childish (AKA Steven Hamper; 1959–), artist (Stuckist)

These are Billy Childish's comments about his brother Nick Hamper's lack of attention from the art world. Childish has achieved worldwide notoriety though he never acquired any qualifications in art. In contrast his brother studied for many years at both the Slade and the Royal College of Art.

Unfortunately, this is a huge problem in the art and design world. I've met many artists and designers who are brilliant, yet they struggle to survive financially. It often isn't made clear during someone's student years how important it is to connect with others, in particular to join or start an influential movement or collective, as Childish did.

If you honestly believe your creative artwork and products are just as good as those getting all the attention, then remember there's a lot of luck and perseverance involved. When developing any arts practice or creative business you should try to obtain constructive criticism about your work from those more established than yourself. No artist or designer became successful without listening to others and adapting their work in relation to feedback.

Other barriers to progress may be the failure to gain a lucky break, or not having the confidence to knock on some doors.

Engage with others

What I have noticed over the last ten years is a dramatic deterioration in the art of conversation. For instance, when creatives arrive for my evening classes they usually make no effort to speak to the person next to them. The whole group just sits there in silence as we wait for everyone to arrive. I always try to stimulate a bit of a chat, to encourage interaction.

This recent phenomenon might have something to do with the growth of communication by email and the internet. Working alone as they do, artists and designers can become used to being quiet. It's worth remembering that quiet people tend not to get very far in the arts or business world. Being able to engage and build rapport with others is essential: talk to people in the queue in the art shop, anywhere, everywhere.

The psychologist Prof. Richard Wiseman, in his books *The Luck Factor* and *Did You Spot the Gorilla?* has proved that being more relaxed and willing to engage people in conversation improves the chances of success.

A photography student who had a job in a famous watch shop in London took on my advice about opening up a bit. When he chatted more to the customers, rather than just selling watches, he found many of them hired photographers regularly and collected photographs! Wherever you are in your career, try to engage with people – you never know what will come of it!

How to connect

When I came to London it took me a while to realise that I wasn't going to succeed in gaining stable representation from a gallery, so I began to approach hundreds of organisations and enter competitions. What I didn't know at the time was that my presentation wasn't good enough. However, despite this, I would say that from 100 cold calls on the telephone, I had three positive responses which generated a couple of thousand pounds in work and sales, though what I really needed were introductions to industry contacts. The problem at the time was that I didn't know who they were.

GETTING IT RIGHT WITH EMAIL

- It's essential these days to have an email account.
- If you don't have an email account, set up a free one for now, and, as soon as you can afford to, subscribe to broadband with a major ISP – say, Virgin or BT. Sign up for email with Outlook Express or Microsoft email software.
- Free email accounts like Hotmail and Yahoo are useful but they can be unreliable, especially if you don't empty the inbox regularly. Email messages from possibly important contacts or clients can be lost due to full inboxes or a rejected loop. The sender will often not have time to chase up returned/rejected emails.
- Join useful organisations and information services. Most now communicate by email loops or subscription to an e-newsletter.
- If you're a Mac user, always invest in a Mac address.
- Avoid writing emails in 'light-hearted' fonts, such as Comic Sans, or with the 'caps lock' button on, and make sure emails are spellchecked.
- Compose a professional signature and insert into all outgoing emails. Include address, postcode, telephone number, website or other web presences.

A common error

I have encountered a great deal of stubbornness from artists and designers about giving up free internet webmail accounts. Believe me, they do you no favours. This kind of solely web-based communication, printed on business cards with a mobile telephone number as the only contact number, give the impression of transience. Hotmail-type addresses are OK for private use. However, oddball email addresses don't build trust or convey a professional image. It's important when moving to the business realm to take yourself seriously and create a professional-looking email address.

A Beginner
Artist

fluffylovepuff21@hotmail.co.uk
07941 74262

Does this look like the business card of a professional artist?

Your networks are developing now

The Creative Networks mind map (see pages 100–101), shows how art schools, professional bodies, art and design periodicals, shops, galleries, studios, clubs and agents are interrelated.

If you are at art college, your art tutors will know influential people in the art and commercial worlds, such as art dealers, directors and critics. Try not to fall out with lecturers or any technicians (especially technicians!), as word of mouth is the most likely method of securing opportunities.

Identify key players

Undertake research in your field. Find out who the agents, agencies, dealers, art directors, buyers, critics, journalists and stylists are and how to make contact with them. If you don't know who they are, how can you make progress?

It can be useful to gain work experience by being an assistant to established artists and designers in their studios, fashion houses or companies. As mentioned earlier, however, avoid being taken advantage of.

What you have to do is find ways of courting interest from people who could help your career or give exposure to your products.

Get yourself invited

Try to get yourself on as many directories, email loops and mailing lists as you can. If you're not on the invitation list then perhaps just gatecrash events. This sometimes doesn't work for ticketed events or for venues that are security-conscious. However, sometimes you have to take a risk and blag your way in!

Get an introduction

Try to get an introduction either at actual events or via an email sent by a colleague, tutor or friend. It's easier to get on people's radar if you are endorsed by someone they know well or respect. We will be covering more about this topic in Chapter 10, Confidence and Negotiation Tactics.

Pubs and private clubs

One must not underestimate the power of socialising with people, wherever this may be. Private clubs in London such as the Groucho, the Hospital, the ICA, the Dover Arts Club and the Chelsea Arts Club are where many opportunities are found. These organisations can be very expensive and difficult to join, but it can be worth it if you can manage it. Around the world there are cafés, bars and pubs which artists and designers frequent, and these can be another way of meeting like-minded people.

Professional associations or bodies

Sometimes it's a matter of what you can do for a membership body more than what it can do for you.

Many students are disappointed when they join a professional body as they may have an unrealistic view of its purpose. Associations can be expensive and will not solve all of your problems or act as a magic gateway to success. They exist to support creative businesses and practitioners.

Make the best use of the organisation's website. Often as part of your membership you receive a directory listing or portfolio page. Professional bodies like the Association of Illustrators or the Association of Photographers have email news alerts, newsletters, guidance on legal matters, training, workshops, e-chat rooms, opportunities and sponsor competitions. Virtually every arts professional body is a not-for-profit affair, so they often rely on membership fees, sales of guides, selling tickets to workshops, and grants.

It's also good to consider the benefits of belonging and contributing to a body with a brilliant network of members. Perhaps put yourself up for election to the board of trustees, or offer to run a workshop, or submit a short article to its magazine.

You're not obliged in the UK visual-art sector to be a member of an organisation if you don't wish to be. However, I thoroughly recommend joining at least one professional organisation which represents your discipline or area of trade, at least during the early years after graduation. Being a member is an important step in creating networks. For more information, see the list of professional bodies, many with overseas membership, in the Useful Organisations section at the end of this book.

Private views and networking events

Talking to people at events can be difficult, especially if you're alone and don't know anybody. If possible go to events with a friend. If unaccompanied, it's really a matter of practice to overcome nerves and engage people in conversation. A good way to approach others is when they're looking at a painting or product. Simply ask the viewer what they think, or just make an interesting observation and they will respond.

Business networking

Moving from networking in the art and design sphere to general business networking is to enter a totally different world. In socialising with peers everyone is visually literate as a rule and understands the language, concepts and reference points in

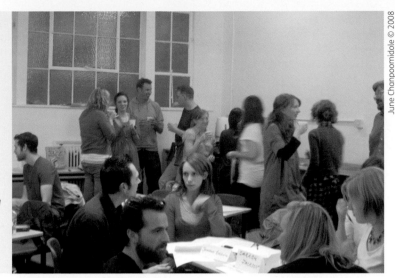

June Chanpoomidole © 2008

Students Networking at an Association of Illustrators Master Class

contemporary art and design practice. In business, this will not be the case.

It's worth considering that many future clients, customers and collectors will be entrepreneurs, small businesses or corporate firms. Some may be local, others based elsewhere in the country or world. Many, but not all of these people, won't respond well to technical design jargon, or dense artistic philosophy or theory. Find a way of speaking about your creative products and services intelligently, without alienating customers by talking over their heads.

Every artist and designer needs the business community. Joining local or regional enterprise networks can be an excellent way to make connections with other businesses.

Expos, workshops and conferences

When you go to such events, whether for a day or several days, it can be an exhausting experience. So make sure your energy levels are high before taking part. If you can't go, for a reasonable fee you might be able to have business flyers included in delegate packs or inserted into guides.

I know a very successful design entrepreneur in London who has built his list of clients and suppliers from visiting, speaking at, advertising and exhibiting his creative products at conferences.

99

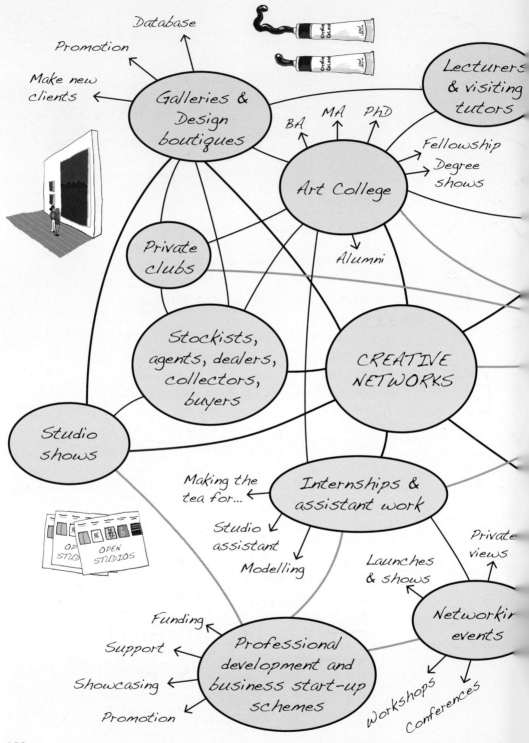

Database

Promotion

Make new clients

Galleries & Design boutiques

Lecturers & visiting tutors

BA MA PhD

Fellowship

Degree shows

Art College

Private clubs

Alumni

Stockists, agents, dealers, collectors, buyers

CREATIVE NETWORKS

Studio shows

Making the tea for...

Studio assistant

Modelling

Internships & assistant work

Private views

Launches & shows

Networking events

OPEN STUDIOS

Funding

Support

Showcasing

Promotion

Professional development and business start-up schemes

Workshops

Conferences

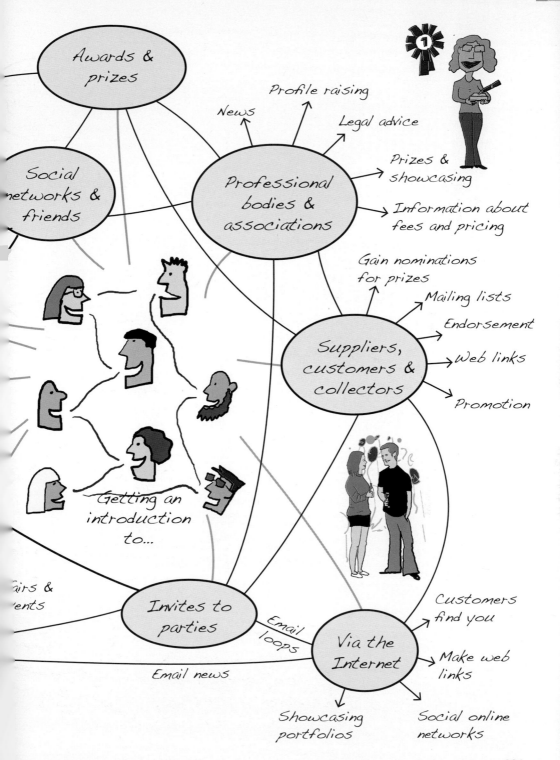

Awards & prizes

Social networks & friends

Professional bodies & associations

Profile raising

News

Legal advice

Prizes & showcasing

Information about fees and pricing

Gain nominations for prizes

Mailing lists

Endorsement

Suppliers, customers & collectors

Web links

Promotion

Getting an introduction to...

Fairs & events

Invites to parties

Email loops

Email news

Via the Internet

Customers find you

Make web links

Showcasing portfolios

Social online networks

Awards

Winning prizes can attract exciting new opportunities and progress your career. However, prestigious and high-profile awards can be very costly to enter. If you've taken part in student awards, have won or been a runner-up, then carry on with this strategy after graduation. Build on this success. Try not to be put off from entering competitions because the entry fees are expensive.

Entering competitions or prizes isn't for everyone, but it can be worth it. To gain attention from potential commissioners or simply to raise your profile you have to take a punt and enter industry awards. To find out more about awards, read your periodicals, check with your professional body, and consult the resources listed in this book.

Magazines

It's essential to subscribe to or borrow several art and design periodicals every month. I would highly recommend, even if you are a student, that you make time to read a number of industry periodicals.

Art-school libraries usually subscribe to a number of magazines and journals. Periodicals are trustworthy sources of information, trends, opportunities and industry developments.

Many artists and designers promote themselves to potential new clients by gaining exposure in editorial features – for example, winning awards, gaining prestigious commissions or launching new products. To find out more about getting free media exposure see the next chapter, Self-promotion.

E-networking and showcasing

> 'The threads of connections run everywhere and to unexpected places.'
>
> *Susan Griffin (1943–), essayist and screenwriter*

Using the internet to network or showcase artwork and products is essential. Speak to any artist or designer over the age of 35 about how life was pre-Photoshop, pre-home printers, pre-digital, pre-scanner, pre-web, and pre-email. To gain any kind of exhibition or opportunity you had to have expensive duplicate 35mm slides made of your work, a carefully typed CV, a statement, price list and covering letter, all weighed at the post office, with an enclosed stamped addressed envelope, so that by law businesses and organisations were obliged to return your precious materials and slides. Such was the expense of it all that artists and designers could only afford to do so much per month.

The 21st-century artist or designer who now seeks attention from a gallery, buyer or client, simply has to include a web link to a showcasing website, or email a PDF portfolio, and that's it. Click Flickr, click Behance, click Coroflot, click Axis to be viewed instantly by anyone in the world. This is a completely different experience from the use of slides and catalogues 20 years ago. It's vital for any older artists and designers who still do not fully engage with the web to get their heads out of the sand and learn about digital technology.

Many women who have taken time out to look after their families return to their practice or creative business to find a new world of presentation and communication that they no longer recognise. The past is well and truly gone, I'm afraid, and the future has to be embraced fully if you are to remain in business.

Communication

It's important to develop a web presence, digital portfolios and market online. At the same time, do continue to phone people and send marketing materials to agents, buyers or clients, and make the effort to go and visit them.

Try not to rely too much on sending unsolicited email. Many agents, dealers, art directors, critics and journalists are snowed under with emails, and often get so busy they will only click on emails they are expecting or those from colleagues or regular clients. They can't cope with the number of emails they receive, so persisting with this approach will only annoy them.

If you still decide to target people by email, phone them up first, to check they would like to receive your images. Make sure JPEG images are low-res, come up quickly, and feature in the body of a very brief email, thus making an immediate impact on the viewer. Always check the agency, business or dealer's websites to see if phoning in is OK – sometimes they only accept enquiries by email.

If approach by phone is acceptable, you will find many deskbound respondents are actually quite relieved when the phone rings, as it gets them away from their computers for a few minutes.

Develop a self-critical eye

A hot topic currently debated in the art and design media is the matter of editorial skills. The reason why I believe editorial skills are declining is, as already mentioned, 20 years ago the preparation of slides to gain opportunities was extremely expensive. Artists and designers had to think long and hard about what to reproduce and why.

Now with the ease and speed of digital technology, creatives are not only able to make and reproduce numerous images at no cost, they can showcase them instantly online. Speedy upload, without proper consideration, can make a creative practice or product range appear weak or confused. Being able to make editorial decisions is vital and demands a period of intelligent contemplation and concentration.

Recently I've met many illustrators and photographers preparing portfolio submissions. They couldn't decide what to leave out. Poor editorial decision-making can give rise to problems during interviews and when working on creative briefs.

A few thoughts

- Think very carefully before putting images online
- Being selective can make a stronger impact
- Make sure all images are of a professional standard
- Check that images relate to one another as a group, body or narrative
- Just because a piece of work is old, doesn't mean it should be dumped
- Remember your images will always be new to the viewer.

Free showcasing

There are so many ways to get your work viewed online for free. It could be argued that having your own domain-named website is now unnecessary. The vast majority of visual artists would agree it's still necessary to have your own website, as you may wish to use it for a number of purposes such as selling products, blogging, and advertising events, as well as protecting your name on the internet.

There are now dozens of social-networking websites, and hundreds of showcasing spaces and online galleries. But you need to think about the following:

- Who is looking at these websites?
- Who judges what is included in the online gallery or portfolio?
- Will you sell anything?
- Is it the right place for you?

At the end of this chapter I have listed some of the key online galleries, agents, e-shops, e-news services, showcasing and portfolio portals which appear to be trusted and well-managed.

Try to showcase your images on high-profile and reputable showcasing or agency websites. Avoid spending time profiling yourself and products on websites which are badly designed and demonstrate no sense of editorial judgement or quality control.

It is also worth bearing in mind that websites like Flickr, Coroflot, Myspace, YouTube, Facebook and Twitter may not always be free.

RESOURCES

Social networking and microblogging websites

If you are a student, before leaving college, or even afterwards, check if there's an alumni network service you can join.

www.facebook.com – achievers

www.twitter.com – microblog

www.flickr.com – images

http://posterous.com

www.creative-enterprise-network.com – all creatives

www.bebo.com – TV, media

www.youtube.com – film

http://shootingpeople.org – film

www.creativeopera.com

www.linkedin.com – professional

www.myspace.com – all

www.sagazone.co.uk – networking for over-fifties

Arts and design email news loops

www.artscouncil.org.uk – arts news and arts jobs

www.artsadmin.co.uk – arts digest

www.creative-capital.org.uk – news

www.artrabbit.com – news

www.creativeboom.co.uk – news and magazine

http://chinwag.com

**Showcasing and web portals
(please note there are crossovers)**

Remember to contact your local council arts officer and regional arts council. They usually have some form of art directory service.

RESOURCES

Arts

To find local art networks:

www.a-n.co.uk (search for the National Artists' Network, NAN)

www.artquest.org.uk (click on Networks)

www.clubbz.com

www.axisweb.org

www.rhizome.org

www.re-title.com

www.midwest.org.uk

www.isendyouthis.com

www.productofgod.net

www.thedigitalartist.com

www.aoiimages.com

www.creativehotlist.com

http://altpick.com

www.folioplanet.com

www.contactacreative.com

www.concretehermit.com

www.illustrationfriday.com

www.theispot.com

www.imagineanimation.net

www.theanimationartgallery.com

www.bbc.co.uk/filmnetwork

www.newwebpick.com

http://ffffound.com

www.chb.com

Design

www.behance.net

www.coroflot.com

www.aquent.co.uk

www.designdirectory.co.uk

www.look4design.co.uk

www.lookupdesign.com

www.creativepool.co.uk

http://designerscouch.org

www.bouf.com

http://mydeco.com

www.seekingdesigners.com

www.hiddenart.com

www.craftscentral.org.uk

www.britishdesign.co.uk

www.archiportale.com

http://designboom.com

Applied arts

www.photostore.org.uk (Crafts Council)

www.designnation.co.uk

www.craftanddesigncouncil.org.uk

www.newdesignersonline.co.uk

www.designshopuk.com

www.gift-library.com

www.britishcrafts.co.uk

www.etsy.com

www.folksy.com

www.misi.co.uk

Business networks

http://aframe.ica.org.uk/index/ (read guidance notes)

www.ecademy.com

www.bni.com

www.prowess.org.uk

www.taforum.org (trade body search)

www.dba.org.uk (Design Business Association)

Books

How to Win Friends and Influence People, Dale Carnegie (London: Vermilion) A classic book about networking, still the best ever written.

Wannabe, Jamie Kennedy (London: Aurum Press) A true story of how an actor became his own agent to gain roles.

The Luck Factor and *Did You Spot the Gorilla?*, Richard Wiseman (London: Arrow Books)

7

Self-promotion

> 'Getting the press to write about a product of their own free will is not like climbing a mountain.'
>
> *Mark Borkowski (1959–), PR guru and author*

Many artists and designers feel uncomfortable about the idea of marketing their work. If this is the case, then I would like the reluctant to accept that 'self-promotion' is simply another creative activity.

In this chapter I'm going to give a structured outline of self-presentation and how to plan a basic media campaign. I will identify which promotional materials are required, when and by whom.

Self-presentation

> 'Sometimes even I think I don't have anything to wear.'
>
> *Vivienne Westwood (1941–), fashion designer*

Appearance and presentation are important. People can make up their mind about someone in just a few seconds. Much of business in all industry sectors is built on trust. Having a professional email, ringing clients, arriving at appointments on time and being reasonably well groomed will increase the likelihood of success even before the first handshake.

A common error

A number of artists and designers suffer from being far too much in the centre of their own universe, often out of synch with the pace of the business world. To participate it's essential to be responsible, to think of others and be able to work with them.

Many artists have difficulty working in teams. This is demonstrated by frequent last-minute cancellations of appointments as 'something better' has come up. It never appears to occur to them that a booking is an agreement.

When making arrangements to meet others, you must be aware that other participants, clients or advisers may have turned down last-minute opportunities to attend. It can be especially annoying to people when informing them of your sudden unavailability by a cursory email. That creates the impression of disorganisation and unreliability. Time is valuable. Wasting other people's time will put them off working with you. It usually contributes to your being quietly dropped.

Body language

Whether making presentations, meeting clients or being interviewed, it's vital to maintain an upright posture. A growing bad habit amongst creatives is adopting slouched standing and sitting positions. This could be a symptom of spending too much time working on laptops, hunched over workbenches or watching television. It's possible to relax either seated or standing with a straight back. Confidence is communicated not just by talking, but also by the way you sit, stand and greet people.

I recall a confidence workshop with a group of children's illustrators, the majority of whom would sit with their feet pushed

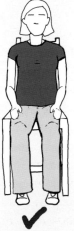 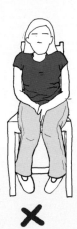

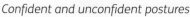

Confident and unconfident postures

back under their chairs, the heels pointing outwards, their toes pointing inwards. Their shoulders were hunched and their hands were either clenched together or pushed in between their thighs. This is almost the posture of a nervous child. Many other postgraduate artists and designers adopt similar poses, especially during interviews.

Such a posture is submissive and looks strange. If you appear stressed during any form of presentation situation, then the client or interviewer will gradually become uncomfortable. This type of body posture is that of an unconfident person. It won't help your gain an opportunity or aid negotiation.

Voice

Developing a creative business or practice in the visual arts does mean attending interviews, giving talks and presentations, and pitching for funding or sponsorship. If you suffer from terrible nerves then I would urge you to attend a public-speaking course or listen to President Barack Obama, whose unhurried delivery lends strength to his words.

A frequent problem among visual artists is that they often speak far too quickly. This is especially the case when they're nervous. This could be due to the fact that they think in images and use more words than are necessary. To maintain this customary speed, they take short, shallow breaths. But it's crucial to slow down so that the listener can absorb what's being said and respond appropriately. Long bursts of rapid speech make it difficult to develop rapport.

For example, when you ring someone up or meet them, don't just say 'Hello' and launch immediately into introducing yourself. Say, 'Hello' and then pause. Let the other person have time to react!

Language

In major UK cities and overseas, English may not be people's first language. In a situation where English is spoken, it can be uncertain whether those who are listening in their second or even third language fully grasp what is going on. They may speak English more fluently than they can understand it. Others can understand English better than they speak it. They may be reluctant to admit that they don't understand what is being said, so you need to encourage interaction to check comprehension.

PRESENTATION TIPS

- Try to keep your back straight and shoulders down.
- Avoid pointing your toes inwards.
- Place your feet about 10 centimetres apart and make sure they are straight and not angular.
- Try not to clench your hands, or force them in between your thighs.
- Maintain eye contact with the whole panel or audience.
- Slow down your speech.
- Pause instead of uttering ums and errs.

Basic publicity materials

'In the future everybody will be famous for 15 minutes.'
Andy Warhol (Andrew Warhola; 1927–1987), artist

Readers of this book may have to undertake regular promotion for all manner of reasons. Some may wish to raise their profile in the media and increase awareness of their creative products and services. Others may focus time and resources promoting a handful of events a year, such as hosting stands at fairs, exhibitions, major product launches or performance events.

The trick with self-promotion is not to rush the development of frontline marketing materials. Many artists and designers tend to focus excessively on the creative process and fail to allow enough time for presentation and advertising. The whole approach to marketing a creative business or practice requires a high level of professionalism. For important shows and events it may be worth hiring in PR expertise.

A key feature of your marketing plan is to identify who your audience is, then decide how to communicate with them. It's easy to make mistakes in promotion. For example, a feature or banner advert in *a-n Magazine* will reach your peers. However, if you're trying to sell products, an approach to the weekend broadsheet supplements – e.g. the *Guardian*, *Telegraph* and *Sunday Times* – will be more appropriate.

The materials included in the marketing checklist (below) may take months or years to assemble in their entirety. You must prepare yourself fully for any engagement with the media. A lack of preparation can ruin any marketing campaign.

Marketing checklist

Photographs
- If possible have them taken by a professional photographer. This is especially important for reproduction in catalogues, on business cards or postcards, and in magazines.
- For web-based images it's possible to use your own photographs. However, there is a limit to how much patching up can be done with Photoshop.
- Have a good-quality portrait head and shoulders shot taken.
- Make sure you also have a stunning, intriguing or dramatic photo of yourself or your creative product, artwork, event or service.
- Include photos of yourself in a studio/workshop space, standing next to your creative products, working at the computer, designing, weaving, painting, etc.
- Include images of recent or important artworks/designs/products, and have these digitally formatted for both print and web quality.
- Have versions in greyscale for tonal print purposes. Some magazines, such as *Art Monthly*, still print in black and white. Marketing materials for large events are often printed in monochrome, e.g. blue, orange, etc.
- Always be selective with photographs.

One-page curriculum vitae or promotional flyer
It's important for artists and designers to have three types of CV: one for employment, one for freelance opportunities, and an edited A4 version for showcasing purposes.

SHOWCASING CV – A FEW TIPS

This type of CV should be used for applying for exhibitions and competitions, and to be available as a PDF on download from your website or email signature.

- Commercial creatives often take a few more risks with their CVs – for example, having them printed on tea towels, embroidered on cushions, or knitted scarves, illustrated on trainers, made into miniature books, etc.
- Take a look in *Creative Review* – they regularly showcase 'self-promotion' items made by designers and illustrators.
- Inject a sense of style and design format into a CV.
- Include clear contact details – your home or studio address and phone numbers. Write a brief profile or statement about your design/artwork/ product or current projects.
- If you're applying for a design job, then a 'mission statement' may be required, but don't include a mission statement on an A4 showcasing CV.
- After any art qualifications, list the awards and prizes you have received, then any exhibitions and commissions.

List the major achievements in sections, with the most recent first.

- If your products are in high-profile stores and collections, or you have worked for high-profile businesses, then include stockists, collections or a client list.
- List web presences and your own website.
- Use strong sharp clear thumbnail images. Be selective – three to five images is enough.
- CVs can be presented in hi-tech acetate wallets or folders.
- You may wish to include on separate sheets, selected quality colour inkjet prints of two to three artworks/ products.
- Alternatively, create an A6, A5 or A4 high-quality profile flyer or leaflet, including portrait photo, profile, micro CV and images of your artwork or products.

Please note that for fine artists, printmakers or sculptors approaching UK galleries, on the whole the convention is not to include images within a CV.

Many creative businesses may wish to move away from 'describing the course of life' and develop stylish brochures or flyers. Commercial creatives usually have a short 'biog' and a few A4 image sheets to send to clients.

Marketing statement

This should be short and sweet, brief and to the point. It sums up (as best you can) what you are doing, why and how, in between 25 and 100 words. Such statements are used for press releases, leaflets, brochures, commercial event listings and for the gallery desk. Concentrate on the relationships between theme, materials, technique and style.

Artist/design statement

A longer and more refined statement, exploring more academic or philosophical themes, e.g. technical aspects, method, issues, ideas, etc. It considers creative strategies – that is to say, the relationship between form and content (artists) or form and function (designers).

These statements explain your practice to an audience. Be prepared to change and adapt statements for different opportunities.

Usually an artist's statement runs to between 100 and 300 words. It's placed next to your work in a public gallery, library or museum. Professional art and design journalists will require a copy if they're writing in-depth articles for visual-arts periodicals.

Marketing copy

This is required by designer-makers wishing to place their creative products and services in style publications, in feature pages or catalogues. An image of the product accompanies the copy. The product appears as a cut-out with a white or black background, or is placed in a relevant environment such as a gallery, trendy apartment or garden, or is worn by a model.

This commercial copy appears as a mini sales pitch. Style magazines are about fashion, retail, trends and consumerism. Look at magazines like Grand Designs or the IKEA catalogue. See how similar products to your own are presented.

Develop an engaging blurb based on your unique selling point (USP). Summarise what is special about your product. Think about form, how the product/artwork is made, what types of materials are used, its purpose and why customers should buy it – and include any eco benefits!

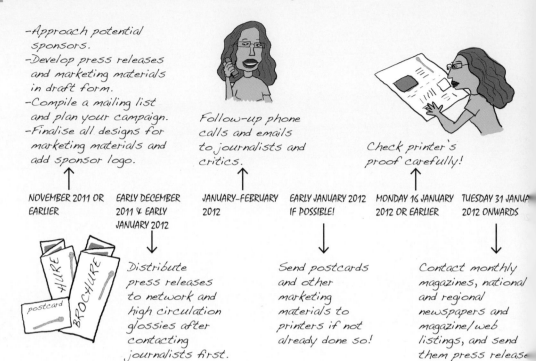

-Approach potential sponsors.
-Develop press releases and marketing materials in draft form.
-Compile a mailing list and plan your campaign.
-Finalise all designs for marketing materials and add sponsor logo.

Follow-up phone calls and emails to journalists and critics.

Check printer's proof carefully!

NOVEMBER 2011 OR EARLIER

EARLY DECEMBER 2011 & EARLY JANUARY 2012

JANUARY–FEBRUARY 2012

EARLY JANUARY 2012 IF POSSIBLE!

MONDAY 16 JANUARY 2012 OR EARLIER

TUESDAY 31 JANUA 2012 ONWARDS

Distribute press releases to network and high circulation glossies after contacting journalists first.

Send postcards and other marketing materials to printers if not already done so!

Contact monthly magazines, national and regional newspapers and magazine/web listings, and send them press release and materials.

Marketing timeline showing a mini marketing campaign

Website
Use websites and email for links to press releases, CV, images, gallery, info, profile or biog, blogs, selling, etc. To read more on websites turn to Chapter 12, What Next?.

Getting free press
Kathleen Hills, who is profiled in this book (see page 140), has never spent a penny on advertising. She's managed to gain media exposure by contacting magazine editors and stylists directly. Many magazines, e-zines and web portals are always eager for news and content as 'features' or 'editorial'.

Press/media release
To gain free press, a media release must convey news. The table on page 117 includes regular feature-page themes covered by style and interior-design magazines. Think which categories fit your creative products. For instance, one month your product may be

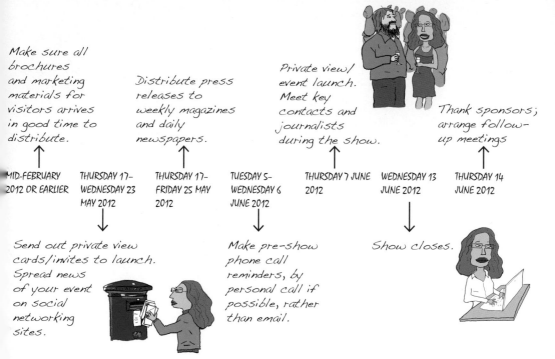

Make sure all brochures and marketing materials for visitors arrives in good time to distribute.

Distribute press releases to weekly magazines and daily newspapers.

Private view/ event launch. Meet key contacts and journalists during the show.

Thank sponsors; arrange follow-up meetings

| MID-FEBRUARY 2012 OR EARLIER | THURSDAY 17– WEDNESDAY 23 MAY 2012 | THURSDAY 17– FRIDAY 25 MAY 2012 | TUESDAY 5– WEDNESDAY 6 JUNE 2012 | THURSDAY 7 JUNE 2012 | WEDNESDAY 13 JUNE 2012 | THURSDAY 14 JUNE 2012 |

Send out private view cards/invites to launch. Spread news of your event on social networking sites.

Make pre-show phone call reminders, by personal call if possible, rather than email.

Show closes.

Please note, always check copy and print deadlines.

included in a magazine as part of a 'living space' feature, then the next as part of a 'gift under £50' piece, and on another occasion simply because it's yellow and it fits in with a colour scheme.

Press releases aren't really necessary to gain the odd spot in a magazine 'wish list'. If you're a newcomer to gaining press, then in the early days, before relationships are made with stylists and journalists, it may be wise to issue a release featuring your product as news – giving a specific angle, e.g. product launch, award-winning, new graduate – in order to attract attention.

You do require releases for fairs, exhibitions, workshops, shows, stunts and for a product or business launch. Local newspapers will feature interesting stories for free, but they will also need good-quality images sent by email that they can reproduce in their evening or weekly paper.

Please note, the table on page 117 is not an exhaustive study of the entire output of lifestyle and consumer magazines, but is simply a guide to help you think about how your creative products and services could fit into different editorial themes. Spaces have been left to pencil in your own ideas.

Be careful about copyright issues in regard to photographs. Make sure you own the copyright to any photos (i.e. you took them yourself) or, if they are someone else's work, you have been assigned the copyright, or have the photographer's permission to use them. Always remember to credit the photographer.

Press releases should be short and punchy, explaining what, where and when. Include contact telephone numbers and email details. Make sure an informed person will always be available to answer any calls.

Convert media releases into PDFs and have a press page on your website where journalists can download images and other content.

To see examples of press releases online, simply visit established artists' and designers' websites or Google 'press release' with the name of a particular event. Observe how others construct their releases and make them stand out. Your press release needs to capture the attention of a busy journalist or editor. Spending time experimenting with making the content and layout more interesting will pay off in the long term.

Remember, as mentioned in Chapter 1, you must distribute notices and announcements in good time, as many magazines have very early editorial and advertising deadlines.

Invest in media guides

For any UK arts or design marketing campaign I would always recommend purchasing a recent edition of the *Arts Press Directory* published by Arts Media Contacts. It costs about £115 but is a worthwhile investment, as it deals with every aspect of issuing press releases, including named contacts and copy deadlines, thereby saving you a great deal of time and energy.

The marketing timeline on pages 114–5 demonstrates that planning a marketing campaign requires the coordination and production of numerous marketing materials. Remember, the earlier you start the better. Make your own timeline for your next show by drawing a line with key deadlines and tasks on a piece of long paper. Then transfer these dates for sending releases and other activities on to a wall planner or personal computer.

Feature pages	Object themes	Key themes	Space	New	Top	Bargain	Festive/Seasonal
	Size: big, small, etc.	Innovation & technology	Storage, space savers		Best pick, star buys, best voted	Salvage, restore, free!	Spring, clean, fresh look, new range, etc.
The wish list, Objects of desire, The It List		Ecology, Ergonomics, Sustainability, recycled, energy-saving		Graduates, ones to watch, rising stars	Award winners, shortlist, nominated	Second-hand, auctions, bargain hunt, money savers, good value	Party season, winter warmers, gifts and presents
	Materials: metal, wood, textile, etc.	Style: vintage, retro, classic, etc.	Rooms: lounge, bedroom, etc.	What's hot? new trends		Gifts under £50, £30, etc.	Valentine's Day, Mother's Day, Father's Day
Articles, news, columns, gossip, spreads, stockists, etc.	Shape, form, function, texture, round, square, etc.		Outdoors, indoors, open space, upstairs, downstairs	New business, product launch, etc.	Top design companies, stylists, designers, etc.		
Profiles: artists/designers		Beauty and glamour	Conversions, architecture	Boutiques, agencies, galleries, etc.		Exclusive offers, etc.	Anniversaries
Up-and-coming fairs, exhibitions, festivals and events	Colour: shades, tones, transparent, translucent, etc.	Mood: light, dark, rich, cool, etc.	Gardens, garden gadgets, ornaments, etc.		Top tips, Top 10, Top 50, Our fab 5	Sales, discounts, vouchers	Summer themes, beach, holiday, sun, fun, etc.
Accessories, fashion, jewellery	Chairs, lamps, cushions, jewellery, etc.	Celebrity, cover star endorsement		New look? What's on?	Top brand, voted best	Make your own, modify, DIY, hobby craft, etc.	Cultural and religious festivals: Christmas, Ramadan, etc.

Examples of magazine themes covered by art and design periodicals and lifestyle magazines

117

When planning a media campaign it's wise to plan well in advance

If your show opens on the 7th June 2012 you may wish to gain coverage in the monthly lifestyle glossies, industry magazines and other media during May and June 2012. In most large-scale events such as your degree show and major trade shows a great deal of marketing is done to promote the event by the organisation's marketing department. However, they may not select your artwork, creative products or services to feature in the campaign. It's likely you will have to approach the media directly to gain coverage of your stand or display space.

If you're marketing your own show either individually or as part of a team you have to be prepared to start as early as possible. The secret to success is to thoroughly plan what you are doing from the outset.

It can be wise to start before Christmas for events opening the following spring or summer. If you seek to gain coverage in the large-circulation glossies, e.g. *Vogue* and *Elle Decoration*, they work four to five months ahead. Other major monthlies, such as the *World of Interiors*, work three months ahead. Even many guides distributed weekly with national newspapers, such as the *Guardian Guide*, may work three to four months in advance.

You could still gain coverage on the web, in smaller circulation industry periodicals, and in weekly, regional and local press if you started a campaign in mid-February 2012 for May 2012 coverage.

Once you have roughed out your timeline you can make a proper schedule in table form or on a year planner.

Key art and design fairs

The table oposite shows the key UK art and design fairs. There are many other fairs hosted throughout Britain and overseas. To find out more information about up-and-coming events see the resources listed earlier and in the Useful Organisations section at the end of the book.

It's always advisable, for market-research purposes, to visit trade and retail fairs. If you wish to exhibit at a fair or festival it's wise to visit in the season or year before you wish to exhibit, to check that it's the right fair for you to take part in.

Table of key art and design fairs

Name of Event	Location	Sector	When	Website
SPRING				
Affordable Art Fair	London	Art, prints, sculpture and photography	March	www.affordableartfair.co.uk
Ideal Home Show	London	Interiors, gifts and furnishings	March	www.idealhomeshow.co.uk
Country Living Magazine Spring Fair	London	Design, applied arts and traditional crafts	March	www.countrylivingfair.com
London Independent Film Festival	London	Film	April	www.londonindependent.org
Grand Designs Live London	London	Interiors, applied arts and design	May	www.granddesignslive.com
Collect: International Art Fair for Contemporary Objects	London	Hi-bred design product and applied arts	May	www.craftscouncil.org.uk
SUMMER				
London Graduate Fashion Week	London	Fashion	June	www.gfw.org.uk
Pulse	London	Applied arts, fashion, gifts and misc.	June	www.pulse-london.com
D&AD New Blood	London	Product and graphic design, illustration, animation and image-making	June	www.dandad.org
Royal Academy of Art Summer Exhibition	London	Paintings, drawings, prints, sculptures and architectural models	June to August	www.royalacademy.org.uk
Art In Action	Oxfordshire	Art	July	www.artinaction.org.uk
New Designers	London	Applied arts, commercial art and design	July	www.newdesigners.com
AOI Images	London	Illustration	July/ August	www.aoiimages.com
AUTUMN				
London Design Festival	London	Design	September	www.londondesignfestival.com
100 Percent Design	London	Applied arts, design and materials	September	www.100percentdesign.co.uk

Name of Event	Location	Sector	When	Website
Top Drawer	London	Applied arts and misc.	September	www.topdrawer.co.uk
Decorex International	London	Interior design, fabrics and accessories	September	www.decorex. com
International Jewellery London	London	Jewellery	September	www.jewellerylondon.com
Autumn Fair	Birmingham	Giftware, prints, greetings cards and stationery	September	www.autumnfair.com
British Art Fair	London	Art	September	www.britishartfair.co.uk
Goldsmiths' Fair	London	Jewellery and silversmithing	September/ October	www.thegoldsmiths.co.uk
BFI London Film Festival	London	Film	October	www.bfi.org.uk
Origin: The London Craft Fair	London	Applied arts	October	www.craftscouncil.org.uk
Frieze Art Fair	London	Art	October	www.friezeartfair.com
Art London Fair	London	Art	October	www.artlondon.net
Affordable Art Fair	London	Art, prints, sculpture and photography	November	www.affordableartfair.co.uk
Designers Block	London	Film, illustration, image-makers and design	November	www.verydesignersblock.com
Christmas Design Fair	London	Applied arts, textiles and gifts	November	www.hiddenartlondon.co.uk
Country Living Magazine Christmas Fair	London and Glasgow	Design, applied arts and traditional crafts	November	www.countrylivingfair.com
WINTER				
National Craft & Design Fair	Dublin	Art, applied arts and design	December	www.nationalcraftsfair.ie
London Art Fair	London	Art	January	www.londonartfair.co.uk
Top Drawer	London	Applied arts and misc.	January	www.topdrawer.co.uk
London Fashion Week	London	Fashion	February	www.londonfashionweek.co.uk
Pure London	London	Fashion	February	www.purelondon.com
Spring Fair	Birmingham	Giftware, prints, greetings cards and stationery	February	www.springfair.com
Ceramic Art London	London	Ceramics	February	www.ceramics.org.uk

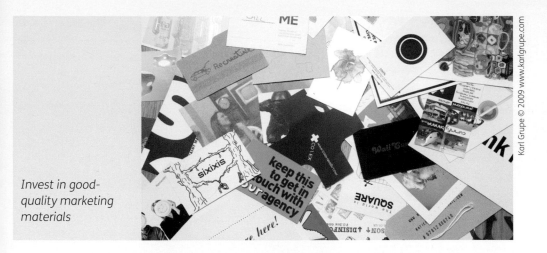

Invest in good-quality marketing materials

Business and postcards

- Make sure business cards and postcards are well designed, using text, graphics or a high-quality image.
- Have at least one postcard made of your work, and always have postcards made of award-winning artwork or products.
- Standardise your design format for all marketing materials including stationery, invoices and website.
- For small runs of handmade gilded or embossed heavyweight paper cards, try contacting a local wedding-invitations supplier, or specialist art printer.
- For reproduction of images on business cards and postcards for degree shows, fairs or mail-outs, always use professional printing firms.
- Never make your own business cards on home printers!

For more about business cards, please refer to page 96 and Chapter 12, What Next?.

Catalogues, brochures and leaflets

- Concentrate on good-quality design. Include marketing statements or copy.
- Avoid printing prices on any marketing materials. Keep trade and retail prices separate, as A5 or A4 paper inserts.
- Check the spelling and grammar. Get all materials proofread!

121

Portfolios

- More contemporary portfolios now take the form of a black 'box' with a white interior, available in various sizes with or without fine clear hi-tech acetate seamless wallets.
- There are also smart leatherbound display portfolios in A2, A3, A4 and A5, with clear modern hi-tech acetate sleeves.
- Bin any old black plastic zip folders with thick old-fashioned wallets.
- Never use black sugar paper as a backing in a professional portfolio.
- Try not to stuff a portfolio. Keep them selective, 12 to 18 images usually being sufficient.
- Store portfolios carefully, away from damp or dusty environments.

Creative marketing

> 'One should either be a work of art, or wear a work of art.'
> *Oscar Wilde (1854–1900), playwright and wit*

Creative marketing takes many forms, from imaginative publicity stunts and flash mobbing to sending promotional artefacts to art buyers and directors.

Celebrated figures in art and design history have succeeded in creating a strong personal identity by adopting curly moustaches, stripy tops and pink hair as memorable motifs.

Others have created their own publicity stunts, such as Yves Klein reproducing his own newspapers, faking catalogues, selling invisible paintings and turning gallery visitors' urine blue. Some may recall Alfred Hitchcock's regular cameos in his own movies or the famous floating of a wax effigy of the director down the Thames.

There are several UK artists today who have courted notoriety through refining the art of the publicity stunt – the likes of Banksy, Mark McGowan and Gavin Turk. In 2003, when Banksy started performing early stunts by planting 'new' exhibits in London museums, it was obvious that his strategy would make him his fortune.

On 25th July 2009, the *Guardian* reported an interesting solution to non-payment from a gallery. When the artist threatened the

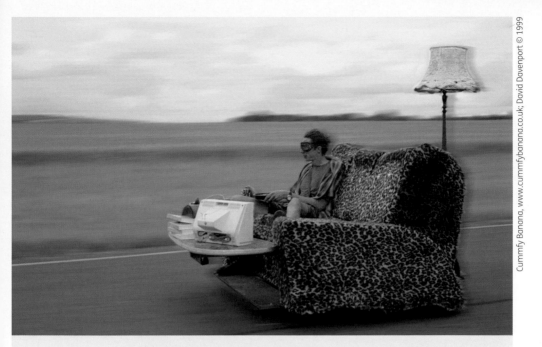

'Casual Lofa': Entrepreneur Edd China driving one of his promotional vehicles

owner with a pavement protest outside the gallery, wearing 'an unpaid artist' sandwich board, the debt was suddenly paid.

The advertising world, as well as entrepreneurs like Richard Branson, have always used publicity stunts, which are usually cheap to produce, as part of their marketing strategy.

Stunts are press-friendly. Before performing your stunt always send a press release to journalists beforehand. If you're relatively unknown it's unlikely the press will turn out. If no press arrive, take high-resolution digital photos of the stunt and immediately email them to your contact or to the news/picture desk.

Mark Borkowski's PR agency has an archive of their PR activities and publicity stunts. *Creative Review* always has news about the latest stunt-like adverts on TV, as well as featuring creative marketing ideas. David Lee, editor of *Jackdaw* magazine, is more cynical about art stunts, and regularly writes a short exposé column in his magazine.

The artist

Rob Pepper

Rob Pepper is a British artist who studied sculpture and photography at Birmingham Institute of Art & Design. He started selling his work at Camden Market at the age of 18 and worked there on and off until he was offered his first solo exhibition in Melbourne, Australia in 2002, at the age of 25.

In 2003, after his second exhibition in Australia, he returned to London to take up a residency at the Florence Trust Studios. This year-long placement led to his being offered another residency and a part-time teaching post at London's Art Academy, where he still works as Head of Studio Practice. Since 2007 he has taken on large-scale commissions with his collaborative partner Aimie Littler. He has recently exhibited his paintings at Liberty of London and London's SW1 Gallery.

You can view Rob's commissions and paintings at www.robpepper.co.uk

His five essential tips are:

1. Be original

Try to be more imaginative when it comes to designing publicity materials. This can be achieved by experimenting with traditional printing techniques or by using modern technology. I've discovered that adding a splash of bespoke printing to my invitations really helps in attracting attention.

2. Find a critic

Find someone you trust who can give constructive feedback. It must be someone who can tell you if a piece isn't any good without battering your ego.

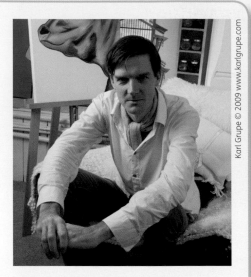

Karl Grupe © 2009 www.karlgrupe.com

3. Discover the art of presentation

When visiting galleries, art fairs and boutiques, observe how products are displayed. Presentation is all about telling an audience that what they are looking at is important. Whether it's a pile of bricks, a urinal or an unmade bed, the artist or art director has considered where an item is placed, how it's mounted and lit.

4. Keep in touch

Keep a database of all your contacts, which should be updated on a monthly basis. A few times a year let people know what you've been up to in an e-newsletter or by sending postcards. When promoting exhibitions, invite everyone you know as well as industry contacts. If potential clients don't come the first few times, be persistent but not a nuisance, then eventually some will turn up.

5. Be newsworthy

Be creative in taking on opportunities. If there's a story behind a project that will be of interest to the media, then that can be another excellent reason to do it.

RESOURCES

For online showcasing please see Chapter 6.

Printers

Most printers will be happy to send you a free sample pack before you place an order.

www.printing.com (good standard quality)

www.urbanprinting.co.uk

www.abacusprinters.co.uk (fine-art quality)

http://uk.moo.com (stylish fun)

www.bladerubber.co.uk (ink stamps made from drawings)

www.beaconpress.co.uk (eco)

www.paperback.coop (eco)

www.st-ives.co.uk (Creative Review's printers)

www.fabricprint.co.uk (Fabpad – digital printers onto banners, materials and canvas)

Specialist printing, finishing and sundries

www.solways.co.uk

www.mirri.co.uk

www.lasercraft.co.uk

www.fedrigoni.co.uk

www.snazzybags.com

www.cyberpack.co.uk

www.progresspkg.co.uk

www.photobox.co.uk

www.awesomemerchandise.com

Presentation

www.paperchase.co.uk

www.muji.co.uk or .com

Online print-on-demand image books

www.blurb.com

www.lulu.com

www.myphotobook.co.uk

www.bobbooks.co.uk

Portfolios

www.londongraphics.co.uk

www.silverprint.co.uk

www.plasticsandwich.co.uk

www.brodiesportfolios.com

Marketing

Arts media directories and database services

Arts Media Contacts, www.artsmediacontacts.com (check out their free press planner, a simplified version of the marketing timeline in this chapter)

www.thehandbook.co.uk

London Calling, leaflet distribution, Tel: 020 7275 7225 (check out the Total London service)

Artupdate, www.artupdate.com

Creative Tourist, www.creativetourist.com (north-west England)

Creative North Yorkshire, www.creativenorthyorkshire.com (north-east England)

Arts Marketing Association, www.a-m-a.org.uk

Writers' and Artists' Yearbook, www. writersandartists.co.uk

Industry directories

These are guides and subscription services that give you details of art buyers and commissioning agencies.

The AOI produce a number of very reasonably priced directories, www.theaoi.com (UK)

File FX, www.filefx.co.uk (UK)

Adbase Inc., www.adbase.com (US)

www.agencyaccess.com (US)

BikiniLists: www.bikinilists.com

Workbook, www.workbook.com (US)

Art and design fair information

Excel, www.excel-london.co.uk

Business Design Centre, www.businessdesigncentre.co.uk

Earls Court and Olympia, www.eco.co.uk

RESOURCES

Wembley, http://.whatsonwembley.com

Graduate Fashion Week, www.gfw.org.uk

London Fashion Week, www.londonfashionweek.co.uk

Pulse, www.pulse-london.com

Top Drawer, www.topdrawer.co.uk

100% Design, www.100percentdesign.co.uk

Art Quest, www.artquest.org.uk/opportunities/fairs (up-and-coming art and design fair news)

Event supplies

www.aeo.org.uk

www.market-stalls.co.uk

Stunts

www.borkowski.co.uk
www.creativereview.co.uk
www.thejackdaw.co.uk

Books

Getting Free Publicity, Pam and Bob Austen (Oxford: How To Books)

Effective Writing Skills for Public Relations, John Foster (London: Kogan Page)

How to Create a Portfolio and Get Hired: A guide for graphic designers and Illustrators, Fig Taylor (London: Laurence King)

The Guardian Book of April Fool's Day, Martin Wainwright (London: Aurum)

101 Extraordinary Investments: Curious, unusual and bizarre ways to make money, Toby Walne (Hampshire: Harriman House)

Improperganda (Art of the Publicity Stunt), Mark Borkowski (London: Vision On)

Freelance Photographer's Market Handbook, (London: BFP Books)

Flaunt: Designing effective, compelling and memorable porfolios of creative work, Bryony Gomez-Palacio and Armin Vit (Texas: Under Consideration LLC)

How to Make It as an Advertising Creative, Simon Veksner (London: Laurence King)

Installing Exhibitions: A practical guide, Pete Smithson (London: A&C Black)

8

Funding and Sponsorship

> 'It is so difficult to mix with artists! You must choose businessmen to talk to, because artists only talk of money.'
>
> *Jean Sibelius (1865–1957), composer*

There are numerous ways to secure funding for projects, research, equipment and exhibitions. The secret of obtaining money, support or resources from grant-awarding bodies, trusts, banks or business sponsorship is to start as early as possible, sometimes months or even years ahead of planned events.

When you're trying to obtain assistance, whether as an individual, a group or an organisation, filling in applications forms, compiling proposals and writing bids for local or regional government funding requires a great deal of skill and patience. Presentation, clarity, and understanding the eligibility criteria for such ventures are paramount.

At the time of writing, the UK and the rest of the world are recovering from recession. Readers must bear in mind that to secure assistance in difficult times other, more unconventional approaches to gaining resources might have to be considered.

How to get a loan

> 'Painting is easy. The hard part is paying for the frame.'
>
> *Andrew Toos (1958–), cartoonist*

Before considering taking out a loan, it's vital to understand why it's required and how much investment is needed. Market research, assessing market demand, calculating costs, predicting cash flow and learning about the legal issues are key elements in underpinning any application for a loan.

No one is magically going to pop out of the ether and write an application for you. Being successful in gaining a loan requires a great deal of legwork. It can be helpful to consult friends and relatives who run businesses, especially if they've previously borrowed money from banks.

It's important to realise that bankers aren't of the same mind as Arts, Film or Crafts Council administrators. Many artists and designers have fed back to me on Arts and Crafts Council grants they have received in the past that have enabled them to make progress. However, awarding grants to individuals or organisations that don't understand how to sustain a practice as a business, or know how to build an organisation, is a complete waste of time. Grants can simply raise aspirations to an unrealistic level, especially if the venture can't become self-sufficient or profitable.

Many readers may have £15,000 or so of student loans and as a result will tend to reject the idea of taking on further debt. You might have to be prepared to borrow further. It's worth bearing in mind that failure to adequately invest in a business will inevitably lead to disaster. If you can't afford to do it properly, then leave it six months and concentrate on finding new ways to stabilise and improve current finances.

UK banks

If only a small amount of savings is available and you can't obtain a grant or support from your parents to set up in business, then applying for a loan can be the only option, since grants for start-ups are becoming few and far between.

As mentioned in Chapter 3, taking out a business loan from a local bank will require you to open a business account and write a business plan. If you're struggling to write a plan, seek guidance from advisers at local enterprise agencies or innovation centres.

Your plan must convince the business bank manager that you can repay any monies loaned with interest. Usually, loans are repaid monthly over a set period of time. It's customary that the lender will give the borrower two months' grace before the first loan instalment is repaid.

For more information about business plans refer back to Chapters 3 and 5, and for bank accounts, see Chapter 11.

UK Government-backed loans

Local enterprise agencies or Business Link (England), Business Eye (Wales), Invest NI (Northern Ireland) or Gateway (Scotland) will have up-to-date information about government schemes. They can advise about grants to partially fund overseas trade fairs, or direct you to local business support and other loan schemes. Government-backed loan provision is patchy. However, many enterprise and regional development agencies can loan businesses money.

UK credit unions

If the idea of applying for a loan from a bank doesn't appeal, then you could try contacting a local credit union. Credit unions are community banking schemes. To be eligible to borrow money for business or personal use, you also have to save. The minimum amount of saving is usually £10 per month. Some credit unions can only loan you three times the amount you have saved; others will issue straight loans of several thousand pounds or more. I've been a member of my credit union for many years. I find my continuing membership is essential, as loans are easier to arrange.

Credit cards and private loan companies

Try not to become entangled with private loan companies. Where possible, avoid using credit cards to fund business expenditure, particularly if you've no business plan. High interest rates and default fines can become an expensive long-term burden, which can quickly lead into unmanageable debt and wreak havoc on credit ratings.

Applying for grants and sponsorship

'As far as a sponsor is concerned, the visual arts is the ideal running mate. It is fashionable and visible, but cheaper than sport.'

From The Tastemakers (2001), by Rosie Millard, journalist, broadcaster and author

Applying for grants, loans or sponsorship can take many weeks and months to complete. It is highly likely that the first application for any form of grant funding will be rejected. It's essential not to be put off and to be persistent in reapplying.

The approach must be focused, and any documents or images included must be to the highest professional standard. It's better to be selective and to target efforts on two or three applications rather than dozens.

UK grants

Common errors include presenting too many different ideas or art or applied-art forms in one application, with poorly constructed statements. If you're not very good at writing seek professional help. Buying in help from time to time will generate more money in the long term. To apply for grants from the Arts, Crafts or Film Council you usually have to be an EU citizen, a UK national, or to have gained British citizenship.

Application forms for grants are effectively mini business plans in disguise. They're all quite generic in format, and some are unnecessarily complicated. The application forms may ask for projected profits or other financial calculations with which you might be unfamiliar. To complete them satisfactorily you may require input from others.

Various organisations provide free advice and workshops on applying for grants. Short summaries of recent successful applicants' proposals can be found on the Arts, Film, and Crafts Councils' websites. If unsuccessful in your first attempt, try to gain feedback from the funders before resubmitting.

Are awards and grants taxable?

Most grants are viewed as taxable income by HMRC where you're already running a business. This is particularly the case if the award or grant relates to your area of trade. This includes entering an art or design competition and winning a cash prize.

However, some grants enabling people to develop business ideas, rather than to aid their existing business, are free from taxation. It's always worth clarifying whether or not a grant is exempt from income tax once you have been notified of a successful application.

Entering for awards or competitions is termed 'a venture in

trade'. If you haven't started your business yet and you enter a competition, then the income won't be taxable.

Sponsorship

In the economic downturn business sponsorship can be hard to come by. A template letter of sponsorship is shown overleaf. This is a model I have given out to many students over the last ten years. I know various artists and designers who've been successful in gaining up to £1,000 in support from businesses by basing a letter on this structure.

Sponsorship works in two ways

One approach, by sending letters, is to ask for small sums of money or specific materials – say, £50, £200 or £500, or other resources such as rolls of paper, pots of paint, collection of frames, expensive materials, drink for guests, services in kind and so forth. Emailing a request would only be appropriate if you knew the recipient well or as a follow-up to a previous conversation. Never send unsolicited email requests, as they're likely to be ignored.

The alternative course is to secure one or two big sponsors donating significant amounts – £5,000, £50,000, even £100,000 – towards the whole event. An approach to a large corporation requires a hefty, carefully structured and presented proposal. This will require meeting potential sponsors and possibly a formal presentation.

If you decide to approach multiple sponsors, check they are compatible – for example, if you manage to secure sponsorship from a vodka company for one part of a project, they may not be happy to find out that a rival firm is also supporting the event.

Approach by letter

Make sure you type on letter-headed paper. Enclose a draft press release and other supporting materials such as photographs or prints. This letter is really designed to enlist small amounts of support in the form of money, materials, equipment or other miscellaneous items.

Make sure you know who to write to. Is it the business owner or the marketing/PR manager?

131

Template letter of sponsorship

*Use business/organisation's
letter-headed paper.*

Don't forget the date.

*Name, title, position, and
address of person to whom
you are sending the letter.*

Dear _____

We are/I am a _____-based (*insert your location, e.g. London*)
artist(s)/photographer(s)/designer(s)/business. We are/I am exhibiting
our/my _____ (*e.g. awarding-winning/latest/innovative/artwork/
range of products*) in/at _____ (*state event and venue*). The
exhibition/event _____ (*title*) will open with a private view/
corporate/event launch on _____ (*start date*) and will run until
the _____ (*end date*) at the _____ (*state venue's name and
address*).

This _____ (*use 'hook line'/title*) show hosts a collection of
work/designs/objects (*e.g. paintings/soft furnishings*) that explores/
captures _____ (*state unique selling point phrase*). (*Then state
any other interesting information such as the role of other funders/
agencies/hosts/partners.*)

At present we are/I am devising a marketing and publicity strategy
that will include catalogue/poster/press releases being sent to
_____ (*state newspaper/media/local/regional/national, etc.*) in
_____ (*state name of town/city; e.g. London-wide publications*).

Adverts promoting the event will be placed in _____ (*e.g. art or design periodicals/and other magazines*). We/I or _____ (*state event organisers*) will also be inviting _____ (*state vast number of people invited, VIP and honoured guests*) to the private view/corporate/event launch and _____ (*quote numbers/other info*) will attend the event/show during the ____ (X number of days) it is open.

(*Remember to link, as best you can, the type of media to public/marketing/product image of sponsor.*)

(*The next bit is up to you. Remember these are rough guidelines. Select relevant items only.*)

We are/I am looking for sponsorship from _____ (*state business name of local/national firms*) in the form of goods/finance, towards the promotion of the event/posters/catalogue/display ware/ framing/materials/wine/refreshments for the private view/event launch, etc.

We all/I would be extremely grateful for your support and will ensure _____ (*state business name*) is/are fully credited in the gallery/display space/exhibition stand/publicity/press release/private view cards/posters and thanked for your donations/gifts.

(*Remember, if you're asking for large amounts of money, you can invite them to attend the event launch or invite them as a 'special' or 'honoured' guest or offer free passes or tickets*).

Yours sincerely,

(*Remember to sign with a high-quality pen such as a fountain pen – avoid cheap biros*)

_____

(*Name of artist(s)/designer(s) with BA or MA letters if appropriate*)

How do I find out more about obtaining business sponsorship?

Arts & Business is an organisation that encourages sponsorship of the arts. They also provide training days on how to write sponsorship proposals.

What sponsors expect

The sponsor will expect that the audience for your event is similar to their own customer demographic and profile, and also that your image fits with their brand value and identity. Goldsmiths degree shows, for example, have been sponsored in previous years by Absolut Vodka, an edgy brand very much associated with younger consumers.

To gain sponsorship, there has to be the promise of advertisement, in all probability featuring the company's logo or trademark. The reason why you need to start approaching sponsors early is to allow sufficient time for obligations to the sponsor to be fulfilled, especially if they're substantial investors. Larger sponsors' logos have to appear on all marketing materials. Events vary in nature, and this affects the marketing materials produced. Here is a shortlist.

Logos or names of major sponsors/funders' must appear on:
- Press releases
- Posters and postcards
- Tickets and programmes
- Brochures, flyers and catalogues
- Advertising
- Large banners.

Most press campaigns start at least eight months before an event. If you're looking for sizeable donors for an event in 2013, it's not unrealistic to start approaching companies in 2011. It may take large firms a while to decide if they're going to offer support – this is why a long lead-in time is vital (see the marketing timeline on pages 114–15).

Remember, major sponsors should be invited to private views or launches.

This list below has been compiled from various sources, including

Artquest, the Arts Council and the *Arts & Business Sponsorship Manual*, which is currently out of print.

What a major sponsorship proposal should contain
- A covering letter – short and to the point.
- A summary of who you are and what you do.
- A summary of who your supporters are.
- A description of the project, including images.
- Who you believe your audience/market to be. Students? Collectors? Local businesspeople?
- Publicity and identity – if you have a website make sure it's up-to-date.
- An outline of the benefits to the sponsor, i.e. what's in it for them.
- The size of donation you are asking for, including VAT if applicable.
- If you have contacted Arts & Business, you should mention them.

Smaller amounts
It's possible to gain small amounts of funding and resources right up until a few weeks or days before the event. If sponsorship comes in late, it might be possible to include the sponsors' details on last-minute press releases sent to local newspapers and weekly magazines. The names of smaller sponsors can be displayed on a sign placed on your stand or in the gallery.

Perhaps acknowledgements can be added to floor plans or pricelists. Supporters can also be given press coverage retrospectively in any post-marketing activities.

Please remember to write thank-you letters to all the sponsors after the event. The best way to secure long-term funding is to build good relationships not only with sponsors, but with your patrons and customers.

The early days
I would advise making your initial approach to local businesses for smaller sponsorship requests between four and nine months before the event. Writing them a letter is the best way to begin.

Alternative fund-raising strategies

> 'August
> And the streets are paved with pavement artists.'
> *Hovis Presley (1960–2005), poet*

If you're currently an art student, you will depend upon additional income to further your studies and mount a good degree show. You might be a recent graduate looking for funding to set up a business, develop a portfolio, make a film or stage an exhibition. Perhaps you're a fine artist working in the community-arts sector, seeking funding for small projects with social and educational benefits.

Whatever the reason for needing money, if you're on a low income, it can be worth spending time investigating state benefits and other less obvious forms of funding.

UK benefits

There are many different forms of benefit you can claim if you're on a low income, unwell or unemployed.

Working and Child Tax Credits

Tax credits are a tax-relief benefit paid via HMRC. They're nothing to do with your local council or Job Centre.

The rules for entitlement are too complicated to explain in a few lines. An illustrative example might be a 25-year-old single designer, self-employed, with no children and working 30+ hours per week, with annual net profits under £13,100. That person would be entitled to Working Tax Credit. If net profits are about £10,000 per year, they would be entitled to payments of £25.54 per week, or £1,328 per year (example based on 2010–2011 rates).

Please note, most people living in the UK can claim tax credits. However, there are certain exceptions for non-EU residents and restrictions for people with particular types of visas.

To find out more, contact the Tax Credit Helpline or visit the Citizens Advice Bureau (CAB). If you've been on a low income for a few years and haven't claimed, you could be losing money. When applying for any kind of benefits always retain a photocopy of the completed form before you post the original.

Local councils

UK Housing and Council Tax Benefits are claimed from your local council to help pay your rent or mortgage interest. Many people aren't aware that Housing Benefit can be claimed when you're self-employed or in a mixture of employment and self-employment. Entitlement depends on a number of issues and where you live. You might be surprised at what can be claimed.

If you're self-employed and have been awarded this benefit, and remain on a low income, it's usual to refresh your claim either annually or every six months. I've met many artists and designers who could be a few thousand pounds better off a year if only they put in claims for Housing and Council Tax Benefits.

To claim you will need to take into the Housing Benefit Office, unless specified otherwise, originals of the following documents:

- Your last tax return (If you have previously filed one with HMRC). The previous tax year's bookkeeping, summaries and audited accounts from an accountant carry more weight. If you're only a few months into self-employment they will look at your current situation, and income earned in the previous tax year. If possible, take along the letter that you will have received from HMRC, informing you of what tax is owed for the previous tax year, if any.
- Six months of business and personal bank statements.
- If you're claiming either Working or Child Tax Credits, bring in the Revenue's calculation sheet and reference number.
- If you're in part-time employment, any P60s you received at the end of the last tax year along with three months of payslips.
- A rent book or tenancy agreement/mortgage payment details.

The advisers will photocopy any original documents. Never post original documents to the Housing Benefit Office – only submit them in person.

Claiming for benefits does take a bit of effort, but if you can't be bothered with bureaucracy, then making a go of a business isn't going to work either. If you do qualify for benefit, then it's also probable that you can't afford to pass it up.

Department of Work and Pensions/Job Centres

As mentioned in Chapter 3, when income is minimal it's possible to claim state benefits, even if you're self-employed or in part-time work. The regulations concerning state benefit change periodically. It's likely that civil servants will knock off your benefit entitlement – Jobseeker's Allowance, for example – any money you have earned in a given week. When declaring self-employed work, always show the full financial details, including the fee, with all relevant expenses deducted to show net profit.

Charities, trusts and foundations

FunderFinder is one of many similar websites and useful services which simplify the process of searching for grants from trusts and foundations. There are hundreds of trusts supporting a wide range of causes. Some charities support educational activities, some research, while others will fund travel costs or childcare or other basic subsistence.

If you're currently a student and in financial difficulty, contact your student welfare officer or union and find out if there are any charitable foundations that you could apply to.

Time banks and barter

Find other creatives or professionals who would be willing to exchange products or skills. I encouraged one artist to swap signed prints in return for web design. I knew a carpenter who did a few odd jobs for an accountant in return for completing his tax return. There are a number of official time banks and barter schemes around the country.

Design and Artists' Copyright Society (DACS)

Register for your 'resale rights' and put in an annual claim for 'Payback' from DACS. UK artists and designers can receive money from Payback if they've had photographs, images of artwork or photos of products reproduced in publications or the media. The registration process for Payback and filling in the application form are straightforward.

Resale rights are a percentage of the resale price of artworks, sculptures, limited-edition prints, collages, photographs, and unique traditional craft or applied-art pieces such as tapestries, textiles, jewellery, furniture, glass and ceramics. For the maker to benefit, artworks and one-off pieces have to be resold though a dealer, agent or auction house. This right lasts your entire life and for 70 years after your death. See the DACS website for registration, more information, and a full list of eligible artefacts.

Street entertainment

Pavement drawing, busking, performance or being a statue can be lucrative ways of making extra cash. HMRC classifies these activities as 'street entertainment'. The coins dropped into your hat are a taxable form of income, as there's a 'profit-seeking motive'. Earnings should be entered into your accounts.

Before doing anything like this, it's best to check with the local council whether there any by-laws that prohibit these activities or require a street trader's licence. As a wise precaution (if not a mandatory requirement in order to secure a licence), I would also take out public liability insurance.

I would suggest that if you're allowed to trade as a street entertainer in your local area then you should set up with a friend who's also interested in having a go, as the streets are not as safe as they used to be. During the few years I did it whilst attending art school I collected many stories with which to entertain my friends. There were a few nasty incidents, so be prepared to deal with the odd problem if undertaking any form of 'street entertainment'.

Other money-spinners

- Money raised by selling raffle tickets (prizes including artworks, prints and products)
- Holding art and design auctions
- Adding on workshops to exhibitions for children or adults
- Charging or asking for donations for wine at private views
- Car boot sales
- Selling sundry items: badges, T-shirts, mugs, postcards and greetings cards
- Flogging off sundry items on eBay.

Please note, if you're holding a raffle you may require a licence and should contact your local council for more details.

The product designer

Kathleen Hills

Kathleen Hills is a British designer who originally studied graphic design, and worked in publishing, before moving into floristry. She set up and ran two flower shops in London before deciding to return to college. Her first degree, from Central Saint Martins College of Art and Design, was in ceramic design, after which she gained an MA from the Royal College of Art.

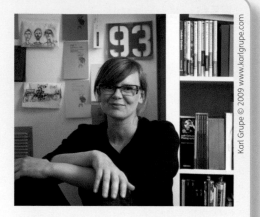

Karl Grupe © 2009 www.karlgrupe.com

Kathleen designs slipcast bone-china tableware and lighting products. These are sold via her website and selected retailers such as Liberty and Thorsten van Elten.

Since graduation she has taken part in a number of trade shows and is a regular exhibitor at 100% Design and Pulse.

You can view her products and stockists at www.kathleenhills.co.uk

Her five essential tips are:

1. Go for sponsorships

When studying at the RCA I spent time at Wedgwood, where they helped me with the production of my first three products. This experience was vital in setting up my business. Take advantage of any sponsorship opportunities whilst you are studying.

2. Find a good manufacturer

I visited manufacturers in Stoke-on-Trent and looked for a company with whom I could develop a good, long-term working relationship. Finding good-quality manufacturers that will support your business is essential.

3. Invest in good photography and get media coverage

Interior design magazine or design portal stylists or editors are usually very approachable, often working on tight deadlines and always looking for new products and designers to introduce. Invest in good photography – strong, clear images – and prepare marketing copy. Be prepared to email high-res images and prose at very short notice. Delays in getting these materials to editors may cost you opportunities.

4. Be creative in your approach to promoting your work

As well as gaining free exposure in the media through the feature pages, try to get your work into the high-street shop windows. This can be done by approaching the store's visual merchandising designer or manager.

5. Make use of all your skills

Having worked in graphics, I understood the importance of branding. My experience of publishing helped me to know how to use the press to generate free publicity. The flower shop taught me to create displays for the window and shop space, which was great practice for designing exhibition spaces. You may not realise it but you probably have lots of skills you can apply to your business.

RESOURCES

Grants

Directory of Social Change
They publish several fundraising directories for individuals and organisations.
www.dsc.org.uk
www.grantsforindividuals.org.uk

UK Trade and Investment
Helps businesses break into overseas markets. For self-employed people or companies that have been trading over 18 months, they can often provide grants towards attending trade fairs overseas (e.g. the Milan Design Fair).
www.ukti.gov.uk

FunderFinder
Search service, partly free. To access the full service you need to find an organisation which has a software licence. Contact large libraries and regional arts organisations (e.g., in London contact Artquest).
www.funderfinder.org.uk

The Association of Charitable Foundations, www.acf.org.uk

Other useful websites

www.trustfunding.org.uk
www.governmentfunding.org.uk
www.j4b.co.uk/www.j4bgrants.co.uk
www.artquest.org.uk (under 'Funding' section)
www.dacs.org.uk
www.artsadmin.co.uk
www.artscouncil.org.uk
www.craftscouncil.org.uk
www.fashioncapital.co.uk
www.ukfilmcouncil.org.uk
www.thedesigntrust.co.uk
www.nesta.org.uk
www.shapearts.org.uk

Sponsorship

Arts & Business, www.artsandbusiness.org.uk

Hollis PR, www.hollis-sponsorship.com (publish the Hollis Sponsorship & Donations Yearbook)
www.uksponsorship.com

Information about loans

www.abcul.org (credit unions)
www.shell-livewire.org.uk
www.businesslink.gov.uk
www.bisgov.uk (Department for Business, Innovation and Skills)
www.gle.co.uk (London only)
www.nfea.com

Free advice about benefits or debt problems

Citizens Advice Bureau, www.citizensadvice.org.uk

For help with paying for dental and prescription costs in the UK, apply for a HC2 Certificate, www.nhs.uk

Barter

http://uk.bartercard.com
www.londontimebank.org.uk
www.timebank.org.uk
www.letslinkuk.net
www.free2collect.co.uk

Free

www.freecycle.org
www.free-stuff.co.uk
www.skype.com
www.blogger.com
www.gumtree.com
www.info-britain.co.uk/uk.art/artweeks.directory

Books

The Tastemakers: UK Art Now, Rosie Millard (London: Scribner)

9

Creative Crimes

> 'If business is not for you, then the art world is not for you.'
>
> *Tracey Emin (1963–), artist*

Some readers may recall Tracey Emin saying this before the start of a famously heated interview with John Humphrys back in 2004 on BBC Radio 4's *Today* programme. At the time, I found it a startling and shocking statement. But having given it due consideration over the years I now think Emin made an extremely astute observation.

The business world, be it art or commercial, requires candidates to possess a mental toughness and a clear understanding of legal and financial matters.

Just about every artist and designer I have met over the last decade is falling foul of the law in some way. But failure to comply with British or European Community standards could have terrible consequences for yourself and customers.

The art and commercial worlds aren't for everyone. However, if you wish to manufacture and sell creative products and services, even on a part-time basis, then it's vital to learn about the legal and regulatory requirements that govern your specific area of trade.

The laws pertaining to the creative industries and the visual arts are of a magnitude that can't be covered in its entirety in this chapter. The Creative Crimes mind map (see pages 144–5) is a visual summary of the key areas of law and current regulations.

It's worth bearing in mind that a vague or loose grasp of the law can actually be worse than knowing nothing at all. It's advisable to take advice from a lawyer who has a proven track record in your particular sector. Indeed, it's sensible when establishing any kind of business to form good relations with a firm of solicitors.

Protecting and exploiting Intellectual Property

> 'Intellectual Property, potentially, is more valuable than any tangible thing you can imagine.'
>
> *Trevor Baylis (1937–), inventor*

As you can see from the mind map on pages 148–9, intellectual property rights (IPR) are a series of rights, both moral and financial, that govern artists, designers, inventors and businesses/brand-name rights.

At the time of writing there is no global standardisation of IP rights, and the laws that govern them vary from one country to another. However, there are international agreements in place, such as the Berne Convention and the Madrid Protocol, which do recognise other countries' IP laws.

The European Union is working towards harmonising a set of IP rights that would ensure protection across Europe. EU design right and trademark registration systems already exist, but the European parliament is now in the process of working towards developing an EU patent right and registration system.

UK copyright regulations are also currently being reviewed. By the end of the next decade it is likely that significant changes will have taken place in this area of the law.

Now let's clarify the basics

Moral and financial rights

When you create a painting, a lamp, a bagless vacuum cleaner or a unique brand, you have created two sources of value: the physical 'object' and the 'intellectual rights' to the use underlying or enabling that object. For instance, when you finish a painting, you have both the painting itself and the 'copyright' in it. You can decide to sell the painting but retain the copyright. Equally you can license or sell (assign) the copyright, while keeping the original painting.

Moral rights govern issues such as the right of paternity, that is to say, the right to be acknowledged as the 'author'. Financial rights recognise the 'labour' involved in the creation of an object and also the right to be paid for the reproduction of artworks or creative products.

PS Don't panic!

Insurance

Risk assessment

Always a good idea & sometimes compulsory.

Contents

Professional indemnity

Equipment

Employer

Product liability

All risks

Stock consequential loss?

Public liability

Health & Safety

Labelling regulations

Health & safety signs

Safe storage

Reporting of Injuries, Diseases and Dangerous Occurrences Regulations (RIDDOR)

Equipment

Risk assessment

Fire and building regulations

Control of Substances Hazardous to Health (COSHH)

PAT (electrical testing)

CE product marking

Fireproof & safety standards

Other Key Laws & Regulations

Packaging & recycling ecology

Indecency & obscurity

Anti-terror

Fine Art Trade Guild (e.g. Giclee Standards)

Late payment regulations

EU Directives

Business names

Fibre content labels

Company regulations

Product liability

Data Protection Act

Distance selling regulation

Trading standards

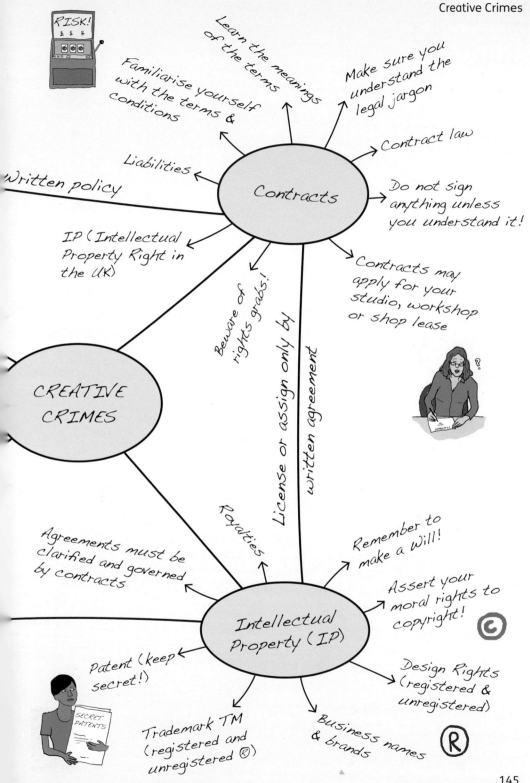

RISK!

Learn the meanings of the terms

Familiarise yourself with the terms & conditions

Make sure you understand the legal jargon

Contract law

Liabilities

Written policy

Contracts

Do not sign anything unless you understand it!

IP (Intellectual Property Right in the UK)

Contracts may apply for your studio, workshop or shop lease

Beware of rights grabs!

License or assign only by written agreement

CREATIVE CRIMES

Royalties

Agreements must be clarified and governed by contracts

Remember to make a Will!

Assert your moral rights to copyright! ©

Intellectual Property (IP)

Patent (keep secret!)

SECRET PATENTS

Design Rights (registered & unregistered)

Trademark TM (registered and unregistered ®)

Business names & brands ®

145

UK copyright ©

This is an artistic right governing the rights of artists, designers, photographers, film-makers, musicians, writers and performers. It is automatic and lasts for life, plus a further 70 years after the author's death.

It is worth understanding that you're the owner of your own copyright unless you're an employee, in which case it's usually the employer who owns the copyright in all your creative output. When you're self-employed, it's vital to retain ownership and avoid 'assigning' or selling rights.

If you're creating artwork or products with other artists and designers, before you begin working make sure any contract you receive is thoroughly checked by an IP solicitor. If there's no contract then it's advisable to seek legal advice about IP matters before collaborating on any joint project. If there's no written contract in place regarding IP rights, then at some later date it's likely disputes will arise between the parties about the ownership and control of rights.

UK unregistered design right

This is like a lazy copyright, which offers limited protection for designers. UK unregistered design right lasts 15 years from the object first being made, and ten years from first marketing. After the first five years since it was first made or marketed others have the right to manufacture your products, after seeking your permission.

Designers must be aware when undertaking commissions that it's usual for the commissioner to have 'unregistered rights' to your designs. It's your responsibility to negotiate the contract and assert ownership of your rights. However, under the implied law clients have a legitimate claim to own the unregistered design right in commissioning agreements.

UK industry know-how

You may have a brilliant trade secret, a method of manufacture, a recipe or a process. When a patent is published, anyone can read the formula or method involved in making a material or product. Sometimes it can be wise to keep inventive processes a 'trade secret' and not to seek patent protection, thus keeping information private far beyond the lifespan of a patent.

UK unregistered trademarks™

This right protects business names, logos, and brands. Business owners use ™ to inform customers, clients and competitors that this is their 'trademark'. ™ is used when a business hasn't officially registered a business name/logo, are in the process of gaining registration with the Intellectual Property Office, or have failed to achieve such registration but are allowed to continue trading using the same name/brand/image.

Everything before this line is an automatic right in UK intellectual property right law. There's no need to register it anywhere; you simply have to keep records, such as sketchbooks, photographs, tapes, recordings, emails, letters and contracts.

Everything after this line is 'registered intellectual property', where through registration an artist, designer, inventor or business owner is enabled to gain further protection in the marketplace. Registration is optional though strongly advisable. To register designs, patents and trademarks, contact a specialist IP solicitor or the Intellectual Property Office (IPO) directly.

UK registered design right

To be eligible for UK design right you must register a design within 12 months of it first being made or its first public display. Protection is only gained after the date when the claim is filed. If this application is successful, a photo or drawing of the product is published on the UK IPO website, with the registrant's details. Design right lasts 25 years but has to be renewed every five years to keep a commercial product protected in the marketplace.

If you have commercially viable products then it's essential to try and obtain UK or EU community design right. If you don't have enough spare cash to spend on filing a design then you are simply not being realistic about the amount of investment required to start a creative business.

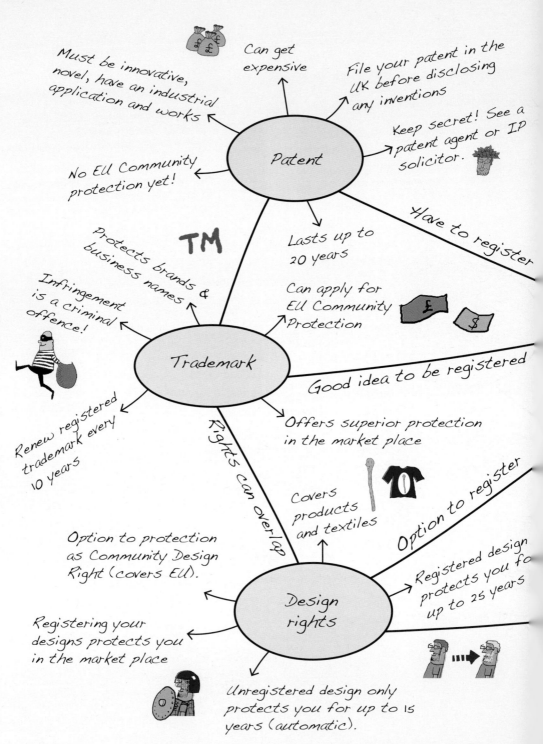

Must be innovative, novel, have an industrial application and works

Can get expensive

File your patent in the UK before disclosing any inventions

Keep secret! See a patent agent or IP solicitor.

No EU Community protection yet!

Patent

Lasts up to 20 years

Have to register

TM

Protects brands & business names

Infringement is a criminal offence!

Can apply for EU Community Protection

Trademark

Good idea to be registered

Renew registered trademark every 10 years

Offers superior protection in the market place

Rights can overlap

Covers products and textiles

Option to register

Registered design protects you for up to 25 years

Option to protection as Community Design Right (covers EU).

Registering your designs protects you in the market place

Design rights

Unregistered design only protects you for up to 15 years (automatic).

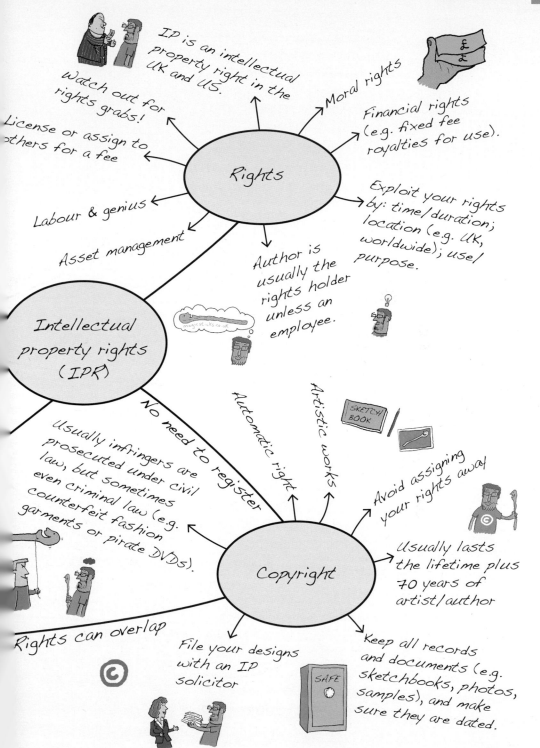

IP is an intellectual property right in the UK and US.

Moral rights

Financial rights (e.g. fixed fee royalties for use).

Watch out for rights grabs!

License or assign to others for a fee

Rights

Exploit your rights by: time/duration; location (e.g. UK, worldwide); use/purpose.

Labour & genius

Asset management

Author is usually the rights holder unless an employee.

Intellectual property rights (IPR)

No need to register

Automatic right

Artistic works

SKETCH BOOK

Usually infringers are prosecuted under civil law, but sometimes even criminal law (e.g. counterfeit fashion garments or pirate DVDs).

Avoid assigning your rights away

Usually lasts the lifetime plus 70 years of artist/author

Copyright

Rights can overlap

File your designs with an IP solicitor

SAFE

Keep all records and documents (e.g. sketchbooks, photos, samples), and make sure they are dated.

149

UK patent

Innovative product ideas, innovative materials or other inventions that have an industrial application can be protected by filing and publishing a patent. **Diagrams, formulae and prototypes should only be shown to an IP solicitor or patent agent. Do not show innovative materials or products at exhibitions or fairs, nor make any public disclosure, before seeking professional advice.**

Once a patent is filed as an 'initial application' for one year (no fee), then you can discuss the invention openly, appear on *Dragons' Den*, etc. The filing remains confidential at the Intellectual Property Office (IPO). It's essential prior to filing that you make use of non-disclosure agreements (NDAs) when speaking with potential investors or manufacturers.

Gaining full registration takes up to three years. Once granted, a UK patent can last up to 20 years. Patent law is one of the most specialised areas of law and can't be picked up simply by attending a few talks. It is essential with any innovative business idea to execute it quickly and not delay in seeking professional advice.

UK registered trademark

Notice the word 'trade'. This area of IP law covers business names, visual images like an illustration or a photograph, logos, brands, 3D objects, sounds (jingles), smells, shapes, even an artist's or designer's name or signature, as with the likes of Picasso, Zandra Rhodes and Damien Hirst.

It's vital to make use of the business-name search engine www.start.biz and to check www.uktrademarkregistration.com. Please note, the trademark search facility on the IPO website is more advanced though very complicated to use, so I would advise undertaking an initial search with the Start.biz search engine.

Intellectual property is an extremely complicated series of rights which can overlap each other. The diagram on page 151 demonstrates some of these quirky crossover areas.

No guarantee of success

When you start the application process to gain protection for a design, patent or trademark there is no guarantee that you'll be granted these rights. It's a tricky process, and this is why it's

Registered design covers the external form and appearance of a design object/product.

Unregistered design covers the external form and internal function of a design object/product.

PATENT
APPLICATION
SOLAR POWER
TOY TRACTOR
MOTOR

Registered patent or secret industry knowledge covers inventions or innovations with industrial applications in core 'materials', like flooring.

Engineers', inventors' or architects' drawings/diagrams are covered under UK copyright.

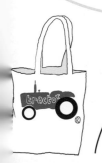

Design Right, registered or unregistered, covers jewellery, silversmithing, glass, ceramics, furniture, lighting, fashion garments, accessories, patterns, toys.

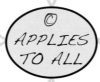

© APPLIES TO ALL

© Copyright covers all artistic works such as drawings, paintings, sculpture, films, plays, written work...

A trademark, registered ® or unregistered ™, covers brands, logos, shapes, names colours, images, signatures...

A drawing can be an artistic work = copyright. A drawing could also turn into a logo or 3D trademark, registered or unregistered.

A drawing can be a logo, the logo could turn into a design and then a functioning product, like a toy, or be repeated as a fabric pattern. This product could be protected under registered design right and as a trademark.

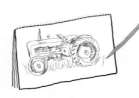

151

usually better to employ an IP solicitor to overcome any objections from the IPO and to guide you throughout the process as to the options available to you.

Avoid selling your rights

In 1971, Carolyn Davidson was paid a flat fee of just US $35 for the Nike Swoosh logo by Nike founder Phil Knight. If only this young designer had been advised to license her logo design to Mr Knight instead of assigning it (selling it outright) for a one-off fee. Had she negotiated a licence, she might have limited how the logo could be used, for a specific purpose, time, and territory – e.g. for use solely on certain kinds of footwear produced by the company, for a period of five years, and only on those products sold within specified jurisdictions. It's a classic example of where a well-drafted contract could have resulted in a more successful exploitation for the designer.

Quoting fees

When an artist or designer ventures into the commercial world of company branding, advertising, merchandising or manufacturing, creatives should be aware of 'above the line' and 'below the line' usage. Always remember to quote your fees on the basis of what, where and for how long the client wishes to use artwork or designs. (Please consult the glossary for more detail.)

A licence

The following checklist sets out typical priorities in a licensing agreement:

- The licence will be a written contract.
- Its payment terms may be either a fixed fee or royalties, or a combination of a fixed fee and royalties that can be negotiated.
- The duration of the licence will be specified, e.g. a day, a week, a month, one year, four years, etc.
- The permitted uses of the design being licensed will be specified, e.g. magazines only, front covers only, t-shirts only, etc.
- The territory in which the licence applies will be specified, e.g. UK only, EU only, Japan only, worldwide, etc.

Stealing ideas

You simply must not take images, lyrics or designs from the web or from books – even with a number of alterations such as colour changes, removing parts, distortion, etc. – and then claim them as your own creative products. It's important to gain permission from the creator or to pay a licensing fee, otherwise you could risk litigation. Unfortunately, artists and designers only realise how damaging this activity is when it happens to them.

What to do if you have been ripped off

Do not communicate with the individual or business who you think may have copied your artwork, designs or products and passed them off as their own. Instead quickly gather all your evidence of research and creation, sketchbooks, photographs of work in progress, catalogues and samples, together with a copy of the offending image or object, and go straight to an IP solicitor to seek advice. Any delay can be fatal to your claim.

It can get messy if you try to be your own lawyer. It's possible to represent yourself and have your case heard in a local small claims court. However, I really wouldn't recommend it unless you are fully conversant with the law.

How to draw up a will

If you are starting to sell artwork and design pieces or you have a number of public and commercial commissions then it is wise to have a will drawn up. Copyright, resale rights and other rights such as trademarks will still be commercially exploitable after your death.

You can leave your rights and the original artworks or designs to your company, family, friends or a charity. As owners of the rights they will be able to benefit from income generated by the licensing and resale of your artworks.

Often only the artist or their representatives and accountant will have inventories of the artists' commissions and sales and the places where original works are stored. When creators die without a valid will drawn up by a specialist solicitor there can be a great deal of unnecessary confusion in the settling of their estate. (For more information consult the books and websites recommended at the end of this chapter.)

The basics of terms and conditions

'The only way to be sure that your terms of trade form the contract is to send them at the earliest opportunity, as a written acceptance of the client's offer.'

Simon Stern (1943–2009), illustrator, author and former director of DACS

If you are working regularly for a number of different clients, supplying numerous shops, taking on commissions or selling products from a website, then it's strongly advisable to invest in your own properly drafted set of terms and conditions. All sorts of calamities can occur when completing an order, so it's vital to limit your personal liabilities.

Most established artists and designers now have terms and conditions on their website. However, as regards trading online, many creatives have one set of terms and conditions governing creative products and services sold through their website and other sets of terms for retailers or private commissions. It is not a case of 'one size fits all', so be careful of simply adopting someone else's terms and conditions to save money.

How to make use of terms and conditions

In Simon Stern's excellent *The Illustrator's Guide to Law and Business Practice*, the use of terms and conditions is described in detail. Though the context is that of an image-maker or illustrator, the general premise is the same for all visual artists.

Sending terms and conditions

Quite simply, if you send terms and conditions to a client and they accept, this can be indicated by silence, i.e. implied consent. They don't even need to respond in order for those terms and conditions to take effect. To avoid any confusion it's wise to double-check confirmation of terms by phoning them or sending them an email.

Receiving terms and conditions

The general rule to remember is if a client sends you a set of their terms and conditions, your silence will be interpreted as

A FEW RULES TO AVOID RUNNING INTO TROUBLE

- Always have professional terms drawn up by an experienced solicitor who understands your sector.
- Alternatively, professional bodies often supply members with model versions but look at them carefully to ensure they meet your requirements.
- Include a handy 'rejection' or 'cancellation fees' clause.
- Reduce personal liabilities by adding a *force majeure* clause – for any situation in which a delay to delivery occurs that is beyond your control, e.g. due to postal strikes, accidents, fires, floods, volcanoes. Such a clause may oblige you to give written/email notice within seven days of the specified deadline, in order to agree an extension of time.
- Read any terms sent to you by a client.
- If something is unclear consult with your professional body or an IP solicitor.
- Avoid signing if the other 'party' wishes to 'own' your rights, e.g. by having you assign the copyright outright.
- A regular trick played by the more mercenary client is to 'acknowledge' in a friendly way that you 'own' your rights, and then state that you agree to grant them a 'worldwide licence, for all time, for all uses, etc.' Beware of such sharp practice and don't let people take advantage of you.
- Also, search for other nasty clauses, e.g. those claiming ownership of original artwork or portfolios, and other unreasonable restrictions of trade.
- Check for any liabilities, e.g. insurance matters, repairs, data-protection issues, image rights of celebrities.
- If there are only a few concerns, raise them directly with the client and request an amended version of the terms. If they refuse, either accept the offer or politely decline it.
- If rejecting a clause, strike through with a black pen and write your initials at both ends of the line. Keep a printed copy for yourself and send the original back to the client. Again, if they refuse to send revised terms or don't mark their initials next to yours, take the work if you're desperate for cash. But bear in mind that if clients treat you shabbily at the outset, relations are unlikely to improve.
- Never start work on a commission or under a contract until you have received and read both the 'terms and conditions' and the 'contract', as they are interrelated agreements.
- If you commence work on a project before reading the client's terms and/ or conditions, and you have also signed a contract, it may mean you consent to their terms/contract, whatever they may be.
- You can't impose your terms after the contract has started.
- Never, ever sign documents without fully understanding them.

acceptance. Moreover, if you receive a set of terms after the client has received yours, then unless it has been agreed to the contrary the last set of terms governs the relationship or 'informs the contract'. This situation is known as the 'battle of the forms'.

Problems occur when artists and designers don't read clients' terms and conditions properly and fail to raise any concerns.

Insurances and other important regulations

'Bonheur also drew attention for sketching at the city's slaughterhouses, dressed in male clothing – a practice that was not only unconventional but technically illegal at that time.'
Rosa Bonheur (1822–99), artist, from Dana Micucci's Artists in Residence, 2001

As I have mentioned, it's impossible to describe all pertinent insurance and legal matters in one chapter. Therefore I strongly urge readers to check the legal situation regarding insurance and any regulations that are relevant to their discipline and country.

If you want to trade or sell products in Britain and Europe, it's important to comply with British Standards and European laws. Readers can undertake further research by visiting the websites and reading the books listed at the end of this chapter.

Health and Safety

Health and Safety, risk assessments and insurance are three areas which interrelate. In 2009, the artist Maurice Agis was fined £10,000 (later reduced on appeal) for breaching Health and Safety laws. His interactive sculpture *Dreamscape* broke free from its moorings during a fair in Durham during 2006, killing several people. He narrowly escaped a manslaughter charge, but died later in 2009, aged 77.

Also in recent years Thomas Heatherwick has been successfully sued by Manchester Council for £1.7 million pounds, once again under Health and Safety legislation, for the unsafe condition of his gigantic sculpture *B of the Bang*.

Many artists and designers have suffered terrible illnesses through failing to consider their own well-being. Since Michelangelo fell from that scaffolding and nearly killed himself, many others have also faced personal tragedies. Sculptor Rebecca Horn ended up in a sanatorium after exposing her lungs and skin to toxic resin, while although she never smoked Patricia Finch died from lung cancer caused by exposure to carcinogenic dust generated from sculptor's materials. More recently, the drum-maker Fernando Gomez died from exposure to anthrax spores after handling animal skins.

The Health and Safety at Work Act 1974, and subsequent amendments, enforces common sense. It's important to realise the dangers to yourself and others if basic risk assessments are not carried out properly. Once creative products are on sale in the shops, mounted for exhibitions or installed on another's property you can be liable if things go wrong. If a product causes a customer, visitor or participant harm in some way, they can sue you.

Insurance

In the UK at the time of writing, *a-n Magazine* promotes inexpensive public and product liability insurance. The policy covers artists and designers in a range of activities including exhibitions, residencies and teaching workshops. Many professional bodies offer low-price insurance deals as a benefit of membership.

It's important to read very carefully any insurance policy, to ensure that it covers your full range of activities. If you're not fully covered then problems may arise in the future.

Public liability (personal)

This is simply a wise precaution, but it can be a contractual obligation for freelancers to take out public liability insurance.

You should seek cover if you are:

- carrying out work on other people's commercial or private property, e.g. mural work, installing sculptures, basic contract work, etc.
- running children's or adult art workshops or private tuition, either at home, on business premises or in other venues such as community centres
- undertaking a residency, exhibiting artwork or products at galleries or fairs, performing, filming, out on a photo shoot or trading on a market stall.

157

Public liability (market traders)

Many councils prefer market traders to sign up to their own public liability insurance schemes. If you're thinking about setting up a stall at a local market, information about the application procedure is usually found on the local or town council's website.

If you're trading at festivals or other events, it's still advisable to take out appropriate cover, as organisers may request a copy of your public liability insurance. Contact the National Market Traders' Federation, which also offers low-price insurance deals for traders.

Winging it

Certain insurances are a legal requirement, while others are simply sensible for any professional creative to have. You may go years and never have an accident or cause any injury to others. Then one day, through a gust of wind, forgetting to check something or becoming distracted, an accident will happen. They do.

If you don't have appropriate insurance, you could be liable for paying damages, hospital bills and replacing expensive objects or equipment. It's possible to be sued hundreds of thousands of pounds if your product is faulty or you have caused an accident.

In October 2009, a school in the UK was fined £16,500 after a 16-year-old girl attending an art class lost most of her fingers after putting her hands in a bucket of wet plaster until it set solid. Most of her fingers had to be amputated due to the severity of the burns.

The case highlights why you must have your own public liability insurance when facilitating art workshops in schools or community centres on a freelance basis. If you're not an employee of the school or local council concerned, then unless their insurance cover has been specially extended for the project you are engaged in, you will need your own. They may try and reassure you that you're covered, but that may not be the case if your specific activities and materials aren't included in the policy.

Read the insurance policy

Another type of 'winging it' is not properly reading entire the insurance policy, including all the schedules – if, say, a public liability insurance policy doesn't cover working at heights over ten metres and a job requires work to be done at 15 metres. Avoid

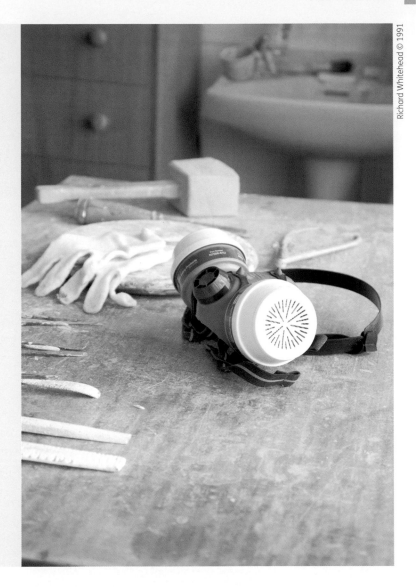

Richard Whitehead © 1991

*Health and Safety
matters*

apathy, and thinking 'It'll be all right'. It might not be. It's far more sensible to contact a reputable independent insurance broker and add extra cover for activities or other risks outside of the current policy. Why lose sleep? Just pay for the extra cover if you need it.

Public liability (buildings)

All buildings open to the public are required by law to have public liability insurance. If you're paying any kind of rent for a studio or workshop to an arts or business organisation, then you might find that public liability insurance for the building is included; but this is not always the case, so you might have to take out your own cover. If the landlord says the public liability insurance for the building is included in the rent, ask to see the policy and take a photocopy for your records. If you're a tenant ask for your interest as a tenant to be noted on the policy.

This type of insurance doesn't cover your personal equipment, tools, materials, stock or artwork. It's up to you to gain extra insurance against theft, fire and flood for your own contents.

Always seek advice from a solicitor and a chartered surveyor before taking on a lease for a shop or other commercial building, especially if you are entering into the lease in your own name.

Trading from home

If you're trading from home then you may require public liability insurance for areas of the property that are used for business. Always seek advice from a solicitor and your insurance broker when planning to trade from home. Activities could include sitting at a computer, private tuition or manufacturing. If you are planning to trade from home, contact your insurance company about the policy that covers your house and contents and notify them.

If you're living in rented accommodation and wish to trade from the property then check your tenancy agreement. You might have to talk to your landlord about amending his domestic policy.

When public liability insurance (on a property) is a legal requirement

If you're converting a garage or part of your home into a gallery or studio purely for business use, and this is open to the public, you are required by law to take out public liability insurance on these areas of the property. Planning permission must first be granted by the local council and business rates have to be paid on the converted part of the property. (Also see page 47.)

Product liability

This type of insurance covers you against claims made by customers for injury or damage caused by your products.

As a separate issue you should always check, before goods go on sale, whether they should be tested to comply with the BSI's British Standards (see pages 164–5).

Equipment

As a general rule businesses should insure key pieces of equipment for their current or replacement value. You need to think carefully about what to insure. I recall a stonemason who had not insured her tools. Individually they were not worth a great deal, but to have a whole bag stolen added up to such a sum that she had to cease trading for a period of time as she couldn't afford to replace them.

Data Loss

Regarding digital files and databases, you can insure against data loss. With all matters concerning data storage, make sure you have good back-up systems in place by backing up files on external drives and storing copies away from your main business premises. It's also worth investigating new virtual back-up systems such as 'cloud computing'.

Other important insurances

- Goods in transit
- Plate-glass window
- General theft, fire and flood
- Theft and consequential loss
- All risks (usually for photographers and film-makers)
- Home workers' package
- Accident and sickness
- Health insurance such as Bupa
- Pension, e.g. stakeholder pensions
- Employers' liability (legal requirement for employers)
- Professional indemnity (architects, and sometimes graphic designers and artists, will require it; it covers any professional advice you may give in the course of your work)
- Infringement insurance (against others who copy your artwork or products) and legal expenses insurance.

Other important regulations

It's incredibly easy to find you have failed to comply with one of the following pieces of legislation. (If you have a knowledge gap, or other concerns, contact the recommended organisations.)

- Health and Safety at Work Act (HASAWA) 1974 (and its many revisions and additions)
- Control of Substances Hazardous to Health regulations (COSHH) 1988
- Reporting of Injuries, Diseases and Dangerous Occurrences Regulations (RIDDOR) 1995
- Electricity at Work Regulations 1989
- The Personal Protective Equipment at Work Regulations 1992
- The Manual Handling Operations Regulations 1992
- The Provision and Use of Work Equipment Regulations (PUWER) 1998
- The General Product Safety Regulations 2005.

It is advisable to go on a short course in Health and Safety, especially if you want to work in studio administration, art colleges, theatres or other hazardous environments. Contact the Health and Safety Executive (HSE) or your local AE/FE college about courses.

- The Sale of Goods Act 1979
- The Sale and Supply of Goods Act 1994
- The Supply of Services and Goods Act 1982
- Trade Descriptions Act 1968
- Unfair Trading Regulations 2008
- Misleading Marketing Regulations 2008
- Unfair Contract Terms Act 1977 (and amendments).

Under the legislation listed above, you have to be careful about how artworks and products are described.

If you sell a painting as a 'unique' piece but fail to tell the purchaser that you plan to make, or have made, 100 limited-edition prints, the purchaser may have every right to ask for his money back. The same scenario applies to all 'one-off' products.

Remember, you have only sold the original artwork, and thus you retain the copyright. If at a later date you decide to make limited editions of any artwork, then it's good practice to let the original purchaser know in a friendly way that this is what you would like to do. It's likely they won't have a problem with your plan if they have been consulted.

The Consumer Protection (Distance Selling) Regulations 2000

These regulations govern selling goods from a website and other e-trading activities. Please note, not all the UK distance-selling regulations apply to products – e.g. paintings, photographs, furniture, textiles, etc. – that have specifically been 'made to measure' or commissioned, i.e. 'made to order'. However, in these cases customers are still entitled to a refund or replacement if the artwork or product is defective in some way.

Contact the Office of Fair Trading for a copy of 'A guide for businesses on distance selling'.

The Late Payment of Commercial Debts (Interest) Act 1998

This Act introduces a statutory right to claim interest on the late payment of debts. If you give a client a credit limit of 30 days to pay, and have sent enquiry letters and reminder emails, their failure to pay allows you to charge interest on the sum outstanding in addition to an administration fee or penalty charge of £40, £70 or £100, depending on the amount owed. (See www.payontime. co.uk for further details and an online interest calculator.)

The Criminal Records Bureau (CRB) and the Independent Safeguarding Authority (ISA)

A Criminal Records Check (CRB) is a check that employers carry out for potential job applicants to discover if they have a criminal past. Generally speaking, in the UK if you wish to join an agency supplying artists and designers to schools, hospitals, care homes or prisons, it's usually the business, arts organisation or local council for whom you'll be working that will run a CRB check on you and charge you a small fee to cover administrations costs. It is only possible in Scotland and Northern Ireland for private individuals to apply for a basic disclosure or 'criminal conviction certificate'.

The Independent Safeguarding Authority is a new registration scheme, for authors, artists and designers who regularly visit or run workshops in schools in England, Wales and Northern Ireland. If it's only a one-off visit you might get away without paying the £64 registration service. If, however, you're heavily involved in community arts projects, and you work regularly in schools, then registration was compulsory from November 2010 onwards. Contact the ISA for more details. A separate scheme has been operating in Scotland since 2011.

BSI British Standards

If you're looking to sell furniture, soft furnishings, toys or other products, it's worth checking whether they need to comply with British and European Standards. Particular products have to be checked to confirm that they are safe for public use, though in certain cases manufacturers might be able to self-certify. Read the regulations concerning your product – it may have to be checked by an independent testing house.

The tests carried out are for durability, strength, stability and fire resistance. For more information contact one or more of the following: BSI education (British Standards), Furniture International Ltd, the Association of Master Upholsterers or, for toy makers, the British Toy and Hobby Association.

CE marking

The CE mark on a product indicates its compliance with Health and Safety and environmental regulations. The main product areas where a CE mark applies are:

- low-voltage electrical products (e.g. lamps, kettles, vacuum cleaners, etc.)
- toys (e.g. characters or ideas fabricated in wood, metal, plastic, rubber, fabric – i.e. soft toys or dolls etc.)
- recreational craft products (e.g. mini stained-glass, tapestry, handicraft or stencil kits for adults or children).

If you're planning to sell particular products, including lights, toys or recreational craft packs, within the UK or European Economic Area (EEA), makers or manufacturers must apply for a CE mark. If you're found to be selling these and other types of products without CE marking you are running the risk of prosecution by your local trading standards authority, although they may give you time to register (unless the product is unsafe). However, not complying with British Standards and CE marking is really not worth the risk.

Failure to comply fully with these regulations – for instance, buying a light fitting with a CE sticker on it to fit into a lamp-holder you have already designed to give the impression an electrical product has CE marking – can result in a hefty fine or even imprisonment. Whatever the product is, the whole completed unit – in this case the shade, the lamp-holder and the light fitting – has to be tested. For more details contact the BSI, the Lighting Association or New Approach.

Textile products
- Indications of Fibre Content 1986 (various amendments 1988, 1994, 1998, 2005).

If you are a fashion designer, dressmaker, costume maker, corset maker, milliner, textile designer, or you make floor coverings, rugs or soft furnishings, then failure to advertise or label products with an indication of their fibre content is a criminal offence. Contact the Office of Fair Trading or The Stationery Office for further details.

Ecology
In this area the following pieces of legislation apply:
- Packaging (Essential Requirements) Regulations 2003 (amended 2004 and 2006)
- Hazardous Waste (England and Wales) Regulations 2005
- Environmental Protection Act 1990.

The key legislation here for most creative businesses is the packaging regulations. It's now a legal requirement for businesses trading within the European Community to make sure that all packaging can be recycled or made from recycled materials.

Design of packaging should eliminate waste, minimising weight and volume. Useful organisations to contact in this context are Friends of the Earth, Recycle Now and Design Track (Envirowise).

Industry regulations concerning limited editions

There are many different types of printing techniques employed in manufacturing limited-edition prints. There are British Standards, rules and general guidelines which auction houses, dealers and galleries observe. These are complicated. I would recommend looking at the Fine Art Trade Guild website, and books written by Annabel Ruston on the subject of the sale and reproduction of artworks.

There is a difference, for instance, between reproductions, on the one hand, and a series of themed works. British Standards categorise the degree of an artist's involvement in creating prints. Printmakers create prints as individual artworks using various means, e.g. linocut, etching, screenprinting, woodblock. These are distinct from purely 'reproduction' copies of an original artwork.

Artists now commonly reproduce paintings as modern giclée prints, rather than by the more traditional fine-art printing methods. It's important to know the various rules and standards attached to them. For example, under the Guild's standards the maximum edition of limited-edition prints should not exceed 1950 but recommends that editions are kept below 850 worldwide. It's also best practice that once an artwork has been reproduced as a limited-edition print, the image should not be re-licensed for other uses such as greetings cards.

The Art Loss Register

The Art Loss Register is where you can report the theft or loss of artworks. If you register missing work and it comes up for auction or is found by the police, you can be reunited with the work. I recommend registration, as many artists, photographers and illustrators have experienced their original work simply 'disappearing' – at the printers, for instance – with the excuse that it's been 'lost'.

Be sure to let the person who has lost your artwork know that you will register it as missing on the Art Loss Register. That way, unscrupulous people won't be able to profit from its sale in the future. The Art Loss Register operates across many countries – refer to their website for more details.

Street Trading Licences

There are all kinds of street licences and it's highly likely one will be required if you're selling goods from a market stall. Even street entertainers such as pavement artists, buskers or human statues are often obliged to purchase a licence from the council or local trading standards office. If you're interested in trading at local fairs, or in town or shopping centres, contact your local council for more information.

Ethics

There are strange sets of double standards operating across the visual arts and creative industries. If we take fashion, we find allegations of exploitation of child labour, of racism (prompted by the dearth of black and other ethnic minority models), and of the industry's insistence on zero-sized models, to name but a few. The only recent positive development in the fashion industry is its embracing of ecology and the creation of clothing made from recycled plastics and fibres. The fashion industry, like the music industry, gets away with a lot.

To avoid the reputation of your industry becoming tarnished, it's vital for all artists and designers to retain a sense of honesty and integrity. Avoid getting involved with untrustworthy characters. It's worth bearing in mind that if clients, agents or dealers discover any dishonesty in their business dealings with suppliers, it's likely they'll end the relationship.

Crime

You must not get drawn into any form of criminality such as tax evasion, fraud, piracy, faking, counterfeiting or taking drugs. These activities are illegal. Criminal convictions can damage your reputation and your business. Even having minor convictions will prevent you from entering the USA and other countries for many years after the event.

The sculptor

Caroline Russell

Caroline Russell is a British artist based in London, where she has a studio. She is an Associate Member of the Royal British Society of Sculptors and has been a professional sculptor since 1993. She graduated from Leeds University with a degree in English and Philosophy and studied sculpture privately under Patricia Finch, FRBS. Caroline makes sculptures with traditional materials, producing work that is mainly cast in bronze as limited editions. Her small-scale sculptures are often used as models for larger pieces.

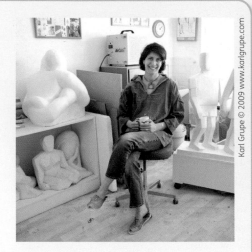

Karl Grupe © 2009 www.karlgrupe.com

Her work has been shown in various galleries, including the Belgravia Gallery and the Limehouse Gallery in London, and at many exhibitions, including the Chelsea Art Fair.

You can view a selection of her sculpture at www.russellsculptures.com

Her five essential tips are:

1. Follow your dreams

Though my first degree was not an art degree I didn't let this limit my options. There's always the possibility of other forms of study. Being tutored by an established artist helped me form my own ideas and visual language. It's vital to discover your own path and believe in yourself.

2. Understand the market

In the beginning I hired stands at art fairs. I now have a website to showcase my work and attract interest from galleries. Part of my success has been not only creating my work, but being able to make it affordable. Make sure your pricing matches the collector's budget.

3. Investment

When I began to exhibit in London galleries I found that the audience and demand for my work began to change. You must be prepared for this if you're aiming for higher-level opportunities such as large-scale public commissions or prestigious shows. If the venture is a success you'll find yourself operating in a very different market.

4. Making time

Studio time is really precious, even more so when you have to look after a family. It's important whatever your circumstances to have a few hours a week prioritised for your own work. I try to work on a piece of sculpture every day.

5. Health and safety

Always take care when working in dusty or fume-filled environments. Keep studios well ventilated or get a dust extractor fitted. Make sure you always wear a dust mask when using plaster or other powdered materials. Always wear protective clothing and use a respirator when handling toxic liquids or materials.

RESOURCES

Legal services

Silverman Sherliker LLP
Free initial consultation session, affordable UK legal document solutions.
www.silvermansherliker.co.uk

Copyright, design right, trademark & patent

Intellectual Property Office, www.ipo.gov.uk (trademarks, copyright, patent and design right)

www.britishcopyright.org

www.start.biz (business names and basic trademark search)

www.companieshouse.gov.uk

www.uktrademarkregistration.com

www.own-it.org (talks, advice, fact sheets, copyright)

www.creatorsrights.org.uk

www.artquest.org.uk/artlaw.htm (art law section and new IP service)

www.a-n.co.uk (under legal contracts and copyright)

Design and Artists Copyright Society, www.dacs.org.uk

Public Lending Right, www.plr.uk.com

www.advicecentre.law.qmul.ac.uk (artists' legal service)

The Fashion and Design Protection Association, www.fdpa.co.uk

Anti Copying In Design, http://acid.eu.com

www.artmonthly.co.uk (see the regular column by Henry Lydiate)

Patent Agents, www.cipa.org.uk

www.trevorbaylisbrands.com

www.innovationuk.org

www.britishinventionshow.com

www.thebis.org

Copyright infringement
http://youthoughtwewouldntnotice.com/blog3
www.counterfeitchic.com

www.spotcounterfeits.co.uk

Wills and Trusts

The Society of Trust and Estate Practitioners,
Tel: 020 7340 0506,
www.step.org

Sources of information about UK trading regulations

The Department for Business, Innovation and Skills, www.bis.gov.uk

Business Link, www.businesslink.gov.uk

Late Payment Regulations, www.payontime.co.uk

Trading Standards, www.tradingstandards.gov.uk

The Stationery Office, www.tsoshop.co.uk

The Office of Fair Trading, www.oft.gov.uk

Health and Safety Executive, www.hse.gov.uk

The Criminal Records Bureau, www.crb.gov.uk

Disclosure Scotland, www.disclosurescotland.co.uk

Access Northern Ireland, www.accessni.gov.uk

Independent Safeguarding Authority (ISA), www.isa-gov.org.uk

Insurance

www.a-n.co.uk

www.saa.co.uk

www.nmtf.co.uk (National Market Traders' Association)

See the Artquest website for more information and a list of art/design insurance brokers. Also check with your professional body.

British Insurance Brokers' Association, www.biba.org.uk

Data storage

Cloud computing
www.google.com/apps

British Standards

www.bsieducation.org

RESOURCES

British Furniture Manufacturers' Association, www.bfm.org.uk

FIRA International Ltd, www.fira.co.uk

Association of Master Upholsterers and Soft Furnishers, www.upholsterers.co.uk

Information about CE marking

www.newapproach.org

www.bsigroup.com

www.businessstandards.com

www.cen.eu

www.iso.org

www.lightingassociation.com

www.btha.co.uk (toys)

Green regulations

Friends of the Earth, www.foe.co.uk

Waste and Resources Action Programme (WRAP), www.wrap.org.uk

Netregs, www.netregs.gov.uk

Ecology

www.recyclenow.com

www.envirowise.gov.uk

www.fsc.org

www.eco-label.com

www.green-mark.co.uk

www.designcouncil.org.uk

www.gpinnovation.org

www.seedfoundation.org.uk

Other standards

Environmental Management Standards, www.iso-14001.org.uk

Industry Council for Packaging and the Environment, www.incpen.org

Art

Art Loss Register, www.artloss.com

Fine Art Trade Guild, www.fineart.co.uk (for access, quality, standards and logo use)

Books

Dear Images: Art, Copyright and Culture, Daniel McClean and Karsten Schubert (eds) (London: UCA and Ridinghouse)

Art & Copyright, Simon Stokes (Oxford: Hart Publishing)

Between A Rock and Hard Place, Lionel Bently (London: Institute of Employment Rights)

The Artist's Guide to Selling Work, Annabelle Ruston (London: A&C Black)

Starting up a Gallery and Frame Shop, Annabelle Ruston (London: A&C Black)

Business Start-up Guide for Designers and Makers (London: The Design Trust); see www.thedesigntrust.co.uk

The Pirate's Dilemma, Matt Mason (London: Allen Lane)

Copyright Law for Artists, Photographers and Designers, Gillian Davies (London: A&C Black)

10

Confidence and Negotiation Tactics

> 'Belief in belief in believing in believing...'
>
> *Tony Kaye (1952–), film director*

In London on 9th June 2009, I attended a seminar being held as a tribute to the maverick art director Paul Arden. A clip of Tony Kaye singing a tribute song to Arden, called *Belief*, was shown to the audience, a lyric from which is quoted above. Paul Arden was sacked from six different advertising agencies during his career. Curiously, he never viewed his dismissal from any of these positions as a disaster. He eventually set up his own film production company and wrote two very entertaining pocketbooks based around the theme of self-confidence.

Self-confidence is essential to make sales and win opportunities. To gain the best outcome requires the ability to think through situations, an understanding of legal issues and a good grasp of the principles of negotiation.

Summary rejection, or receiving the brush-off, can lead to self-doubt. One solution might be mere dogged persistence. However, there might also be problems with your approach – for example, inadequate presentation in the form of amateur photographs, poor English, unimaginative materials, and so on. A rebuff could be due to having no endorsement, no top art school, no reviews by critics, no references or no stockists. It could simply be the case, as any actor, dancer or musician will tell you, that supply outstrips demand.

It's essential to realise that the business side of any creative profession is built on the invisible foundations of trust and reputation. This is why engineering introductions or gaining

171

endorsements from other more established creatives, grandees of the art and design worlds, or other famous achievers is vital. You may not like this proposition, but unfortunately it's a reality.

How do I minimise the likelihood of rejection?

As with legal matters, a bit of 'wising up' is required.

Always try to gain an introduction to established figures such as art entrepreneurs. If this isn't possible, then be bold and make an approach yourself.

If you're trying to gain representation or a show at a particular gallery and you're unknown to the dealer, search through back catalogues and find anyone you know who's exhibited at the gallery before. Then make contact with them, turn on the charm a bit and hopefully they will introduce you formally or informally at some future event. If not, at least they may be willing to put your name on the gallery's mailing list.

If you're seeking to place products in large stores, visit the buyers, if they're willing to see you. Invite them to your degree show or trade fair and send them sample products. If necessary, pick up the phone and call them. However, be careful to avoid over-pursuing buyers, as they don't like to be stalked.

If you're lucky enough to be invited to attend prestigious events with a guest, don't automatically issue the spare invitation to a friend. Consider whether there are potentially useful contacts who may not have an invitation and would like to go. Build relationships with people who might assist you in getting a lucky break.

Call in favours. Ask your friends, or friends of friends, if they would put in a word for you or recommend a contact. Many artists and designers feel nervous about asking for assistance from friends as they think it's unethical. This is total nonsense.

If friends don't wish to help, are they really your friends anyway? Gradually bring your creative, business and future hopes into everyday conversations with friends. Then, eventually, real friends will always help out.

The art of persuasion

> 'Any fool can paint a picture, but it takes a wise man to be able to sell it.'
>
> *Samuel Butler (1835–1902), author*

As you can see from the mind map on pages 182–3, many aspects in improving confidence and related skills are interwoven with one another. Behavioural scientists and psychologists have explored the subject of persuasion in a number of published theories, research papers and books. Long before such research began, writers such as Napoleon Hill and Dale Carnegie in the 1930s had already hit upon many of these now widely accepted theories solely on the basis of their own observation, practice and experimentation.

Good interpersonal abilities and being able to engage people in conversation are central to securing opportunities. (Please refer back to Chapter 6 for more on this subject.)

Collectors

Individuals who buy art for their homes are not to be confused with professional collector-speculators, as some collectors are now called. Seasoned collectors very rarely buy work to hang in homes. It's more likely they will buy paintings, prints, sculptures or unique design pieces as investments. They will be concerned to know whether you have attended a prestigious college or studied under a well-known artist, and whether you have exhibited at established galleries, won awards or sold work previously at similar prices.

Making any comments along these lines will help convince a collector that the artwork is really worth the asking price. Collectors require an invoice, as well as your CV, as part of their archival documentation and also for insurance purposes.

Swap roles

Many artists and designers have found they feel more at ease selling or recommending their friend's artwork or creative products than their own. If this is the case with you, then team up with others whose work complements your own and share the task of selling each other's goods.

HOW TO IMPROVE THE LIKELIHOOD OF GAINING SALES OR CONTRACTS

- Undertake as much research as possible into your potential clients or customers.
- Understand what they want or desire.
- Why will/do your customers/clients buy your creative products and services? It's crucial to know this.
- Develop an enquiring mind.
- After an approach to an agency, or when a potential client responds to a mail-out, if they say, 'You must come in sometime', reach for your diary and make an appointment.
- If you're selling at fairs, stand up as much as possible and maintain a presence on your stand.
- Invest in a high stool with a small back, to sit on during short breaks. This helps to maintain eye contact with passing visitors.
- Have press packs, CD ROMs, CVs, pricelists, business cards and postcards, brochures, etc., all to hand.
- If there's space on the stand, make a quiet area, perhaps in a corner, furnished with a laptop, calculator and order forms, for conducting private discussions with customers.
- Never eat in exhibition spaces, and don't read the newspaper or appear bored. You don't know who will pop round the edge of your stand.
- Engage with visitors all the time.
- Try not to jump on floating browsers and attack them with an over-rehearsed sales pitch.
- Learn to be relaxed about talking to people by asking open questions such as:
  – Is this the first time you have visited this fair? How did you hear about the show?
  – Are you looking for a gift for a friend or for yourself?
  These types of opening questions will help you to discover more about customers, by engaging them in light conversation. This can be initiated by asking the first question, which will help you open a short friendly discussion about the person's interests. 'Casual' conversation gives your visitor the chance to steer discussion in a congenial direction.

In commercial sales, there is usually one person who is informative, who talks to customers about the artwork or product, technically, intellectually or practically. A second person manages the sales process and admin. If you're on your own at trade or retail fairs, it's essential to learn both these skills.

Finally, if you're really hopeless at making sales, then hire people to sell or pay them on commission. Many artists and designers have successfully adopted this strategy, and it's common for creatives working in the fashion industry to work with a partner who looks after the business side.

Understanding contracts

> 'A contract is only as good as the people who sign it.'
>
> *Ivan C. Karp (1926–), art dealer*

It's essential that artists and designers grasp the basics of contract law. *The Illustrator's Guide to Law and Business Practice*, by Simon Stern, is suitable for any creatives who have gained commercial commissions such as CD cover designs or images reproduced as patterns or transferred to other merchandise such as books, magazines, advertising, etc. This book demystifies legal terms and explains how to license rights.

Most professional bodies offer some form of advice service, and I highly recommend all the books and resources listed at the end of this and the previous chapter. If you really want to avoid being ripped off, then investing in textbooks and memberships is paramount.

When you first receive a contract

Think through what you want from the deal and make a list.

In Chapter 9, Creative Crimes, we discussed the subject of terms and conditions, and explained the phrase 'battle of the forms'. (Please read Chapter 9, if you haven't yet.)

After you have checked that there are no conflicting clauses between the two sets of terms, or after any amendments have been agreed, further commissions are usually agreed by separate contracts. It's worth knowing that intellectual property rights can only be legally assigned (sold) or leased by a written contract.

What is a contract?

A contract is defined as an 'offer' and 'an acceptance' with something 'in consideration', which is usually 'money', i.e. a fee.

If a contract is emailed to you, print it out and read it carefully. If there are clauses you don't agree with or understand seek advice from your solicitor or professional body. Then contact the prospective client directly and talk through your concerns in an objective way.

Once again, as with terms, the prospective client may issue an amended and more acceptable contract, without your having to go through the rigmarole of posting documents back with clauses struck out or amended. If the contract is acceptable make sure that both parties sign it, to avoid any risk of ambiguity. It's far better to have a retyped agreement than one with crossing-out all over it.

If there are outstanding issues you may be asked to return the original hard-copy version with your amendments. If so, sign it and then write clearly next to your signature, 'Agreed subject to the striking out of clause x, y & z and amendments to a, b & c, etc.'. Double-check that you have struck out or amended the clauses concerned, and initialled them at both ends of the line. Then return the document with a friendly covering letter, making it clear that you would like to proceed subject to the amendments suggested. They will either accept your suggestions or start negotiating with you. With any luck, an agreement will be reached and they will either send you a revised contract or post you back your original with their signature and initials added to your own next to the struck out or amended clauses.

Be alert to 'rights grabs'

Many firms practise what is known in the trade as 'a try-on'; they will literally 'try it on'. Sometimes these contracts are called 'standard' contracts. If you note the word 'standard' then it's likely the contract states the creative firm wishes to 'own' your copyright, i.e. they want you to 'assign' or 'transfer', or they want to 'buy', your 'rights' or 'copyright'. These are known as 'rights grabs'.

Once copyright is assigned, that's it. You can't even use the commissioned work for your own purposes, apart from being able to sell the original artwork (if the contract doesn't demand ownership of that too). You won't be able to negotiate on future uses or further fees, as the commissioning party will own the copyright outright.

As mentioned in the previous chapter, be aware of granting an all-encompassing worldwide 'licence' for all time. This is more or less effectively the same as 'assignment'.

If you don't understand the contract or you just sign it without reading it, you are storing up problems for later on. I have met many artists and designers who agreed to contracts that restrict their ability to trade and cause them to relinquish copyright of their own portfolio. Whilst there is a law against putting unfair terms into contracts, unfortunately, this doesn't stop companies from being ruthless and greedy. If a contract isn't a good one, then don't sign it.

Oral agreements

Across the visual-arts sector, it's usual that established agents and dealers represent artists and designers upon trust and a 'gentlemen's agreement'. This is often how misunderstandings can occur over time between artists and their representatives as the artist becomes more established. It's always best to confirm any trading agreement in writing with the agent or dealer.

Beware of the sharks

Always be aware of claims from individual agents that they can represent your interests worldwide. Only large agencies can cover a wide number of areas of trade and territory, and there are very few agencies or dealerships in the world large enough to be able to justify such a claim.

A further warning

If you do receive a contract from an agent or dealer and find it's a long, complicated affair, it may mean trouble. They may be trying unjustifiably to restrict your ability to trade. This can take various forms, such as, for example, clauses that disallow studio sales and the supplying of other businesses. Only very big fish indeed can demand exclusivity, so bear this in mind.

Avoid the wool being pulled

Remember, agents and dealers work for you. They're intermediaries between yourself and the client or collector. Professional agents and dealers do not claim any rights over your copyright or original artworks.

The perils of not reading the contract

Recently, an illustrator showed me a contract with an 'agency' that was the worst contract I had ever seen. He had met the directors of a so-called agency. He told me the directors had been really fun and he had signed the contract without reading it. The contract had locked him into an exclusive relationship with the agency for three years, for all advertising and editorial work, and claimed all worldwide rights. The contract also stated that they, the agency, would own the originals of any work produced, along with his entire portfolio including all work produced before the contract period.

The money he had been paid for work he had done up to the point when I met him was about 20% of the going rate. Yes, he had been well and truly stitched up. I suggested that he consult with a solicitor and extricate himself from this deal. Beware charmers bearing contracts.

Public and private commissions

Public art commissions, community projects, private commissions and residencies are usually very different areas of trade from the commercial sector. I would urge artists to take these matters very seriously, in the first instance by subscribing to and exploring the an web guides.

In public art commissions large sums of money can be offered – £20,000, £40,000, £100,000, even £1,000,000. I've met many artists who have been trundling along for years earning profits of anywhere between £16,000, to £25,000 per annum. Then after many attempts at being selected for larger projects they suddenly get a big break. If this happens or is currently happening to you, the size of your game will begin to change dramatically.

Some thoughts on how to deal with a large contract

- Understand all financial and Health and Safety liabilities.
- It's likely the scope of your insurance cover will have to be increased and expanded.

- What are the provisions stated within the proposed contract? Are they reasonable?
- Who is responsible for any maintenance? For how long?
- Are you personally liable if injury is caused to a member of the public?
- If you're accepting a large commission, consider whether to form a private limited company and get VAT-registered even for a one-off project.
- Negotiate for your own terms and conditions to be those that govern the contract.
- Insure that a proportion of the fee is paid up front as well as having interim payments scheduled for different stages of the project. If they are not met on the due date stop work!

In the beginning

When you start out as an artist or designer you may find that getting your own contracts drawn up isn't necessary. Professional bodies should be able to furnish you with the basics. However, I do think it's extremely wise, if you don't manage to gain representation from agents or dealers, at least to have terms and conditions drawn up. As commissions or sales pick up, you can purchase other appropriate contracts or legal documents, such as the following, from a reputable firm of solicitors:

- model release form
- order forms
- sale and return
- terms of hire
- licensing agreement/contract
- acceptance of a commercial commission
- private commission contract
- non-disclosure agreement (NDA)
- Other agreements particular to your area of trade.

Always use an IP solicitor to draft contracts if you are unable to obtain up-to-date versions from your professional body which meet with your specific requirements.

HERE ARE A FEW USEFUL TIPS

- Avoid making up your own terms or contracts; use the services of an IP solicitor.
- If there is a problem with a client's terms or contract, speak up, as silence will be viewed as acceptance.
- Don't be frightened about negotiating for better terms in agreements.
- Avoid relying solely on verbal agreements even if these are with well-established and reputable agents or dealers.
- After you have signed an agreement, you should always post two hard copies back to the other party. These they should sign and return to you (if the copies are not already pre-signed by them, in which case only return one of the original signed copies).
- Always keep a hard copy with your other business records.
- Don't start work until a contract has been signed by both parties, and any deposits due have been paid.
- Beware of free or budget-priced model contracts downloaded from the internet. Always pay for such contracts to be checked by an IP solicitor.
- If a big opportunity comes along and you're without representation, then approach an established agent or dealer. Many agents will be very pleased to negotiate a one-off deal for and may want to represent you on an ongoing basis, if substantial contracts are forthcoming. Most agents charge between 20 and 30%. However, commissions vary for different markets – for instance, 30% for advertising and 40% for work outside the UK.
- When you're undertaking regular commissions for a particular business, try to agree a standard term contract so that follow up commissions can be quickly arranged by phone and email. Agree that all future business will be conducted according to previous working arrangements unless an unusual request is made – it's still good practice to have the arrangements in writing, even in an informal email.

The rules of negotiation

> 'After fourteen trades with people from all over North America, one red paperclip had just become a house.'
>
> *Kyle Macdonald (1979–), maverick negotiator*

The quotation above is from *One Red Paperclip*, by the brilliant Kyle MacDonald, who traded up from one red paperclip, using

Craigslist, going from one deal to the next, until he owned a house. I highly recommend sparing an afternoon to be thoroughly entertained by his book.

Business culture

A businessman with worldwide experience of conducting meetings once said, 'For the Americans it was best to arrive early, for the Chinese it was customary to be prompt, and for the Italians, be prepared to wait...'

Over the years I have heard many strange stories about conducting business in Italy. I recall one artist who arrived on time for a meeting in Milan. She walked into the curator's office to find the gallery owner naked, laid out on her desk having a massage!

Business culture differs in every country. However, securing the best deal for all parties is still the aim of every business meeting around the globe. Many artists and designers are not prepared for the rigours of negotiation – as they are often so pleased to have work, they say yes to everything and consequently lose out.

Don't just say yes

I recall a story a businesswoman told me about visiting a degree show. She saw a painting and asked the art student the price. He said £1,000. The woman offered £400, expecting him to haggle the fee up to £850. Instead the young artist scratched his head and said, 'All right then', and accepted the first and lowest offer.

Overview of the negotiation process

We now have to turn our attention to some of the principles and tactics of negotiation.

Firstly, negotiation is a creative intellectual skill. Secondly, negotiation skills only improve with practice. After gaining a bit of experience you'll become more comfortable about the process.

Presentation

- Make sure to look the part. Pay a visit to the hairdressers, for example.
- Arrive early for meetings.
- Have extra cash to pay for a taxi, in case your car unexpectedly

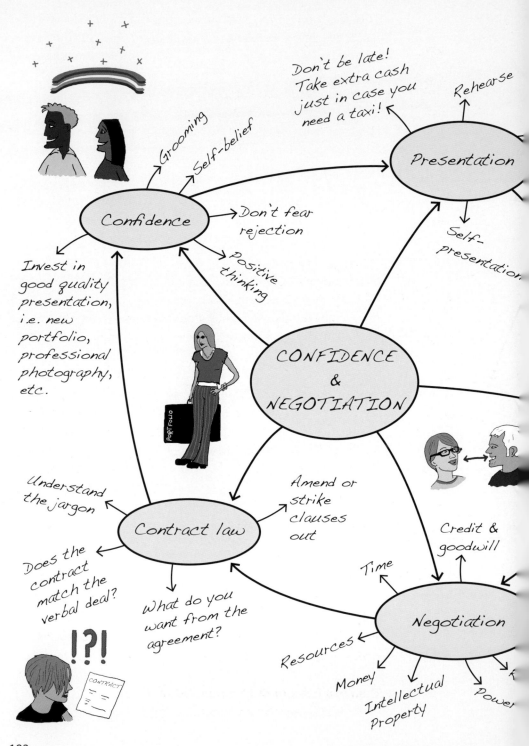

Grooming

Self-belief

Don't be late! Take extra cash just in case you need a taxi!

Rehearse

Presentation

Confidence

Don't fear rejection

Self-presentation

Invest in good quality presentation, i.e. new portfolio, professional photography, etc.

Positive thinking

PORTFOLIO

CONFIDENCE & NEGOTIATION

Understand the jargon

Amend or strike clauses out

Contract law

Credit & goodwill

Does the contract match the verbal deal?

Time

What do you want from the agreement?

Negotiation

Resources

Money

Intellectual Property

Power

!?!

CONTRACT

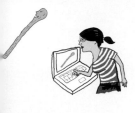

breaks down or you have problems with public transport.

- It's vital not to be late or to become stressed from panic.

Think about the client's needs

- Have a list of useful questions to ask, to clearly establish what they want, and to avoid misunderstandings.
- Think about your strengths and qualities, and interesting aspects that are particular to your work.

Confidence

- Make sure your portfolio looks contemporary – no heavy clips and dusty wallets.
- A refreshed portfolio often boosts self-confidence.
- Think positively about the meeting.
- Eat properly beforehand.
- Believe in yourself, even if you feel a bit unconfident.
- Be ready to talk confidently, and make sure your body posture is open, though not over-relaxed.

Preparation

- Do some research into the business, organisation or person you will be meeting.
- Think through the whole process and make a mind map® or notes on index cards.
- Use coloured cards and theme them. Put them in your pocket, so you can refer to them before the meeting starts.

Familiarise yourself with the principles of negotiation

- Think through what the other party will want to achieve in the negotiation.
- What's important to you? What's unimportant?
- What could be important to the other party and what is not?
- Think about the best and worst offer you will accept, e.g. the best fee, the most time and resources, versus your bottom line, below which you won't go.

Then you need to think about tactics

- Hopefully the other party will be up front about fees or

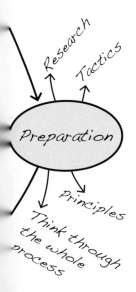

Understand your client

How to sell

Research

Tactics

Preparation

Principles

Think through the whole process

budgets. If they're vague about these issues, don't quote a price until you have had time to discuss and consider the brief.

- When quoting fees, go in high. Remember it's likely you will be haggled down.
- Show a willingness to negotiate and agree to compromises with clients. Stubbornness may get you a fat fee, but if it's at the expense of goodwill, then the working relationship may be a short one.
- Never reveal what is important or unimportant to the client. Use unimportant matters as bargaining chips. Unimportant matters could be time (if you're at a loose end), or transport (if you own a van), or space (if you're already renting a studio), etc.

THE SEVEN RULES OF NEGOTIATION

1. Time
To make life easier, always negotiate as much time as possible. Extra time means less pressure and the chance to take on other work. Remember, things can go wrong, so getting the maximum time will prove useful to allow for mistakes, corrections, illness or being let down by suppliers.

Time is of the essence, usually to the commissioning party. They will desire creative products and services completed by a deadline. If it's a short deadline, like 'tomorrow', you're within your rights to charge an extra 'rush fee', if it means working unsociable hours or turning down other opportunities.

2. Resources
Resources can easily be overlooked or undervalued. The commissioning party may have access to all sorts of resources which they would be happy to offer

you. The key aspect here is to think creatively about what could be useful to you. Gaining extra resources could save money elsewhere in the budget. These resources could include:

- Help with marketing or raising your profile
- Postage
- Photocopying
- Use of an empty space, e.g. a shop
- Venues
- Accommodation
- Temporary storage
- Software
- Equipment
- Transport
- Materials
- Models
- Costumes
- Props
- Archive materials
- The assistance of skilled technicians.

3. Money

It's easy to make the error of focusing on only obtaining the largest fee. Try to think about the bigger picture. In the longer term there can be alternative approaches to gaining money, valuable endorsements or raising your profile.

I agree that one of the main points of negotiation is to get a decent fee, but fledgling negotiators must look at all seven parts of the negotiation mind map before rejecting any deal.

4. Intellectual Property (IP) – *licensing or assigning rights, copyright, design right, patents or trademarks.*

If clients wish to own the copyright or registered rights to your creative products then charge them a substantial fee. If they don't wish to pay a large amount, offer them a licence.

'Selling physical artworks or products' and 'licensing rights' are two separate arrangements. If a visitor to your show says, 'I would like to buy that picture and put it on t-shirts', purchasing an artwork doesn't mean they can reproduce it. You could sell, or more wisely license, the visitor with 'limited merchandising rights'. They could purchase a licence and buy the original artwork to hang in their office, if they wish.

More money in the long run can sometimes be made by licensing, while at other times it can't. This is why it's best to talk to other industry professionals to help you decide what to do.

If clients wish to own the copyright, and aren't willing to pay a commercial fee, then the stock phrase you utter is 'I only undertake commissioned work on a one-use basis'. This means you only license rights and never assign them.

5. Risk

A cunning negotiator will put the burden of risk on you. An instance of this is offering you a deal with no fee, with only the promise of royalties. This is fine if products sell like hot cakes, but what if they don't?

Another example is a college or arts organisation offering you art courses to teach. They advertise the course with no guarantee of enrolment, nor a cancellation fee. Yet you can't book work on the dates advertised. This is common practice in the arts, I'm afraid. If you're unsure whether the marketing will be done properly, in the first year only commit to teaching the odd course.

6. Power

When you're on your own, and not part of a partnership, professional body or collective, it's easy to feel powerless. This is especially the case when you're without an agent or dealer, as representation by respected figures empowers your own reputation.

Open body language, formal posture and a clear speaking voice will make a good impression. If you exude confidence, then others will treat you with respect.

Knowing your rights, and being prepared to negotiate over rates, editorial decision making, retaining artistic control, etc. will gradually improve your position.

Saying no to a bad deal demonstrates you won't be taken advantage of. If you're worth it, they'll come back to you with something more reasonable.

7. Credit and goodwill

Always gain acknowledgement as the author/originator on any reproduction of your artworks or creative products.

Make sure any individuals, organisations or sponsors are properly credited. Taking all the glory, when it's not yours to have, can become a sore point if the input of others is ignored. It's unlikely they'll support you again.

Goodwill is the principal factor in all business relationships. Once rapport or trust evaporates then relations can deteriorate. Always do your best to maintain goodwill in any business dealings.

However, this isn't a green light to give in to unreasonable additional demands from clients, which are often preceded by the phrase 'could you just'. If 'could you just' is a great deal of extra work, then the commissioner has to pay more money or agree a further contract. Reputation is important. Be helpful, but not subservient.

RESOURCES

For other useful websites regarding legal matters and negotiation please refer to the Resources at the end of chapters 1, 2, 3, 4, 5 and 9. But see also: http://clientsfromhell.tumblr.com

Books

It's Not How Good You Are, It's How Good You Want to Be, Paul Arden (London: Phaidon Press)

Whatever You Think, Think The Opposite, Paul Arden (London: Penguin Books)

How to Develop Self-Confidence and Influence People by Public Speaking, Dale Carnegie (London: Vermilion)

Words That Change Minds: Mastering the Language of Influence, Shelle Rose Charvet (Iowa: Kendall/Hunt Publishing)

The Definitive Book of Body Language, Allan and Barbara Pease (London: Orion)

The Mindgym: Give me time (London: Time Warner Books)

One Red Paperclip: The story of how one man changed his life one swap at a time, Kyle MacDonald (London: Ebury Press)

Contract Law, Ewan McKendrick (Hampshire: Palgrave Macmillan)

Graphic Design: A User's Manual, Adrian Shaughnessy (London: Laurence King Publishing)

Against the Odds: An Autobiography, James Dyson (New York: Texere)

11

Records, Tax and Basic Bookkeeping

Co-authored by Dean Shepherd, Creative Industries Accountant, www.taxbydesign.com

> 'Accountancy is a profession whose idea of excitement is sharpening a bundle of No. 2 pencils...'
>
> *Anonymous*

Artists and designers new to business who haven't sought the advice of an accountant may be failing to maintain their records properly. I've seen notes of sales jotted down in the back of diaries, or scribbled on scraps of paper. Others have greeted me with a jumble of documents and receipts in plastic bags.

The disorganised can become quite huffy when informed that this isn't a professional way to maintain records. You should be aware that failure to keep proper records is a fineable offence. If you've a heap of receipts under the bed, it's now time to buckle down and get organised.

This is a long chapter. For anyone new to the subject of invoicing, tax and bookkeeping, it might be advisable not to read this chapter in one sitting. HM Revenue and Customs will be abbreviated to HMRC. Please remember to consult the glossary for any terms you don't understand.

Invoicing and getting paid

> 'Bill-making times of course were busy; yet it was only at Christmas that the bills were sent out...The idea was that farmers might have some money at that season.'
>
> *From The Wheelwright's Shop (1923), by George Sturt (George Bourne; 1863–1927), wheelwright*

As mentioned in Chapters 9 and 10, it can be helpful to adopt your own terms and conditions of trade. Issuing them to clients is the first step in ensuring you'll be paid for the provision of creative products and services.

An invoice is a bill. This can be a 'pro forma' invoice, which is what you send to clients if you need money up front to start work, e.g. for a substantial commission. The client may agree to stagger payments, e.g. part payment on presentation of roughs, with subsequent payments as later stages of the work are completed.

It's vital for any major undertaking that you minimise any financial liability to yourself by agreeing regular payments. Avoid heavily weighting an invoice (especially with clients you don't know very well) towards substantial payments on completion of a project. This could cause you cash flow problems or, worse, lead to bankruptcy.

How to send

An invoice can be sent by email as an email attachment, e.g. a PDF, in the body of the email or by post. I tend where possible to hand the invoice to the client when delivering work. Other artists and designers may require payment up front or on delivery of a painting, for example. Every creative business is different. The example on pages 190–1 is a template for what should be on a basic invoice. The design of invoices can vary. Suppliers of design products may select an elongated table format, so there's room for a list of products; other creatives may prefer no table at all. What's important is the following.

Dealing with late payment

I would strongly urge all UK readers to download and read the late-payment guidelines from the www.payontime.co.uk website, as mentioned in Chapter 9, Creative Crimes. They explain what to charge as an administration or penalty charge for late payment on invoices.

It's generally advisable to make payment terms 30 days, unless the custom is payment on delivery of goods. You can add the following phrase to your invoice and terms and conditions. Including any terms on your invoice will only act as a reminder

IMPORTANT TIPS TO KEEP YOU OUT OF TROUBLE

- Make sure that hard-copy invoices are printed on letter-headed paper.
- Avoid using carbon books unless at trade fairs. If you do, remember to retain the copy.
- Many creative businesses record payments by issuing receipts at retail or local craft fairs.
- Make sure every invoice sent is numbered and dated.
- Include the name and address of the client and if necessary any 'delivery' address, to avoid any confusion.

- You can only charge VAT if registered for VAT with HMRC. Note that this is a common error. If you have been charging VAT without being registered, seek advice from an accountant.
- Terms and conditions on an invoice only serve as a reminder and can't be legally enforced.
- Always print out two copies of invoices – one copy for your records and the other for the client.

to the client, as terms and conditions have to be agreed before any trading commences. Please refer to Chapter 9 for more on this issue.

'Payment to be received within 30 days of date of invoice. We understand and will exercise our right to interest and compensation for debt recovery under the late payment legislation if we are not paid according to agreed credit terms.'

To avoid running into problems with clients regarding late payments, always clarify the agreed credit period before accepting the work. If you're allowing 30 days, and no cheque arrives by post or any deposit appears in your business bank account, phone and email clients around the 25-day stage and enquire as to whether the client received your invoice, and if so how the payment is progressing. With telephone and internet banking, clients can pay any bill in a few seconds. So the cheque is in the post routine doesn't wash any longer, and is thus unlikely.

If the enquiry yields no results, send reminders by email and by post on day 27. Only after the 30-day period should you start issuing invoices with penalty fines. I have done this a few times over the years and it hasn't gone down well. Corporate firms can bully small suppliers, as they know smaller suppliers are dependent on them for business.

At the time of writing the UK government is exploring the idea of making late payment to small businesses a criminal offence. If they do pass this law, life for the self-employed will be a lot easier.

I would advise joining the Federation of Small Businesses (FSB), as they have extremely good deals on debt collection if things get to this point. The FSB also runs a legal helpline, which can be a lifeline when things go wrong. However, if the amount owed is under £100 it may not be worth the effort in chasing or taking it to the small claims court.

What to put on an invoice (sample layout)

Letter-headed paper

Your name, address or set letterhead/logo
Include your telephone and a fax number (optional)
e-mail and website address (especially when
sending electronically)

All these things need to appear, though not necessarily in this order!

INVOICE NUMBER/REF: Type number (first invoice would be 0001)

INVOICE TO: Name and address of client

DATE: Today's date

If a limited company include registered place and number (These details should be included in your letterhead)

If VAT-registered, VAT registration number

PAYMENT TERMS: Usually 30 days from the date of the invoice, but it may be 10 days, if you wish, or even cash on delivery, for example.

TERMS & CONDITIONS: You may want to state that you will:
- retain the right to copyright and right to be credited on your designs/artwork/film/script/learning material, etc.

- charge fees for cancellation/rejection/liability/storage of late pick-ups
- charge interest on late payments at 8% over current base rate plus administration fees.

Remember, printing terms on invoices only acts as a reminder.

INVOICE				
Date	**Quantity**	**Order Ref**	**Description**	**Amount**
State date of sale or service	Number	Special code or reference number (Purchase Order no.)	Description of sale or provision of a service	£s, or €s
		Subtotal		£s or €s
		Handling/Transport/Packaging/Delivery		Your own charge if applicable
		VAT 20%		N/A If not registered
		Total Due		£s or €s

- Insert logos of any business or membership of any professional bodies, e.g. FSB, ACID, etc.
- Think about how your invoice is designed in terms of style and practical use.
- For example, you may not need a purchase order reference.
- You can include your business bank account details (bank name, account number and sort code) on your first invoice to a client or include it every time.
- Always keep a copy of any invoices sent to clients or customers for future reference.

Taxation demystified

> 'In particular, I enjoy nothing so much as the moment, in the help sheet IR35 when, after a drill on the intricacies of National Insurance contributions, one is suddenly asked the question, apropos nothing: Are you a deep sea diver?
> I am not.'
>
> *Ross Clark (1966–), author and journalist*

Many readers may regard the subject of taxation as really boring. Well, it can be, if you don't try to understand it. Running a business requires a reasonably good grasp of maths and, sadly, many artists and designers are not very good at this subject. I wasn't very good at maths when I was younger. However, I have learned, like many business owners, that you can only acquire wealth when maths and common sense are applied to fiscal matters.

In this section I hope you will grasp the basics of what profit is and what kind of costs can be claimed as business expenses.

The UK tax year

The tax year runs from the 6th April (e.g. 2011) to 5th April (e.g. 2012) every year.

Timeline of deadlines for tax year 2011–2012

6th April 2011	5th April 2012	31st October 2012	31st January 2013
Start of the tax year	End of the tax year	Deadline for tax return for HMRC to calculate any tax owed	Final deadline for tax return submitted electronically and pay a proportion of tax owed

UK tax returns

Tax returns or self-assessment forms, also known as paper returns, must be completed and returned to HMRC, or filed online, before 31st October following the end of each tax year (e.g. 2012), and a cheque, or online payment, for any tax owed must be paid by the following 31st January (i.e. in the year 2013).

It's advisable if you're filling in the tax return yourself to send it to HMRC well before the first deadline of the 31st October.

If you fail to submit your tax return by 31st January 2013, HMRC will charge a penalty of £100. This penalty will rise to £200 if your tax return is still not submitted by 31st July 2013. If the tax due is not paid by 28th February 2013, there will be a 5% surcharge in addition to any interest. This surcharge will rise to 10% if tax remains outstanding at 31st July 2013.

Please note, if you're late and you have made a loss from your business, penalty charges will be withdrawn. However, it's better to file tax returns on time to avoid running into problems.

If your income is under £16,000 free advice is available from Tax Aid, who have offices in London, Birmingham and Manchester.

How UK income tax is charged

Income tax on net profits = income less business expenses and personal tax allowance. (See Business Expenses Chart, page 196.)

Your personal tax-free allowance (PTA) for the tax year ending 5th April 2012 is £7,475. (Please note this allowance is applicable

How is Profit Taxed?

Note: Personal tax allowance changes annually. Remember you only get your annual tax allowance once!

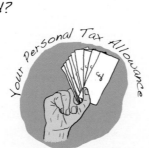
Your Personal Tax Allowance

P.T.A. £7,475 (2011-2012)

EXPENSES

PTA
First £7,475 income tax free

Only pay income tax on what's left!

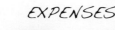

 Overheads

Variable costs

Petty cash

Dual use

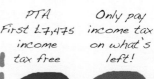 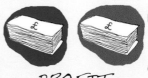 PROFIT

TOTAL INCOME

for 2011–2012 but changes annually, and is reduced if your income exceeds £100,000 in any one year.)

Meanings of basic bookkeeping terms
- *Overheads* – regular or fixed business costs
- *Variable costs* – irregular and less predictable costs
- *Petty cash* –expenses in cash, e.g. stamps, taxi fare, art sundries
- *Dual use* – tax relief claimed on a percentage of costs that are part business/part domestic, such as a car or a flat

The term '*offsetting*' means reducing your 'net profits' by subtracting all your overheads, variable and dual-use expenses from all business income. You offset expenses to reduce the tax liability on your profits. See example below and the chart on page 196. This summarises what can be counted as business expenses.

The more evidence of business expenses you have, such as paper invoices and receipts, the less tax you will be liable for. However, it's not wise to spend money on a business simply for the sake of paying less tax. On the other hand, if you understand how taxation works and are making a lot of money, it can be beneficial to spend money on equipment or vehicles before the end of the tax year.

UK tax bands

The self-employed have the same tax bands as employees.

Income tax is paid on any earnings over and above the personal tax allowance. The PTA can be set against your business earnings or employment if you have a job. Remember, you cannot claim your personal tax allowance of £7,475 twice (2011–2012). It's worth noting, the PTA, along with income-tax bands and National Insurance contributions, increases slightly every year.

For the tax year 2011–2012 for self-employment
- The first £7,475 of profit (your PTA) is income-tax-free.
- On the next £35,400 earned above that, income tax is paid at 20% (20p in the pound – known as basic rate).
- For earnings over £42,875, income tax is paid at 40% (40p in the pound – known as higher rate).
- For income over £150,000, income tax is paid at 50% (50p in the pound – known as additional rate).

Some pre-trading expenses can be offset against any profits made in the first year of trading. Usually, the pre-trading period is 18 months before registration. The pre-trading and start-up costs that can be counted are items such as business courses, equipment, computers and vehicles. See Business Expenses Chart, page 196.

National Insurance and personal allowances (2011–2012)

Class 2 National Insurance (NI) is set at £2.40 per week (or £124.80 per year) unless you have a Certificate of Small Earnings Exception. Predicted profits need to be less than £5,075 (in the tax year 2011–2012) to be eligible for such an exemption. If they are, fill in HMRC form CF10.

If profits are predicted to be over £5,075, you should instead set up a direct debit and pay Class 2 NI. This is payable every calendar month – fill in HMRC form CA5601.

Class 4 NI is payable at 9% if profits are between £5,715 and £42,875, and at 2% above £42,875 per year. This is paid with any income-tax payments due, after a tax return is submitted to HMRC.

A simple example

You have earned £16,000 income from your business.
£6,000 of this is made of business expenses: travel, insurance, post, materials, studio rent, marketing, etc.
This leaves £10,000 net profit.
Take away your personal tax allowance of £7,475 and you are left with £2,525.
The first £37,400 of income is taxed at 20p in the pound (20%).
   20% of £2,525 = £505.
Thus the total income tax you will have to pay on your net profits of £10,000 is £505.
Class 2 National Insurance at £124.80 per year applies to net profits over £5,075.
Class 4 National Insurance is 9% of any net profits over £5,715.
   So £10,000 – £5,715 = £4,285.
   9% of £4,285 = £385.65
Thus there is £385.65 to pay in Class 4 National Insurance contributions.
So the total National Insurance you will have to pay is £124.80 (Class 2 NI)
   + £385.65 (Class 4 NI) = £510.45.

Business expenses chart for offsetting against profits and tax

Materials	Services	Fees/other	Equipment/tools	Premises	Advertising	Admin.
Costs of goods bought for resale	All services: photocopying, film developing, framing, casting fees, printing costs, renting equipment	Fees for professional organisations, conference fees, periodicals/newspapers, gallery/other visits	Hand tools, paintbrushes, power tools, benches, any piece of equipment you need to make your work with	If your business is registered at a studio/office/workshop/shop, 100% of your rent, all electric & gas	All marketing cards, postcards, postage, adverts, exhibition costs	Stationery, envelopes, faxing, postage
Costs of manufacture						Cleaning expenses
Raw materials used	Expenses for hiring equipment	Travel (business), motor expenses, insurance, servicing repairs, petrol, parking, RAC/AA travel fares, hotel accommodation	100% tax relief on larger purchases, (see Annual Investment Allowance, AIA)	% of Council Tax bill	Setting up website/paying fees	Office sundries
All materials: e.g. paper, fabrics, card, chemicals, inks, cartridges, fabric, printing, plinths, display cases, films/videos, zip discs, CD-ROMs				% of telephone bill & rental (depending on location)	Printing stationery, compliments slips, rubber stamps	Notebooks, folders
	Accountant's fees, solicitor's fees, photographer's fees, web-design fees		Presses, easels, cupboards, storage boxes, maintenance repair, books/portfolios, bags	As a rough guide, if your home, % of use – so if you have 4 rooms and use 1 you can claim 25% of your tax back + % of utilities	Promotional gifts (small cost items)	Storage units, binders, pens/ink
	Repair fees, servicing fees, training fees	Licenses, insurances, private pension, bad debts, bank charges		Cost of repairs to business premises	Gifts up to £50 per year with branding on	Year-planners calendars, diaries
	Wages for employees	Registration fees	Food-business trips subsistence only (depends on where business is registered also)			Petty cash book/receipt book
		Special clothing				
		Certain research grants				

Services, materials, equipment, premises, sundries, and other costs, that you can claim as business expenses to reduce your tax liability.

Other information

- Tax rates and administrative requirements for registered companies are different from those for individuals. Companies pay corporation tax on their profits and income tax and National Insurance on directors' salaries.
- At the current time in the UK the self-employed can claim tax relief on mileage for cars at 40p per business mile for the first 10,000 miles, and 25p thereafter; for motorbikes it's 24p per business mile, while bicycles can claim 20p per business mile (a green initiative!).
- There are special rules for the claiming of expenditure on premises, large plant, equipment and cars called capital allowances. They are designed to spread the cost of the asset over its useful economic life to the business. There are a number of different rates of capital allowances, the most common being the Annual Investment Allowance or AIA.

Annual Investment Allowance (AIA)

This is a scheme whereby from April 2008 you have been able to obtain 100% relief on equipment, plant and machinery costs (except cars, though vans are included) up to £100,000. This limit will be reduced to £25,000 from 1st April 2012.

Cars

If you buy a car and wish to offset it for tax purposes, the calculations can be complicated. Cars emitting no more than 100g/km CO_2, and registered between 17/04/02 and 31/03/13, will have 100% tax relief, meaning that you can deduct the whole cost as a business expense.

Capital allowances

Other non-eco cars and vehicles are subject to a special capital allowance, where 20% of the balance of costs are claimed annually over the lifetime of the asset or until the vehicle is sold on. This rate will reduce to 18% from 1st April 2012.

A note to artists and designers who are currently not registered as self-employed

What if I'm making a loss?

If you are employed either part- or full-time, it can be worth registering as self-employed even if your business is making a loss.

How so?

If over the course of a year, you spend more money on materials/equipment than you receive from ad-hoc sales, you could offset any losses from being self-employed against the income tax paid in the course of your PAYE employment.

How is it worked out?

Suppose that you have a part-time job paying £10,000 gross, and your PTA (the first £7,475 earned) is allotted to your employment. The income tax on the remainder will be charged at 20%.

If you make a loss in your business of, say, £3,000, you can offset this loss against any tax paid under PAYE. Thus 20% of £3,000 is £600, meaning that if you are registered as self-employed and fill in a tax return, you will receive a cheque from the HMRC for £600.

The vagaries of VAT

VAT-registered business to VAT-registered business

Value Added Tax or VAT is a transaction tax charged on most products and services. The standard rate of VAT is currently 20%. There are also reduced rates and zero rates, but these only apply to a limited number of goods and services. Businesses can only charge VAT if they are VAT-registered. Then they will usually be required to complete a VAT return every three months.

Output tax

When a VAT-registered business supplies products or services and charges VAT on their invoices, this is termed 'output tax'.

Input tax

When a VAT-registered business receives an invoice or bill from a VAT-registered business and pays the supplier, this is termed 'input tax'.

VAT returns

VAT-registered businesses complete four VAT returns annually, when they are expected to pay the output tax, minus any input tax, to HMRC. This can become complicated. It requires you to complete forms and keep your accounts up to date.

Should your business have a good quarter, you'll have to pay HMRC all the VAT charged to other businesses (output tax). Against that, you'll deduct VAT paid on bills received (input tax). If you are charging more VAT (output tax) than you receive in relief on VAT paid on supplies or incoming bills (input tax), you will owe more VAT to HMRC overall.

The reverse is true should a business have a poor quarter, i.e. your VAT-registered business has paid a large quantity of bills to other VAT-registered businesses (input tax) and has not generated many orders or sales. Then your business will be paying more VAT on bills (input tax) than it's issuing to other businesses (output tax). In consequence you'll receive a welcome VAT refund from HMRC, of the difference between lower 'output tax' and higher 'input tax'.

When should you register for VAT?

- Only businesses whose turnover is greater than £70,000 (figure for 2010–2011) in any 12-month period are required to add VAT to their prices.
- Any business whose turnover is below £70,000 can choose to register for VAT voluntarily or not deal with VAT at all.
- The general rule is that if all your customers are VAT-registered businesses themselves (e.g. if you are a freelance designer working for a range of companies), then you will be better off financially if you register for VAT voluntarily.
- However, even if you deal only with VAT-registered businesses, if your income is low you may be better off not registering for VAT in order to keep your financial affairs simple.

Selling to the general public

If all your customers are members of the public (e.g. if you are selling your own products on market stalls) then you will be better off financially if you avoid registering for VAT until your turnover exceeds £70,000 in any 12-month period (limit for 2010–2011).

Payments

A variety of schemes are aimed at helping smaller businesses, such as the Flat Rate Scheme, the Cash Accounting Scheme, and the Annual Accounting Scheme. It's worth discussing these three options with an accountant to see if they would be beneficial to you.

Introduction to bookkeeping

> 'Bloom, do me a favour. Move a few decimal points around. You can do it. You're an accountant. You're in a noble profession.'
> From the film The Producers (1967), Mel Brooks (Melvin Kaminsky; 1926–), screenwriter

Bookkeeping, cash flow (money management) and working out tax liability are three separate sets of calculations. You may not fully grasp how to undertake these mathematical feats immediately after reading this book. These are activities that warrant demonstration by a trainer or being understood in one-to-one guidance from a sympathetic accountant.

Creative industries accountant Dean Shepherd and I have done our best to try to provide as much explanation as we feel we can in this section. With any luck, if you grasp the basics of tax and how to use a business bank account, then begin writing up your sales/commissions and noting expenses, that will be a good start.

How to use a business bank account

At the current time in the UK it's not a legal requirement to have a business bank account if you're self-employed. However, it is a legal requirement for a registered company.

Opening a business account is what any professional artist and designer should do if they're serious about managing a business properly. In other countries, not having a business bank account is illegal even for sole traders.

A business account will help you keep your accounts accurately, builds trust with clients and suppliers, and helps in the management of finances. Having a business account also acts as a buffer if you should find yourself investigated by HMRC. If you're self-employed with no business account, the Revenue can delve straight into your personal current account and examine transactions going back over many years.

'How to manage a business bank account' demonstrates how business accounts work. Once you have worked out your Personal Survival Budget (PSB), the annual amount is divided into 12 monthly amounts. Remember, these are known as your 'drawings' – what you are taking out of your business to live on.

If your business account can stand the strain of regular payments to your personal bank account, set up a monthly standing order from your business account to your personal account. In the beginning, when earnings are unpredictable, this could well cause difficulties. Don't set up such an arrangement until you have a few thousand pounds in your business account.

Drawing money randomly from your business account, or worse still trying to trade from your personal current account, will lead to cash flow problems and confusion in your financial affairs.

If you have a part-time job and are claiming Working Tax Credit, Child Tax Credit and/or Housing Benefit, you may wish to pay these monies into your personal current account. You might find you only need to draw a fraction of your monthly budget from your business account, especially if there's other income coming in from a job, a lodger or benefits. Remember, should you have a lodger or should you be renting a room in your house, you must include this income in your tax return.

With all business matters, it is best to be honest and straight. Tax evasion is a criminal office. Being dishonest can leave you open to blackmail or to spiteful people reporting you to the authorities.

Ask yourself if it is really worth the risk? If you're currently stretching the elastic of truth, there could be consequences, such as professional suppliers and clients deciding not to trade with you.

Bookkeeping

There are two main reasons for keeping an accurate record of your business income and expenditure. You are legally obliged to complete a tax return each year and disclose business profits to HMRC. Secondly, monitoring your incomings and outgoings is essential for making informed financial decisions.

HOW TO MANAGE A BUSINESS BANK ACCOUNT

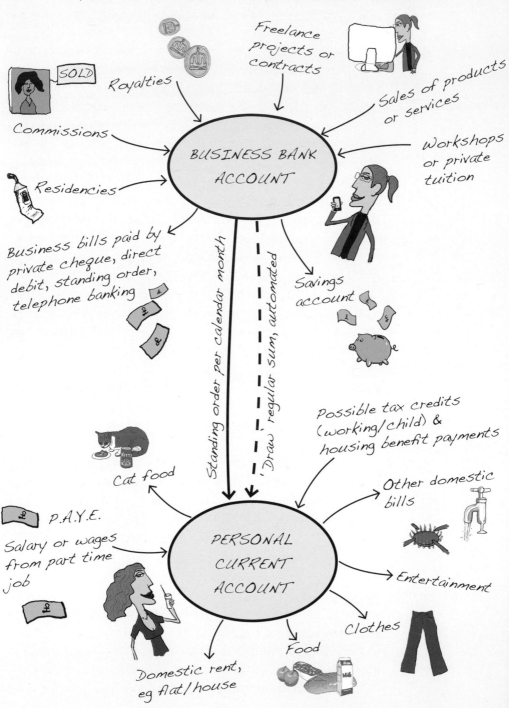

Royalties

Commissions

Residencies

Freelance projects or contracts

Sales of products or services

BUSINESS BANK ACCOUNT

Workshops or private tuition

Business bills paid by private cheque, direct debit, standing order, telephone banking

Standing order per calendar month

'Draw' regular sum, automated

Savings account

Possible tax credits (working/child) & housing benefit payments

Cat food

P.A.Y.E.

Salary or wages from part time job

PERSONAL CURRENT ACCOUNT

Other domestic bills

Entertainment

Clothes

Food

Domestic rent, eg flat/house

There are a variety of methods for recording business income and expenditure. The three most popular methods are as follows:

1. *Manual bookkeeping in a paper cashbook.* These types of books can be found in quality stationers. You record every item of income and expenditure that you earn or incur. At the end of each month, add up the rows and columns to calculate your total net income for that month. Then repeat the process until the end of the financial year. Be careful to avoid errors by double-checking entries.

2. *Computer-based spreadsheets (Excel)* offer a significant advantage over their manual counterparts. The software calculates everything for you. A good spreadsheet will mimic the manual-based cashbook that you may be used to. Many accountants like spreadsheets because they are flexible. They can easily manipulate, collate and, if necessary, correct mistakes.

To avoid data-entry problems have spreadsheets set up by an accountant, tailored to your own requirements. Basic spreadsheets are all that the vast majority of artists and designers require.

3. *Accountancy software packages (Sage/Tas/Quickbooks)*
A good software package can tell you how much money is in the bank, which customers still owe you money, and which bills need paying.

One could be forgiven for thinking that this would be the best option. Many software companies market their programs as really simple to operate. However, I have yet to use one that I can wholeheartedly recommend as the perfect solution for the smaller business.

Bookkeeping explained
You may find that Option 2 is the best place to start. A good spreadsheet designed by an accountant will make bookkeeping easier to do and is a good first step.

Let's use the example of 'A Beginner' to explain how a good bookkeeping spreadsheet should work.

Explanations follow about the three separate spreadsheets

that should be completed every month. The three separate spreadsheets record:

- sales invoices raised
- income as it arrives into your bank account
- business expenses

Record of sales invoices

Once it has been set up, you can use a spreadsheet like the Record of Sales (see page 205) to add amounts up automatically. If you've different income streams for your business, such as product sales, commissions or workshops, then you may find it useful to separate them out in columns, as shown opposite.

If your business is much more straightforward and has only one source of income, such as design fees, then simply use a single column.

An important feature of this record of sales is the 'Date paid' column on the right. If you complete this date each time you're paid for an invoice then it's very easy to see who still owes you money and how long customers take to pay.

Record of income

The Income spreadsheet (page 206) is very similar to the Sales spreadsheet. However, this time, instead of recording invoices as you issue them to customers, you record only cash physically received.

As you will see in the example, any cash received from customers can go in the sales column. (This information is gained from looking at your invoice records and business bank account statements.) This should hopefully match any invoices raised. If not, then somebody owes you money!

You can check who has not paid by looking at the 'Date paid' column of your Sales spreadsheet as mentioned earlier.

Sales receipts are unlikely to be the only source of business income. You may have interest paid to you by the bank, or you may have taken out a loan or put some savings into the business account. All these different sources of income must be correctly recorded in the Income spreadsheet but listed in separate columns to your Sales.

A Beginner 2011-2012 – Year End 5th April 2012

SALES   **OCTOBER 2011**

Invoice date	Customer/Event	Invoice no.	Total	Sales	Commission	Workshops	Other	Date paid
1 Oct 11	Arts Arts Centre/drawing workshop	0014	200			200		1 Nov 11
10 Oct 11	Mr Saatchi/Large canvas 33 'Eggs'	0015	1,400	1,400				5 Nov 11
15 Oct 11	Arts Arts Centre/drawing workshop	0016	200			200		14 Nov 11
TOTAL			1,800	1,400		400		

Record of Sales. Available on request from www.taxbydesign.com

A Beginner 2011-2012 – Year End 5th April 2012

INCOME NOVEMBER 2010

Date	Detail	Total	Sales receipts	Bank Interest	Owner's funds	Other income
1 Nov 11	Invoice 0014	200	200			
5 Nov 11	Invoice 0015	1,400	1,400			
14 Nov 11	Invoice 0016	200	200			
28 Nov 11	Interest received	5		5		
29 Nov 11	Savings from Halifax Building Society	500			500	
TOTAL		**2,305**	**1,800**	**5**	**500**	–

Record of Income. Available on request from www.taxbydesign.com

EXPENSES **NOVEMBER 2011**

Date	Payee	Receipt no.	Ref.	Total	Business Bank	Other	Materials	Studio costs	Travel & subsistance	Advertising & marketing	Research & subscriptions	Postage & stationery	Telephone fax & internet	Bank charges & interest	Loan repayments	Equipment & tools	Drawings & salaries	Other expenses	Description
					PAYMENT METHOD														
2 Nov 11	Mr Fab's Art Shop	001	Debit	100	100		95									5			Materials & tools
5 Nov 11	Tracy's Stationers	002	Cash	5		5	5												Paper
10 Nov 11	Local transport pass	003	C/card	80		80			80										Bus pass
17 Nov 11	BT	004	C/card	50		50							50						Landline
20 Nov 11	Publishers	005	Chg	38	38						38								Periodical subs.
22 Nov 11	Mr Fab's Art Shop	006	Cash	40		40	40												Paints
24 Nov 11	Colour Arts E-Shop	007	Debit	60	60		60												Canvasses
24 Nov 11	Reds Repo Graphic	008	Debit	65	65					65									Flyers
28 Nov 11	Miss A Beginner	009	Tfr	1,700	1,700												1,700		Drawings
29 Nov 11	Post Office	010	Cash	2		2						2							Stamps
30 Nov 11	Bank	011	Debit	200	200										200				Start-up loan
TOTAL				2,340	2,163	177	200	–	80	65	38	2	50	–	200	5	1,700	–	

Record of Expenses. Available on request from www.taxbydesign.com

Record of expenses

The final spreadsheet (page 207) is the Expenses spreadsheet, and this is slightly more complex. The layout should look familiar in that there is a date column and a space for your supplier's name and the receipt number. You can number receipts sequentially – 1, 2, 3, 4, etc. – by writing on each receipt with a pen. This will make it easy to locate any receipt in future in case you or your accountant need to look at it again.

One notable difference when entering data into this sheet is that you need to enter the same figure twice. This is called double-entry bookkeeping.

First of all enter the amount paid in one of the two grey columns, which denote how the payment was made – either from the 'business bank account' or 'other' sources such as cash or credit card. Then the same figure has to be entered again under one of the appropriate expense headings, so that we can analyse where our money is being spent over the course of the year.

Note, for example, that on the 2nd November at Mr Fab's Art Shop, materials costing £95 and tools to the tune of £5 were purchased. These two amounts are shown under the appropriate columns, as a 'debit' in the reference column, and entered as a total of a £100 in the 'Business Bank' grey column.

The 'Reference' column (or Ref.) is where we enter a description of the payment method – credit card, debit card, cash or cheque. The 'Description' column to the far right details what it is we have bought, such the 'materials and tools' on 2nd November.

In summary

If you use the above three spreadsheets then you shouldn't go too far wrong. Any mistakes you make along the way should be easily rectified by your accountant.

What about PayPal?

As more and more people are buying products and services via the internet it's advantageous to have a facility for accepting payments online. Accepting online payments can improve your cash flow significantly.

If you're unsure of the level of online sales you are going to make then PayPal is a quick and easy method for collecting payments from customers. As PayPal is a recognisable brand, many of your customers will already have confidence in using it as a payment method.

Key points
- Your customer doesn't have to be registered with PayPal themselves and can pay using a range of credit and debit cards, bank transfers or even their own PayPal account balance.
- There are a range of business-account options depending on whether you want to accept multiple currencies, integrated website buttons or even payments over the phone.
- The fees per transaction can be higher than having your own merchant banking account, but PayPal is quick and easy to set up.

Bookkeeping and PayPal
- It's vital to retrieve your total income, fees, charges paid and balance transfers every month. These can be easily downloaded from PayPal in the form of a bank statement.
- To keep things simple, open one PayPal account for any purchasing transactions you make for your business, and have a separate account to accept payments from customers.
- You must keep all personal expenditure away from the business PayPal account, just as you would from your business bank account.
  Read more about trading online in the next chapter.

Records to be kept
Records must be kept for six years. So if you start trading in 2011–2012 you would have to retain your records until January 2018. That means storing all your records, labelled, in large lever files, or A4 archive boxes.
- Keep all receipts/invoices of sales and expenditure in good order, bagged by month, labelled and organised, i.e. not in a massive heap on the floor.
- Keep evidence of all expenditure and sales, such as all

supporting documents relating to business transactions including business and personal current-account bank statements, as well as deeds, contracts, insurance records, important email correspondence, vouchers and receipts.

- All creative businesses should keep stock and work-in-progress records, and details of money introduced into the business from savings, grants and loans from relatives or banks. Also make a record of money taken from the business for personal use, usually referred to as 'drawings' for artists and designers who are sole traders.

- Keep a full set of accounts in Excel, with spreadsheets, if possible, or manual records of all payments coming in and any going out. You may require two to four spreadsheets for each month.

- Keep summaries and documents relating to any indirect or dual-use expenses, including, fuel/petrol, domestic rent, domestic mortgage, Council Tax and utility bills such as electric and gas.

RESOURCES

Please view websites listed at the end of chapters 1, 2, 3, 4 and 5.

HMRC, www.hmrc.gov.uk or www.hmrc.gov.uk/students

Companies House, www.companieshouse.gov.uk

Tax and Accounting Services

Tax By Design: Accountants for creative people, www.taxbydesign.com. See this website for current updates about taxation matters. Digital versions of the accounting spreadsheets featured in this book are also available on request.

UK tax calculator, http://appshopper.com/finance/tax-calculator-uk

'Credit Card Terminal' and 'Timeworks' invoicing application, www.apple.com/uk

Association of Chartered Certified Accountants, www.accaglobal.com

Institute of Chartered Accountants in England and Wales, www.icaew.com

Tax Aid, www.taxaid.org.uk

Federation of Small Businesses, www.fsb.org.uk

Pay on time 'Late Payment Guidelines': templates and interest calculator, www.payontime.co.uk

Books

Tax Answers at a Glance, H.M. Williams (London: Lawpack Publishing)

101 Ways to Pay Less Tax, H.M. Williams (London: Lawpack Publishing)

Bookkeeping Made Easy, Roy Hedges and Roger Walkley (London: Lawpack Publishing)

How to Label a Goat, Ross Clark (Hampshire: Harriman House)

Please note that details of tax rates and allowances given in this chapter are subject to change. Please visit www.taxbydesign.com for the latest rates.

12

What Next?

> 'Your horizon always grows.'
>
> *Gareth Neal (1974–), furniture designer*

At the 2009 Hidden Art Forum, Gareth Neal spoke about how he nurtured relationships with collectors and had successfully raised his profile by showcasing his work at prestigious design fairs in London, New York and Milan.

He talked about how aspirations change as a practice or creative business develops. This is true: as a third-year student you're hopeful that sales or offers of work will arise from your degree show, whereas after graduation an ambition may be to have a solo exhibition or host a stand at a trade fair, while other creatives may aspire to gain commissions, contract work, representation from an agent and so on.

To make progress, it's essential to pursue new initiatives. Larger-scale ventures are more risky and costly, and may not yield immediate benefits. Yet to move a creative business forward, you have to seek fresh direction, and take some risks.

Keeping up to date

> 'As soon as you become complacent in any creative industry, then there is somebody in the fast lane overtaking you...'
>
> *Paul Smith (1946–), fashion designer*

The relentless pace of change in styles, software and technology is an additional challenge. Many designers can't even afford the expensive software that is termed 'industry standard'. Another difficulty for the new graduate is maintaining access to expensive or hi-tech equipment.

When establishing a business, it's vital to develop your skills base and keep abreast of technological advances. In major cities there are innovation centres or universities where local creative businesses can access technical expertise, equipment and prototyping facilities.

There are Arts and Crafts Council programmes, available throughout the UK, which provide placements for artists and designers in universities or businesses, as well as supporting research activities. Numerous government-funded organisations offer advice and funding. (See the resources listed at the end of previous chapters.)

So what if I get a bit behind, it's not the end of the world

If you fail to keep up to date with current trends you'll lose out to competitors. Many artists and designers struggle financially because they have failed to adapt their methods since the early 1990s. They may continue to retain a few longstanding clients. But what happens when old clients retire from business? Traditionalists may find they can't complete orders quickly enough and lose clients to the competition.

As Paul Smith declares, the next generation and those hungry for success will always be there.

How to keep up to date

Periodicals – read them
At least once a month, read a selection of industry periodicals. Quality publications are trustworthy sources of information. Reading only one periodical every so often is not enough; in fact it can be damaging, as you won't gain a balanced or informed view of what's going on.

Industry events
Attend conferences, workshops and networking events. It's only when diverse, accomplished speakers and interested audiences come together that new knowledge and deeper understanding about your industry will be acquired.

Courses

Take courses, whether technology-based, theoretical, vocational or more to do with learning about contemporary issues in your field. If you're too short of time, pay other people to undertake complex, highly skilled or technical tasks. Remember, you don't have to do everything yourself. From Michelangelo to the Mike Smith Studio, creators have always employed assistants and skilled technicians.

Access to resources

Find ways of gaining access to essential software, hi-tech digital printing or other equipment. Contact local business support agencies, innovation centres, universities, the Arts, Film and Crafts Councils, and local-council arts and business-development officers. If you're still at college, chat up the technicians, turn detective and track down hidden resources.

In the know

Keep informed about market trends, as well as business, fiscal, legal and political developments around the world. Listen to or read the news, and subscribe to legal email newsletters sent out by the Intellectual Property Office (IPO) or other memberships bodies such as Anti Copying in Design (ACID).

Google provide a number of free business services. One of them is a currency converter. You can install it onto your Google page. This device is especially useful when calculating pricing for overseas sales, jobs or orders.

Trading via the internet

'With the ascendancy of Etsy.com and other e-commerce sites aimed at the new wave of crafters, it's not far-fetched that today's artists tailor their work to look good on an LCD screen.'
Garth Johnson (1973–), ceramicist and lecturer

There are many ways of promoting, showcasing and trading online such as Etsy, Bouf, Hidden Art, Ispot and even eBay. There are also popular social networking websites, including LinkedIn, Facebook and MySpace. Images can be placed on portfolio websites such as Axisweb, YouTube, Behance, Coroflot, etc. Blogging sites such as Twitter, Illustration Friday and Creative Opera are also now very popular methods of attracting attention, and it is also worth considering other online creative business directories, e.g. Image Animation, The Interior Design Directory and Photostore (Crafts Council).

As well as having your own website it's wise to have a number of other web presences. However, most arts practitioners and creative businesses use their own websites for the majority of e-trading transactions.

The improved security for processing card payments has increased consumer confidence. The public now expects, in most cases, to buy products directly from business websites.

The basics of setting up a website

There are several types of software for setting up an e-commerce website. These include Adobe Dreamweaver, Freeway Pro, and Golive. Other less expensive and easier options are purchasing template packages such as Mr Site. It's tempting to use these budget solutions, and they can work when constructed with minimal composition and a subtle palette.

The downside of any template website is that they restrict design flair and stifle presentation. It's easy to tell the difference between a site built with a standard package and one that's been professionally designed.

If you're selling limited-edition artworks or niche products, it's advisable to use the services of an experienced web designer. It's better to have a three-to-five page stylish layout than dozens of pages using a cheap, unimaginative template format.

Checklist for e-trading

Information technology and web-design language is full of jargon and anachronisms that can easily confuse the beginner. Please read this section carefully, especially if you are unfamiliar with some of these terms.

Internet Service Provider (ISP)
It's sensible when embarking on setting up in business to invest

in a broadband connection with an ISP such as AOL, BT or Virgin. This will enable you to set up, for example, a Virgin Media or BT Internet email address, and to use the Outlook Express or Microsoft Outlook email software installed on your computer.

Buy a domain name

The first task is to purchase your domain name or URL (Uniform Resource Locator). If you're not ready to build your website, at least register so you can 'park' the domain name to ensure it doesn't get taken by a competitor.

Try to buy the .com domain name, as well as the domain name applicable to your country – .fr, .au, .es, .co.uk, etc. If you're using a business name, keep it short, memorable and easy to spell.

Domain names are only licensed from domain/hosting providers and can never be owned outright. When you buy your domain name, ensure that you provide a reliable contact email address, so that the domain-name company can always contact you to remind you when to renew the domain. It's essential to register the domain in your own name or company name. Remember, it's only the registrant who owns the rights to rent that domain name.

The whole package – domain name and web hosting

To reduce complications, it's easier/advisable to buy both the domain name and the hosting (meaning the rental of web space on a server) from one company at the same time.

Setting up your email address

The domain/hosting company you bought the domain name from usually provides you with access to an online control panel. This can be used to create email addresses and set up 'forwarding rules' for your business email address – so that, for instance, Alison@alisonbranagan.com forwards to your ISP email alison.branagan@virgin.net. You will be able to send and receive emails from your ISP's webmail service online from any computer with internet access.

Then it's wise to configure your MS Outlook or Outlook Express email software so you can also send and receive emails from your own PC.

215

If you set up an email forwarding rule to an internet-based email service like Hotmail, in the first instance people will think that they are emailing, say, a@abeginner.com at their own website; but when you reply to their email the sender will be your Hotmail email address. This doesn't look professional. One way around this is to choose a web-hosting company that offers the facility to set up a webmail service provided by the hosting company itself. One disadvantage is that webmail accounts usually have a restricted capacity, which means that email in the webmail system must be periodically deleted. If the capacity allowance is exceeded then emails will stop being received and will bounce back to the sender.

In any case it's not very sensible to set up a business using a free web-based service. To avoid making life complicated, simply set up an email account with your ISP provider.

You can set the sent/reply email address in your Outlook mailbox to include your domain name, e.g. a@abeginner.com. This will mean the receiver of your email will not view the sender as a.beginner@virgin.net

Establishing the forwarding means you can avoid making elementary mistakes on marketing materials (see below).

A Beginner
Artist

w. www.abeginner.com
e. abeginner44@hotmail.com
07941 74262

A business card without a professional email address

This is a common mistake – a mobile phone number, with no professional email address such as a@abeginner.com. Also, not including a business address, e.g. studio, workshop, office or home, does not help potential clients to trust you.

Search engine optimisation and registration

Meta tags
Meta tags are an aid to search-engine optimisation. They consist of a title, a description and keywords/phrases. When a user searches for a website, the search results will feature the title as a link and the description below. When visiting a website, the title also appears within the top bar of the browser. Note that keywords/phrases are not visible to visitors.

Keywords/phrases are terms that a user would enter into a search engine such as Google in order to find your website. Meta tags are placed within the code on each page so that the pages are accessible to search-engine spiders. If budgets allow, hire a web-optimisation company to analyse the best keywords/phrases to target. If you're short on funds, you can decide on your own key words. To view examples of meta tags, go to any established website and look to the top left of your browser menu bar. Click on View, and a dropdown menu will appear. Then click on Source.

Other techniques to improve your search engine ranking include having specific keywords within web pages, headings and subheadings. A 'Links' page to relevant websites will increase traffic. Include your keywords within the link and ask related websites to link back to your website (called 'reciprocal linking').

World Wide Web Consortium
For best results your website should pass the W3C validation at http://validator.w3.org.

Search-engine registration
Once your website is online, it's crucial to register it with search engines and directories. You can do this yourself by visiting search engines individually, or you can hire a search-engine registration company. If finances allow, it's best to employ professionals.

Selling online

Check your hosting provider supports PSP
If planning to sell products online you'll need to set up an account

with a payment service provider (PSP) such as PayPal. An account can be easily set up by visiting any of these websites.

SSL – shopping securely

If you are collecting customer data such as names and addresses then it's advisable to collect this data on a secure page, loaded via an HTTPS connection. To achieve this, you must purchase an SSL certificate, dedicated to the site domain name, which is normally available via your hosting company.

SSL (secure socket layer) certificates create a secure connection between the visitor's browser and the server, protecting any data being transferred, such as address details. Your PSP will have their own SSL certificate to protect credit-card information.

With the rise of credit-card fraud, the payment card companies have issued the Payment Card Industry Data Security Standard (PCI DSS), which requires all organisations that take payment card information to audit their IT systems and procedures, and secure their servers. To minimise the potentially huge costs relating to the PCI DSS requirements for websites that handle payment card information, most businesses use a third-party PSP such as PayPal, Sage Pay or Google Checkout to collect online payments.

If you're gathering and retaining customer data (collecting and storing it digitally or even as paper records), you must also comply with the Data Protection Act 1998 and register with the ICO (the Information Commissioner's Office) by visiting www.ico.gov.uk. Fill in the notification form and post it back to them. Alternatively, you can phone 0845 630 6060. The annual fee is currently £35 per year.

Other regulations to comply with are the Consumer Protection (Distance Selling) Regulations 2000. You also need to have terms and conditions for e-trading drawn up and included on your website.

Don't panic

For most readers, to minimise the audit overhead, it's recommended simply to use the services of a secure payment gateway such as PayPal, Sage Pay or Google Checkout for the collection of payment details.

Typically, the shopping cart checkout will collect the customer's address details, confirm the order details and transfer them to the payment gateway. The customer will be returned to the site once payment has been collected. However, if you retain customer information in emails, it's likely that you'll still need to register with the ICO. The rules and regulations are complicated, so if you're unsure you should phone them to clarify your situation.

Other online payment gateways
Please note, if you're using a payment gateway other than PayPal or Google Checkout then you will need to open a merchant bank account with a separate business bank account set up specifically to collect online payments. This option is usually only appropriate if you are expecting multiple orders every day as there are setup and monthly fees involved.

For more about PayPal, please see the previous chapter and also below.

Options for setting up an e-commerce website

eBay store
If you're only selling a few products and operating on a shoestring budget, an eBay store will allow you to sell products online. However, the store can be limited in terms of customisation and there can also be hidden fees.

Google Checkout
Google Checkout works in a similar way to PayPal Standard in the sense that the user is transferred to the Google website during the purchase process.

PayPal Standard and Pro
The easiest option for a beginner is to set up Paypal Standard. This allows you to add 'buy' buttons to your website. The customer is redirected to the PayPal website to make the purchase. The purchaser does not need to have a PayPal account, as payments can be made via a PayPal account or a credit/debit card.

Paypal Pro will allow you to integrate a seamless shopping

cart into your website so that the user remains on your website throughout the purchase process.

Pre-built shopping carts

There are a number of pre-built shopping carts available such as Zen Cart (free), osCommerce, Cubecart, Magento and CRELoaded. Please note this option should only be set up by an experienced web designer.

Custom-built shopping carts

If funds allow, having a custom-built shopping cart is the way to go. A web developer will be able to design and build a customised online store tailored to your branding and requirements.

Some final thoughts

To avoid running into disputes, always register the domain name yourself. If you commission a web designer, check that there is a proper contract clearly stating which services have been agreed, with a breakdown of fees and a deadline for completion.

Innovation and future trends

'Designers always need to have a foot in the future while also having the other foot in the present...so they can make the future happen by pushing innovation.'

Paola Antonelli (1963–), senior design curator, Museum of Modern Art, New York

As well as the advancement of technology, there are many other issues of which artists and designers must be aware. It's impossible to ignore innovation, ecology, economic factors, fashions and trends, even if you wanted to. It's crucial to find time to think and cultivate a vision for the future.

Trends

If a you're a product, furniture, textile, fashion or interior designer or architect, predictions for colours, materials and textures can be obtained from trend-forecasting reports. These publications also outline consumer attitudes and interests. In 2011, trend forecasters will be working on 2013 and beyond. These reports are taken very seriously by pigment, paint, wallpaper, carpet and textile firms. Major fashion and home-styling firms will already know what they will be stocking over the next six to 24 months. They have to know what raw materials need to be produced, the basic ingredients and materials. between two and fours years in advance.

These industry reports are very expensive to buy, so a less expensive option is to buy colour and trend magazines. They give a general outline of what's happening in the next six to 24 months.

No time to waste

When establishing a business, train your mind to think between one and three years in advance. What's in your sketchbook today may take more than a year to develop into a realistic product. If it's late 2011, then realistically your first trade fair could be the spring of 2013, where buyers will be placing orders for autumn and winter 2013.

If large orders are taken, they may have to be honoured in a very short space of time, sometimes in a matter of a few weeks. Preparation is paramount to be able to meet the quotas requested.

Art trends

Artists, commercial artists and image-makers have also to be aware of trends, both current and some way off. If a style magazine requires an illustration of funky teenage girls, would you be clear about what they should be wearing? I recall meeting an illustrator friend outside H&M, who was quickly drawing a shoe in his sketchbook and taking a few photographs on his mobile phone. When I enquired what he was doing, he said, 'Look, see the shoes – they are now round, not pointed,' he replied.

Artists and designer-makers will find similar patterns of trends within the art market. It's predicted that, following the current period of economic gloom, by 2011 the art world will have fully recovered. In fact the crashing of the auction price of contemporary artists' work may provide new openings for less well-known artists.

It's worth bearing in mind that Sotheby's, Christie's and Bonhams are establishing new auctions for one-offs or limited edition pieces of contemporary art and design. The antiques trade is a shrinking market. If auction houses are to survive they have to develop new markets. I'm convinced that over the next ten years regular auctions for new artworks and design pieces will spread beyond the major cities into the regions.

Rise of handicraft

Trend forecasters predict that consumers will become more interested in craftsmanship and the handmade. It's likely there will be a crafts renaissance, with adults and children becoming more interested in physically making things for the home themselves. There may be openings in 2011 for the provision of more art and craft workshops, or for kits for adults, children and families (information from Future Laboratory).

Cult of the amateur

A big problem facing new and established artists and designers is the 'cult of the amateur'. Blogs and virtual noticeboards are replacing the output of experienced writers and journalists. With the growth in 'micro-stock' websites fuelled by Flickr, novices are destroying the market for stock images by professional photographers. Illustrators and designers are being equally damaged by the availability of cheap stock and the recent phenomenon of 'crowdsourcing' (outsourcing tasks by advertising online for free or low cost assistance). Illustrators, for instance, have suffered a fee freeze on most commissions since the 1990s.

Free art fairs, giveaway art projects and public participation events such as the One and Other Trafalgar Square plinth project in 2009 deny opportunities to professional artists. TV reality, video-clip and quiz shows are being commissioned ahead of more traditional, but more expensive, light entertainment or drama serials. These developments are a serious challenge to those who have paid to study at art school.

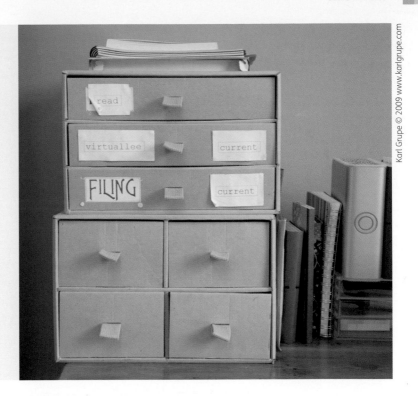

Eco filing system

Why not give art away for free?

A senior graphic designer I met recently said that an increasing number of his clients are making their student interns undertake work he used to do as a freelancer. This rise of a 'free culture' is problematic. When you're young, making work for 'free' can appear to be fun. However, this trend of young creatives working for nothing is destroying the market, just as the rise of DIY in the 1970s undermined the skilled tradesman.

Ecology

Recycling, minimising waste, reducing carbon footprints, ergonomics, eco-friendly materials and sustainability are aspects of a huge problem facing the world today. Consumers around the world are becoming increasingly aware of climate change, pollution and the poor working conditions endured by workers in developing countries. Businesses and consumers are now paying greater attention to these concerns, as are an increasing number of artists and designers.

223

Reflection and innovation

Experimentation and innovation are activities that require time and a environment conducive to the development of new ideas. The artist, designer-maker or traditional craftsperson should consider applying for residencies as a means of widening their horizons. Residencies take various forms, such as teaching workshops, the creation of a mural or public artwork, or staging an exhibition. They are usually community-based, in schools, hospitals, arts organisations and universities. Although some businesses and larger corporate firms offer residencies, these are essentially for aesthetic or social purposes.

It's usual when undertaking a residency to be provided with a studio space and to be paid a fee. These types of opportunities can vary in duration from a few days to a year.

Holidays and travel, or simply taking proper time off to rest after a busy period, are further ways to renew your perspectives. Thinking is the only way you can reflect, find solutions, and originate new ideas.

Well, goodbye...for now

I hope you've enjoyed reading this book and now feel more confident about how to start and run a successful creative business. The chapters in the book have been designed to take you on a journey providing an overview of key business skills and industry resources.

Most people who set up in business are surprised to find it's more complicated then they first anticipated. This is why researching, planning and sketching mind maps can help you make more informed decisions.

I wish you the best of luck with your practice or creative business. A&C Black is always interested in recommendations from readers about useful books, websites and organisations that may have been missed from this first edition. Please email any suggestions about new content for inclusion to me at alison@alisonbranagan.com

The web designer

Lee-Ann Olivier

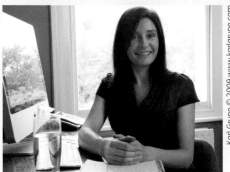

Karl Grupe © 2009 www.karlgrupe.com

Lee-Ann Olivier is a British, South African-born web designer who came to live in London 15 years ago after completing a language degree at Durban University in South Africa.

In 1998 her husband was transferred from London back to South Africa for two years. Lee-Ann returned with him. Determined not to work in formal employment, and without any experience, Lee-Ann started a business designing sleepwear. She hired patternmakers and dressmakers to make up stylish sleepwear and linen, and then supplied local boutiques with her collection. The customer base grew from one shop to several retailers throughout South Africa.

She sold her business in the year 2000 when she and her husband returned to London. Ten years ago the demand for websites from small businesses as a form of advertising and communication was increasing. Lee-Ann spotted this opportunity. She taught herself basic website design from a book and then studied for six months on a full-time advanced web-development course. To learn more about how to set up a creative business she also enrolled on a series of workshops at a local community centre.

Lee-Ann's websites are custom-designed with meticulous attention to detail. To view her portfolio visit www.virtuallee.co.uk

Her five essential tips are:

1. Is an art or design degree really necessary?

Try not to be put off by the fact that others may have spent years studying what you want to do. If you have the ideas but not the skills, then outsource to someone who can make your ideas become a reality. When I started the sleepwear production business, I didn't even know the difference between a hem and a seam – but the patternmaker and seamstress did.

2. Improve your business skills

Fill knowledge and skills gaps. Do short courses in business, marketing and presentation.

3. Don't procrastinate

Don't use the excuse that before you can promote yourself it's necessary to build a large portfolio or product range. Have confidence – a small selection demonstrates editing skills and a clear focus.

4. Network

I built my business through networking. I found most of my customers by joining local business clubs and women's networking organisations.

5. Be the first to reply to an enquiry

Respond quickly to any enquiries, the client may be contacting a number of designers. Stand out, be efficient and respond promptly.

RESOURCES

Innovation

www.newscientist.com

www.sciencemuseum.org.uk

www.innovation.rca.ac.uk

www.hhc.rca.ac.uk

www.london-innovation.org

www.londoninnovationmap.com

www.nesta.org.uk

www.apple.com

www.adobe.com

www.wacom.com

www.artcam.com

www.google.com/finance/converter

www.google.co.uk/intl/en/exportadviser

Distance-selling regulations

Office of Fair Trading, www.oft.gov.uk

Trading Standards, www.tradingstandards.gov.uk

Information Commissioner's Office, www.ico.gov.uk

Technical

www.w3.org

www.seo-blog.com

Trends

Mix, the magazine for colours and trends published by Global Colour Research, www.globalcolour.co.uk/magazine.php

The Future Laboratory, www.thefuturelaboratory.com

Worth Global Style Network, www.wgsn.com

www.style.com

www.modeinfo.com

www.thetrendboutique.co.uk

Books

Tomorrow's People, Susan Greenfield (London: Penguin)

Techno Textiles 2: Revolutionary Fabrics for Fashion and Design, Braddock Clarke and Marie O'Mahony (London: Thames and Hudson)

British Design 2010 (Amsterdam: BIS Publishing)

Future Systems, Deyan Sudjic (London: Phaidon Press)

The Cult of the Amateur: How blogs, MySpace, YouTube and the rest of today's user-generated media are killing our culture and economy, Andrew Keen (Boston and London: Nicholas Brealey Publishing)

Cradle to Cradle, Michael Braungart and William McDonough (London: Vintage)

In The Bubble: Designing in a Complex World, John Thackara (Cambridge, MA: MIT Press)

Your Ethical Business: How to Plan, Start and Succeed in a Company with a Conscience, Paul Allen (London: Ngo Media)

Artists in Residence: A Handbook for Teachers and Artists, Sally Manser and Hannah Wilmot (London: St Katherine and Shadwell Trust)

ANSWERS TO THE COSTING AND PRICING QUIZ
IN CHAPTER 4, MONEY MANAGEMENT

1. What is an acceptable daily rate for artists?

Artquest recommend no less than £30 per hour plus 7.5% for London Market Allowance which makes £32.75 per hour, so about £180 to £260 per day. They also suggest £175 to £300 per day for experienced artists for a project lasting between one and five days.

a-n Magazine has a number of articles and reports about what to charge featured on their website. They have created a daily rate table, basing costing on 177 days. The daily rate is in the range of £183 to £290 per day depending on experience.

In further published research they give examples of arts projects where the fee offered for a 30-day art project was £250 per day and £300–£350 on other, shorter ad-hoc projects.

2. For designer-makers, what is the most popular price range for their products?

In the Crafts Council 'Making it in the 21st Century' research report published in 2003, 63% of applied artists and craftspeople said the most popular price range for their products was £51 to £100. An earlier report in 1994 found that the most popular price range was £5 to £20. This demonstrates how bespoke and handmade items have become more valued by the public in the period of time between the two reports.

3. What is a freelance photographer's daily rate working for national magazine?

These rates have been sourced from the NUJ website: for a half day at least £300 to £500 and at least £800 for a day. National magazines with large circulations are *GQ*, *Marie Claire* and *Management Today*. To source information about the circulation of newspapers and magazines have a look at the NUJ website or www.abc.org.uk

4. What is the national average daily rate paid to creative freelancers in the UK?

In the Marketing, Advertising and Design (MAD) Freelance Survey of Professionals (2007) it found that men earned an average of £260 per day, whereas women earned an average of £232 per day. The average daily rate was £244. This research was based on feedback from commercial creatives, and 80% of the respondents were based in London.

5. What is the average salary for a junior designer in London and what is it outside London?

In the '*Design Week* London Salary Survey 2009' a junior designer in London earned an annual salary of £19,200 and those based in the regions earned an annual salary of £17,821. Please note at the time of writing rates and salaries in London are declining due to the recession.

6. What is the hourly freelance rate charged by a senior artworker inside London and what is it outside London?

According to *Design Week*'s 'Freelance Salaries Survey' (September 2009) a senior artworker earns £25 per hour inside London and £19 per hour in the regions, with a national average of £22 per hour. (Please note at the time of writing freelance rates are slightly down due to the recession.)

7. What do freelance illustrators charge for a book jacket for a mass-market fiction paperback, commissioned by a major UK publisher?

When illustrators are commissioned to illustrate book jackets the publisher usually requires the rights to use the image for the length of copyright for the book only. However, sometimes it's for a specific length of time such as three to five years or ten years.

The fee should be around £1,000 to £1,500, but over the last few years £800 appears to have been the going rate. Illustrators should always try to persuade the commissioner to be a bit more generous. If you're uncertain about fees and rights, seek advice before agreeing any deal.

8. What's the recommended hourly rate for a freelance graphic designer?

According to *Design Week*'s 'Freelance Salaries Survey' (September 2009) an hourly rate for a freelance graphic designer is between £19 and £20 per hour. In the blogosphere many graphic designers discuss charging £20–£40 per hour, and vary their rates depending on what the designs are for.

In the 2007 MAD 'Freelance and interim Salary and Benefits Survey' on average male freelance graphic designers were paid just over £200 per day and women appear to earn around £180 per day. (Please note, these rates may since have been affected by the recent recession.)

9 What are the hourly PAYE rates for lecturers working in adult, further and higher education?

Rates vary around the UK but generally employed lecturers in AE and FE earn between £15 and £30 per hour before tax; in HE it's between £30 and £60 per hour, with most lecturers earning between £32 and £41 per hour.

10. What is the UK national minimum hourly wage if you are 22 years of age or over?

From October 2009, if you're aged 22 and over, the hourly rate is £5.80 (2009–2010 rates).

If you're aged 18 to 21 then the hourly rate is £4.83, and for employees aged 16 to 17 it's £3.57. From Oct 2010 21-year-olds will have the statutory minimum wage. Thus if you're aged 22 or over, for a 37.5 hour week at £5.80 per hour, you will earn £217.50 before tax. (Please note these figure are correct at the time of writing.)

Glossary

Meanings of business, financial and legal jargon

AAT The Association of Accounting Technicians is a professional body for bookkeepers and accountants with over 100,000 members. www.aat.org.uk

Above the line/Below the line 'Above the line' is a term used to describe the commissioning or buying of artwork, usually for advertising purposes, that appears within 'paid' or 'rented' space, e.g. adverts in magazines, billboards or on TV. When agreeing fees for 'usage' this type of use is charged at a premium rate.

'Below the line' is a term used to describe commissioning or buying of artwork for non-rented advertising space. This sort of publicity is in the form of mailshots, packaging, artwork for the client's own website, business cards, flyers, posters and signage. When quoting fees for 'below the line' you should make it clear in your agreement that the artwork can only be used for the purposes agreed. If the client desires to reproduce the artwork for other purposes outside the agreement then the client will need to negotiate another licence.

For example an illustration for a leaflet promoting a local attraction may earn you a fee of £250–£450 (below the line); whereas a commission from an advertising agency for a national or regional billboard campaign would gain you a commissioning fee plus a fee of around £5,000–£10,000 for usage (above the line).

Remember, there are two issues: a fee for originating the artwork, if a new commission, and then other fees for 'usage', i.e. the rights to reproduce artwork on leaflets (on a local level) or on billboards (on a regional/national level).

Some illustrators often quote fees including usage. However, it's better to keep commission and licensing rights separate.

This is a complicated area, so I suggest you read more about this subject. Please refer to the Association of Illustrators' 'Fees and Pricing Report' and Simon Stern's book *The Illustrator's Guide to Law and Business Practice* (see www.theaoi.com).

ACCA The Association of Chartered Certified Accountants has more than 345,000 members and students in 170 countries and is one of the six chartered accountancy bodies in the UK. www.accaglobal.com

Accountant A professional person able to assist with your tax and financial affairs. Most professionally qualified accountants fall into one of these categories:

Chartered accountant – www.icaew.com
Certified accountant – www.accaglobal.com
Management accountant – www.cimaglobal.com
Tax accountant – www.tax.org.uk

There is little difference between a chartered and a certified accountant, and both qualifications entitle the practitioner to prepare the accounts of any business. However, there is no statutory requirement for an accountant to be professionally qualified, so do check their credentials.

Accounts/Accounting These are detailed financial records of your business, usually set out in spreadsheets on a computer, written down in a book or on a recognised accounting package such as Sage. They show, usually on a weekly or monthly basis, for each year, money flowing into and out from the business. These translate into annual summaries showing end-of-year profit or, in a bad year, loss. They form a major part of your business records and must be kept for six years. You should also ensure that all receipts are retained with your accounts.

Annually/Annum Usually 'per annum', meaning each year, or 'annually', meaning once every year.

Assignment/Assigning A legal term usually employed in the transference of rights in property and intellectual property. In the UK rights can only be 'assigned', i.e. given over in writing. An assignment of rights means a total sale of all rights concerning the property or artwork. Artwork assignment means giving away to another business all rights for all uses, territory and time until the end of copyright. This could be as long as 100 years if the artist is still alive at the time of the buyout.

Bankruptcy When a court of law decides a person cannot pay their debts to suppliers or other financial commitments and is served with a bankruptcy order.

Bank statements These are quarterly, monthly or weekly bulletins from the bank showing your deposits, transfers and withdrawals to and from your business account. Don't throw these away – keep them, as they are part of your business records. You should also retain your quite separate personal current account statements.

Basic rate (BR) The main rate of income tax in the UK, which at present is 20%. There are higher rates for higher earners. Tax rates are reviewed each year and are subject to change.

BIS The Department for Business, Innovation and Skills (formerly the BERR).

This government department manages matters to do with business and regulations within the UK. It has useful resources, reports available on its website – www.bis.gov.uk

Bookkeeping/Bookkeepers Bookkeepers ensure that businesses' financial records are accurate and are kept up to date. They maintain records of basic business transactions, including receipts and payments, and may be involved in the preparation of sales invoices.

Although it is not necessary to gain one to operate as a bookkeeper, a recognised formal qualification can be obtained. Many bookkeepers have joined professional bodies such as the International Association of Bookkeepers (IAB) or the Institute of Certified Bookkeepers (ICB). You can find lists of registered bookkeepers on these sites – www.iab.org.uk and www.bookkeepers.org

Branding This refers to the logos, motifs, design formats or sounds that are part of the distinctive identity of a product or service. Branding aids in building a recognisable image, builds trust with the customer and 'ownership of mind'. You can apply for recognised protection under the trademark route via the UK Intellectual Property Office.

British Standards If you plan to sell particular products within the UK and the European Union then your products may have to be tested by you or be independently verified to check they are safe to sell. For more information refer to Chapter 9.

Business bank account This is a bank account for people who are in business, i.e. in self-employment. It demonstrates that you have a professional trading status, and allows you to trade with a business name as well as electronically via the internet.

Business library A business library is a resource through which you can access business information. The most famous in the UK is that based at the British Library in London. You may find a business library in your local town. If not there will be a business section within the public library where you can borrow or access reference books.

Business Link This is the brand name used for a government-funded network of business information and resources across Britain. Business Link has an outstanding website with thousands of useful fact sheets, and will signpost you to local business support.

NDR business rates If you are planning to rent premises such as a retail unit or convert part of your house into a gallery with public access, you need to be aware about business rates.

Arts organisations that lease studios to artists and designers should include any business rates within the rent. However, they may not do this, so check carefully before agreeing to take on a lease. If rates are not included, you'll pay rent to the landlord rent and business rates separately to the local council.

Business rates are also known as Non-Domestic Rates. Although similar in principle to Council Tax, business rates are calculated in a different way. A separate rateable value is determined for each individual business property, and this value is multiplied by a rate per pound (the Uniform Business Rate or UBS), which is set by central government.

You will only be liable to pay business rates on your home if you have made structural alterations to your property for business purposes. If you are only using a room in your home as a studio or office, you will not be charged.

If you have turned part of your house into a gallery or shop, for instance, then valuations are undertaken by your local Valuation Office Agency. You can gain relief on the rateable value of a property under certain amounts on the Small Business Rate Relief scheme. Contact your local authority for more information.

Capital This is a complex word with many meanings. In its simplest form it's money used or accumulated in a business by a person, partnership or company. For start-ups it usually applies to grants, loans or savings being put into the business.

Cash book A cash book records the flow of cash in and out of your business. Any transaction that involves the inflow (receipt) or outflow (payment) of money in cash from your business should be recorded in the cash book.

Cash-flow forecast A cash-flow forecast is a prediction of when cash will be received and paid out by a business. This allows the business to anticipate any potential cash problems and make arrangements to reduce spending, to speed up payment by those who owe money, to borrow money or to inject more working capital. Usually, a twelve-month forecast is enough when you start out, but many businesses plan up to between three and five years ahead.

CE marking (European conformity) Quite a number of products now have to display a CE mark so that they can be legally sold in the UK and across the European Union. For more information on the procedures you should follow to obtain a mark, please refer to Chapter 9.

CF10 (Small Earnings Exception form) If profits from your business are very low you may be able to apply for a Small Earnings Exception form from HM Revenue and Customs. You can be exempted from paying Class 2 National Insurance by filling in this form. Don't forget, however, that prolonged non-payment of NI might affect your State Pension and other entitlements.

Chambers of commerce Your local chamber of commerce is an official association for people in business; it supports and promotes trade within the local area.

Class 1 National Insurance This is for individuals in employment. (Employees are those under a contract of service, or those employed in an office with earnings subject to tax at source.) There is no liability on employee or employer National Insurance Contributions (NICs) on wages at or below the earnings threshold, known as the Personal Tax Allowance (PTA). On all earnings above the threshold, both employee and employer have to pay contributions.

Class 2 National Insurance This is paid by self-employed people whose profits exceed the small-earnings threshold, at a flat rate either once a year or by monthly direct debit (see Chapter 11). (Please note at the time of writing the PTA and small earnings threshold are set at different levels; they may be set as the same amount in the future).

Class 3 National Insurance These are voluntary payments made by people who for one reason or another have not paid other forms of National Insurance payments or who have a shortfall.

Class 4 National Insurance This is paid by the self-employed as a percentage of their profits that exceed a set threshold. The amount is calculated at the end of each tax year. The threshold varies from year to year.

COSHH (Control of Substances Hazardous to Health) Part of Health and Safety legislation, employers have to comply with these regulations to control, minimise or eliminate employees' exposure to hazardous chemicals or materials.

Commercial As well as its connection with advertising, e.g. a TV commercial, it also means 'a business venture' with the main aim being to make a profit.

Commission (1) This kind of commission refers to a person being offered business or a work opportunity in the shape of a project or an order being placed, e.g. a sculptor commissioned by their local council to create a memorial for a civic park, or a writer being commissioned by a publisher to write a book. Commissions are usually one-off events. Some creative businesses rely heavily on attracting commissions, while others don't need them at all.

Commission (2) This second kind of commission is when an intermediary or agent takes part of the income from a sale in exchange for their

services. For example, if a shop takes an item made by a potter and agrees to sell it, the vendor will deduct a percentage from the final sale price of the piece to cover the costs of their role in the deal. In an art gallery, it's common for the business owner to take between 33 and 50% of the retail sale price of a painting, with the artist receiving the rest.

Consequential loss (insurance) Usually referred to when insuring stock, consequential loss means goods or stock are covered for the full sale price of the products rather then the trade/wholesale price, so if your stock is stolen, badly damaged by flood or destroyed in a fire you can make a claim for the full amount. Bear in mind, though, this does mean you will pay a higher insurance premium.

Contract A contract is an agreement where there is an offer and acceptance of an offer, with something in exchange (known as consideration), usually money, and the desire of both sides to form legal relations – meaning to enter into this arrangement. A contract can be oral, but is best put in writing with both sides having a signed copy. Contracts can be very difficult to understand, and I advise seeking professional advice before agreeing and signing any contract.

Copyright Copyright is part of what we refer to as intellectual property. In the UK it means any author (not an employee of a business) who creates an artistic work – a painting, sculpture, photograph, drawing, performance, film, story, song or musical score which exists as an object, drawing, tape/video, 2-dimensional design or craftwork, recorded on CD/film/tape/video or stored in a computer – has automatic protection. If you're an employee your employer will usually own the copyright to your creative work.

Council Tax Benefit Just about everyone has to pay Council Tax, but there is a certain amount of relief you can claim if you are not earning enough from your business. You need to make an application to your local council for

Housing and Council Tax Benefit (please refer to Chapter 8).

County Court Judgment (CCJ) This arises when one of the organisations you owe money to takes you to court. If a County Court Judgment is made against you, as well as having to find a way to make some payments to the creditor you will have what is known as a bad credit rating. This means it could be difficult, sometimes for a number of years, to get a credit card, open a business bank account or take out a mortgage.

Credit check This is where a lender and sometimes an employer looks into your credit history to check you don't have any outstanding unpaid loans and recorded County Court Judgments against you.

Credit terms This phrase describes how much time you agree to give your clients/customers to pay. It's usually 30 days or longer. Payment may be required on delivery of goods or services.

Creditor A business to whom money is owed by another business. For example, Jack is owed £30 from Jane, so Jack is a creditor of Jane.

CWF1 (included in the leaflet known as SE1) The CWF1 is the form you need to fill in to become self-employed. You can call HMRC to request an SE1 leaflet or you can download the CWF1 form from their website. You can also phone HMRC to register. For more information, please see Chapters 3 and 11.

Debit An entry on a financial statement which reflects payments or disbursements made on behalf of a party for which the party is responsible (the opposite of credit), i.e. money being taken out of a bank account to pay bills for goods and services.

Debtor A debtor is a person (or a business) who owes another business money. For example, Jack is owed £30 from Jane, so Jane is one of Jack's debtors.

Depreciation Decrease in the value of equipment from wear and tear and the passage of time. Depreciation on business equipment is calculated to provide a truer profit figure. This is a complex subject that is best discussed with an accountant or business adviser.

Design format This means applying a range of design rules to the presentation of your product, packaging, marketing material, website, stationery and business cards. It feeds into a recognised design style, using preferred fonts, sizes, colours, shapes, lines and their arrangement. This not only makes your documentation look distinctive, it can also assist with the development of your brand identity.

Design Within business culture it is well understood that design is not simply a matter of branding. Nowadays business people are working with designers in every aspect of their enterprises. Design is being incorporated into office and factory spaces as colour schemes, furniture, administration systems, communication methods, working practices saving resources and minimising waste through recycling (see Ergonomics).

Design right This is part of what is known as intellectual property and is a right similar to copyright. UK design right applies to works of 3D and 2D design. Areas such as fashion, product design, furniture, textiles, glass, ceramics and jewellery are included. Unlike copyright, design right has two distinct areas of entitlement: registered design right and unregistered design right. If you can gain a registered right to your design you can secure a higher level of protection than if it's not registered.

Design right is meant to protect works of design which usually have some function – e.g. a lamp, table or dress – and are intended to be reproduced as multiples for sale. To find out more and to see a full list of design classifications, contact the UK Intellectual Property Office (www.ipo.gov.uk).

Direct debit This is a UK payments system designed to allow other businesses such as utilities – e.g. telephone, gas or electricity – on a regular basis to collect variable amounts due to them from your business, current or savings account by electronic funds transfer. A direct debit is different to a standing order (see standing order).

Domestic Usually we refer to 'domestic' when we are referring to mixing business matters with issues such as using part of our home for business activities. For example, if you work from a rented flat you can claim tax relief on the percentage of the flat you use for business expenses. Please refer to Chapter 11, Records, Tax and Basic Bookkeeping.

If you are planning to run a business from a rented flat or house, you need to check your tenancy agreement. If you're unsure, check with your landlord that he is OK with you working from home as a self-employed person. The property will have 'domestic insurance' so if a business is based there, the landlord's insurance company will need to know. This is the same situation for home owners: if you plan to register your home address as your business address, you should discuss these plans with your insurers.

Drawings (similar to your Personal Survival Budget) This is the word we use to describe the monthly payments self-employed people draw from their business to cover personal living expenses. Drawings are based on the financial exercise of working out what your annual Personal Survival Budget is – your drawings are actually your profits, which you draw from your business to live on. Unfortunately, you can't offset these against tax and claim them as a business expense. It's also difficult as the year proceeds to know how much tax you will need to pay on your profits, and therefore how much you need to be putting aside for your tax bill. The best tip is to store away between 15 and 25% of all your income to help you pay tax when it is calculated at the end of the tax year.

Dual use This phrase, often used by accountants, refers to things such as premises, clothing, equipment and vehicles that are used for both business and domestic purposes. Sometimes, for instance in the use of cars for business and personal use, a percentage of petrol and maintenance costs can be offset against profits, thus reducing your tax bill. It's always best to seek the advice of an accountant to clarify what you can and can't claim for.

eco- Abbreviation for ecology or ecological. 'Ecology' is about the delicate balances between life forms and the environment. There are many environmental regulations, which have become law. They affect all businesses and their relationship to waste disposal, emissions, packaging, and recycling. Please refer to Chapter 9, Creative Crimes.

Economics Is classified as a social science – the study of the relationship between the production, distribution and consumption of goods by the population. It's a study of the rate of growth or recession in these activities and their relationship with such factors as unemployment, government spending and inflation.

Employment PAYE Employed work for which you are paid for on a full- or part-time basis. Earnings above a certain threshold are subject to prior deduction of National Insurance and income tax. Income tax bandings are the same for employees as they are for the self-employed.

Enterprise Agencies These are business support organisations that offer advice, training and sometimes access to loans. To find your local one, contact the National Federation of Enterprise Agencies (www.nfea.com) or call Business Link.

Ergonomics Ergonomics is the study of the relationship between people and their working environment in terms of efficiency, safety and ease of action. Ergonomics is often associated with the design of buildings or products, where the design minimises waste, and maximises efficiency through saving energy and using recycled materials.

Exporting Exporting is where a business sells products or services to foreign countries.

Factoring Factoring is a form of short-term financing whereby the lender, also known as the factor, will purchase the value of an invoice debt from you at a discounted price. For example, if you raise an invoice for £1,000 that would normally take 30 days to be paid by your customer, a factor will pay you £900 immediately in exchange for collecting the £1,000 directly from your customer. It can be a very expensive form of financing but very useful for cash flow if you have a large number of debtors who take a long time to pay.

Federation of Small Businesses (FSB) This is a fee-paying membership service open to anyone who has started a business, whether self-employed, a partnership or a company. The FSB is really a lobbying organisation for business people's rights. However, their support services are another reason to join, and these include a free legal helpline, a tax line, insurance and banking deals, a web package and phone offers, plus much more.

Finance This is the commercial activity of providing funds and capital, usually in the form of obtaining a loan from the bank.

Finance raising In a very real sense raising small amounts of money (less than £10,000) can be just as difficult as searching for larger sums. For small investments, approach family, friends, banks, join credit unions or contact local enterprise agencies first. (But be careful about friends and family; you must formalise the arrangement with a repayment schedule.)

Larger business ventures may often require more than one source of finance. For example, say you need £100,000. One investor may agree to put £50,000 into your business on condition you can find another investor or source of finance for the balance. The essential

tool in raising money is a detailed business plan. Seek professional help from a business adviser before approaching investors and applying for loans.

Forwarding This is a term used to describe a service that enables emails to be sent using a business email address and forwarded to your personal email account. So, for example, my email is alison.branagan@virgin.net but my business address is info@alisonbranagan.com. Forwarding means you can have a number of emails, e.g. info@, alison@, john@, etc., at alisonbranagan.com, all being diverted to a standard email account.

Freehold/Freeholder When you buy a property freehold it means that you own both the building and the land it occupies. A freeholder is a person who owns the freehold of the property/land.

Freelance/Freelancer Preferred or customary term for someone who is self-employed and works for a number of different organisations on an occasional basis. The legal term is 'sole trader'. One thing you need to learn is what to charge for a daily or hourly rate, for which please consult the reports and websites listed at the end of Chapters 1 and 4.

Gross profit Gross profit is the total income from sales less any variable or direct costs incurred. For example, 100 vases bought wholesale cost £1000. The cost of packaging required before these are sold on to the customer is a further £300. This is a variable cost. If all the vases are sold at £30 each, the seller makes £3,000, leaving a gross profit of £1,700 (£3,000–£1,300). This excludes overheads or indirect costs such as rent on premises, advertising, insurances, etc. (see Net profit).

Health and Safety Executive (HSE) The government organisation you turn to if you need information or leaflets about risk assessments and all Health and Safety matters. I would always advise seeking professional advice from you local council, the fire brigade and Health and Safety consultants before taking on any large buildings. www.hse.gov.uk

Housing Benefit If you are on a low income, either from self-employment or a mixture of paid employment and self-employment/employment as a company director you can apply to your local council for Housing Benefit and Council Tax relief.

HMRC Her Majesty's Revenue and Customs is the UK tax collection service. This is where you register yourself as a sole trader when you are ready to start trading. HMRC also administers tax credits.

ICAEW The Institute of Chartered Accountants in England and Wales (ICAEW) has more than 132,000 members in 165 countries and is one of the six chartered accountancy bodies in the UK. www.icaew.com

Importing Importing is where a business brings into the country products and services from another country.

Income tax A tax levied on employees, partnerships and the self-employed.

Inland Revenue The former name for the tax office, which in 2005 merged with the department of Customs and Excise, the new body being called Her Majesty's Revenue and Customs (HMRC).

Invoice An invoice is a bill issued to a customer or client seeking payment for the supply of products or services which have been provided. Please refer to Chapter 11 for more details.

Intellectual property rights (IPR) The term 'IP' or 'IPR' includes within it all intellectual property rights, whether moral or financial: that is, copyright, design right, trademarks and patents.

Large firm A large firm can be defined a business that employs over 250 people and has a turnover of over €50 million per annum.

Lawyers For Your Business (LFYB) Under this scheme, sponsored by the Law Society, more than 1,800 solicitors across the UK will offer half an hour of their time to outline the legal needs of your business at no cost or obligation to you. If you do take advantage of a free 30-minute consultation, make sure you can convey the essentials of your business query in just a few minutes so as to maximise the advice time. Bring with you a few images or samples of products or services. Make sure you target an appropriate solicitor. Solicitors often specialise in different areas, such as contracts, employment or intellectual property.

Loan Before you approach a bank to borrow money you must first set up a business account and then seek a loan separately. Make sure you have a business plan with financial forecasts showing how you intend to pay back money to the bank with interest. The bank usually has business-planning software to help you develop a plan (see Finance).

Market/Marketing The word 'market' has many meanings. Here we define 'market' as a particular section of the population who are likely to be the customers or audience for a particular work. They could be of a particular age, gender, occupation and location. Other factors that may be of interest are social class, income, distribution, lifestyle and aspiration. The analysis of such data is known as creating a demographic profile, whereby the population is divided up into distinctive consumer groups.

Before you start targeting your publicity at particular groups of people, organisations or businesses, you have to understand who and where your customers are, and why they might be interested in your creative products and services.

Micro-enterprise A micro-enterprise is a business made up of less then ten employees with an annual turnover of less than €2 million.

Net profit Net profit is what is left after all your variable costs and overheads have been deducted. For example, 100 vases bought wholesale cost £1,000. The cost of packaging required before these are sold on to the customer is a further £300, which is a variable cost. Then there are overheads, such as a proportion of the marketing budget, insurance and the rent of a market stall, totalling £200. If all the vases are sold at £30 each, the seller makes £3,000, leaving a net profit of £1,500 (£3,000 – £1,500) (see Gross profit).

Non-disclosure agreement (NDA) A non-disclosure agreement or confidentiality agreement is a document you can present to investors, manufacturers, advisers or other businesses with whom you are discussing commercially sensitive proposals. If you download a model contract from the internet, make sure it's governed by the law pertaining to your country, e.g. England and Wales, or that of Scotland.

Always make sure NDAs are checked by a solicitor and signed by them as well as yourself. You will also require the signature of the person you plan to discuss matters with before revealing any designs, plans or prototypes. If the other parties refuse, then it's advisable to withdraw.

Offsetting expenses This can be a difficult phrase to explain. When running a business you only pay tax on your net profits. If you're self-employed you pay tax on your profits only after your personal tax allowance has been exhausted. The more receipts and evidence you can provide of business expenses, the less tax you will pay. So when business people say, 'I'm offsetting the expenses of this research expedition to China against my tax,' they mean they are counting the costs of the trip as a business expense, in the process reducing their net profit by the same amount and thus their tax liability. See Chapter 11 for more explanation, and always check with your accountant what can be legitimately claimed as a business expense.

Orphan works At the time of writing there is growing concern about proposed legislation to amend US copyright law. The Orphan Works Bill/Act would make it possible in the US to commercially exploit artworks where the author can't be identified or traced. There is already legislation in Canada to deal with 'unlocatable works'.

In the UK permission has to be granted by the author for exploitation of their artwork. It remains an infringement of copyright to commercially exploit a living artist's work without gaining their prior permission. The UK Government is investigating potential ways of managing the use of orphaned works, and there may be legislation to come in this area in the next few years. Please visit the AOI's website for more details. www.theaoi.com. (Refer to Chapter 5, Business Planning, and Chapter 9, Creative Crimes.)

Overheads Overheads are expenses to your business which are indirect but pretty much fixed and predictable. Each business will class their overheads differently, though as a general rule expenses such as studio rent, insurances and other regular payments are classed as overheads.

P45 A P45 is the document you receive after you resign or are made redundant from any PAYE employment. Keep documents relating to your employment with your business records.

P60 A P60 is a document sent annually by your employer which informs you about how much income tax and Class 1 National Insurance has been deducted from your wages. You need this form to help you fill in your self-assessment form/tax return at the end of the tax year, which always ends on 5th April. Employers are legally obliged to send this to you before the end of the following month, 31st May.

PAYE Pay As You Earn or PAYE simply means that you are in a job where income tax and national insurance have been deducted at source by your employer.

Patent Patent is part of the group of intellectual property rights that protect inventions. It's a legal instrument giving the patent holder the sole right to sell or license an invention. It also protects your rights in the country or countries where you have filed and published a patent. Refer to Chapter 9 and contact the IPO for more information. www.ipo.gov.uk

Payment terms Your payment terms should be included in your terms and conditions. If you're operating without terms, you need to check the terms of your clients and suppliers and confirm you are happy being paid, or making payments, within a specific number of days or months.

PEST (also known as STEP) PEST is an analytical tool to help you understand the growth or decline of markets by discovering the relationships between politics, economics, society/social trends and technological advancement. Other areas to consider in this mapping exercise are ecology, culture, law and innovation LICE. The exercise helps you to think about how external factors such as changes in the law could help or hinder you business.

Petty cash This is a money spent on incidental business expenses such as taxis, buses and postage.

Personal Survival Budget (PSB) A Personal Survival Budget is what all self-employed people should compute before going into business. You need to include all your personal living expenses. See 'Drawings' and refer to Chapter 4.

Personal Tax Allowance (PTA) The government allows everyone in the UK to earn a certain amount of money every year free from income tax. This amount varies depending on your age and the amount changes slightly each year. If you are under 65 the PTA for 2011–2012 is £7,475 per year. Refer to Chapter 11, Records, Tax and Basic Bookkeeping, for more details.

Profit Profit is what you are left with after all your business expenses have been taken away from your business income (see Gross profit and Net profit).

Profit forecast A profit forecast is similar to a cash-flow forecast. The key differences are you do not show any data to do with drawings, grants or loans. It is purely an exercise in predicting business profit.

Receipts When trading at retail fairs or on market stalls, it is good practice to issue customers with receipts. This can be via a till, a PDQ machine or a small receipt book.

Records of trading As well as recording all your financial dealings in your accounts, you are also required by law to keep all your receipts together with invoices, contracts, bank and HMRC documents, business and personal bank statements. Please refer to Chapter 11 for more details.

Royal Institute of Chartered Surveyors (RICS) RICS is an organisation with information and free guides about property, leasing and surveys. www.rics.org

Self-Assessment Self-assessment tax returns are completed annually by the self-employed, by partnerships and by those with mixed incomes or investments. Please refer to Chapter 11 for more details.

Self-employed Being self-employed is a preferential or customary term for people who wish to enter into business and trade. (See Sole trader.)

Small business A small business is a technical term for a partnership or company which employs fewer than 50 people and turns over less than €10 million per annum.

Small claims court This is where you need to go if you wish to take a creditor to court for non-payment of an invoice, and where you might also find yourself if you have outstanding debts. You can use the online small claims court service. www.courtservice.gov.uk and www.moneyclaim.gov.uk

Small Earnings Exception certificate (CF10 form) If profits from your business are very low you may be able to apply for a Certificate of Small Earnings Exception from HMRC. By filling in this form you can be exempted from paying Class 2 National Insurance contributions.

SME 'Small and medium-sized enterprises' is a term for a business which is either small (10–50 employees and an annual turnover of less than €10 million per annum) or medium (50–250 people and turning over less than €50 million per annum).

Sole trader Being a sole trader is a legal status reference for being self-employed. (See Self-employed.)

Standing order This is where the purchaser sets up a regular payment from their bank account to pay their suppliers. Only the purchaser can alter the amount the supplier can be paid. You may choose to use a monthly standing order to pay, for example, rent to the landlord of your business premises. Both purchaser and supplier need to agree to the arrangement, as the purchaser requires the supplier's bank details. A standing order is different from a direct debit. (See Direct debit)

Tax Aid Tax Aid is an organisation based in England which gives free advice to businesses who have profits of less than £16,000 per annum. www.taxaid.org.uk.

Tax There are many different forms of taxation for businesses and private individuals. For most readers the basics have been covered in Chapter 11. However, to check you are aware about other taxes you maybe liable to pay, I would always recommend discussing business matters regularly with your accountant.

Tax bands The tax bands for employees, partnerships and the self-employed are the same. See Chapter 11 for more details. Please remember, thresholds and bands usually alter every year.

Tax credits Working Tax Credit and Child Tax Credit are available to people – whether employed, running a business or a mixture of activities – who are on a low income. Please refer to Chapter 8 and the HMRC website for more details. www.hmrc.gov.uk

Tax return See Self-assessment.

Turnover Turnover means the amount of money which a business brings in from sales of products and services over a particular period of time, usually a 12-month period.

Usage When quoting for any commercial projects, commercial artists and photographers need to divide their fee into two parts. One part, a fee for undertaking the work, is usually based upon an hourly rate, while the other part of the fee quoted is for licensing the copyright of the artwork or photographs for particular uses. Refer to Above the line/Below the line for more detail.

Unique selling point (USP) A unique selling point is a sentence which sums up the key features and benefits of a product or service. USPs can turn into slogans or can be incorporated into marketing statements.

Unique Taxpayer Reference (UTR) The UTR is also known as your self-assessment number, tax reference or self-employment number, and can still be referred to as a Schedule D number. The ten-digit number appears on the front of your tax return and is printed on the top of any correspondence from HMRC.

Variable costs Variable costs are business expenses relating directly to the creation, manufacture or sale of your product or service. These could be the costs of production, materials or commission on sales.

VAT Valued Added Tax is a tax that is added onto the sale of a wide variety of goods, products and services. The rate can vary depending on what you are selling. The obligation to register for VAT is dependent on your turnover, though in some areas of trade it's advisable to do so in any case. Please refer to Chapter 11 for more details, or contact HM Revenue and Customs.

Warranty This is a written statement that a business gives to a customer undertaking to repair or replace faulty items. You also find the term 'warranty' in commissioning contracts, which could mean that you as a supplier or contractor are liable for repairs to, or even the replacement of, damaged parts of artworks or sculptures.

Useful Organisations

UNITED KINGDOM

Key organisations

Artists Information Company, www.a-n.co.uk
The Artists Information Company publishes a-n *Magazine, a UK-wide artists' periodical. A small subscription provides access to their resource centre.*

Artquest, www.artquest.org.uk
Though a London-based service, the Artquest website includes lists of professional UK art and design bodies.

Crafts Council, www.craftscouncil.org.uk
A support service covering England and Wales, their website includes a list of professional guilds, agencies, organisations and societies.

Craft Northern Ireland
www.craftni.org

Rural Crafts Association
www.ruralcraftsassociation.co.uk
A UK-wide organisation providing advice and resources.

Arts Council England (ACE)
www.artscouncil.org.uk
A support organisation for artists based in England, their website includes links to regional councils, as well as information about funding and resources.

Scottish Arts Council
www.scottisharts.org.uk

Arts Council of Wales (ACW)
www.artswales.org.uk

Arts Council Northern Ireland
www.artscouncil-ni.org

Design Council, www.designcouncil.org.uk
Promotes effective design to UK businesses, and has a useful website, with links to other sites and case studies.

British Fashion Council
www.londonfashionweek.co.uk

Film Council
www.ukfilmcouncil.org.uk

British Council
www.britishcouncil.org/arts
UK organisation for international cultural relations.

Department for Culture, Media and Sport
www.culture.gov.uk

Key professional bodies and associations

Federation of British Artists
www.mallgalleries.org.uk
The Federation of British Artists is based at the Mall Galleries in London. It comprises the following organisations:
Hesketh Hubbard Art Society
New English Art Club
Pastel Society
Royal Institute of Painters in Watercolours
Royal Society of British Artists
Royal Society of Marine Artists
Royal Institute of Oil Painters
Royal Society of Portrait Painters
Society of Wildlife Artists

Hilliard Society of Miniature Artists
www.art-in-miniature.org

Royal Society of Miniature Painters, Sculptors and Gravers
www.royal-miniature-society.org.uk

Medical Artists' Association of Great Britain
www.maa.org.uk

Society of Equestrian Artists
www.equestrianartists.co.uk

Society of Botanical Artists
www.soc-botanical-artists.org

Guild of Aviation Artists
www.gava.org.uk

Guild of Motoring Artists
www.motorart.co.uk

Guild of Railway Artists
www.railart.co.uk

Society of Wood Engravers
www.woodengravers.co.uk

Royal Watercolour Society
www.royalwatercoloursociety.co.uk

Royal Society of Painter-Printmakers
www.royalsocietyofpainter-printmakers.com

Printmakers' Council
www.printmaker.co.uk

UK Association of Print Specialists and
Manufacturers
www.prismuk.org

British Art Medal Society
www.bams.org.uk

Royal British Society of British Sculptors
www.rbs.org.uk

British Association of Modern Mosaic
www.bamm.org.uk

Association of Illustrators
www.theaoi.com

Society of Architectural Illustration
www.sai.org.uk

Institute of Medical Illustrators IMI
www.imi.org.uk

Cartoonists' Club
www.ccgb.org.uk

Federation of Cartoonists' Organisations (worldwide)
www.feco.info

Professional Cartoonists' Organisation (Feco UK)
www.procartoonists.org

Society of Authors
www.societyofauthors.org

Design and Art Direction
www.dandad.org

Institute of Practitioners in Advertising
www.ipa.co.uk

Chartered Society of Designers
www.csd.org.uk

British Computer Society (Chartered Institute
for IT), www.bcs.org

Computer Arts Society
www.computer-arts-society.org

UK Web Design Association
www.ukwda.org

Design Business Association
www.dba.org.uk

British Sign and Graphics Association
www.bsga.co.uk

Sign Design Society
www.signdesignsociety.co.uk

British Interior Design Association
www.bida.org.uk

British Interior Textiles Association
www.interiortextiles.com

Association of Interior Specialists
www.ais-interiors.org.uk

Royal Institute of British Architects
www.architecture.com

Royal Incorporation of Architects in Scotland
www.rias.org.uk

Institute of Engineering Designers
www.ied.org.uk

British Design Innovation
www.britishdesigninnovation.org

Association of Photographers
www.the-aop.org

British Institute of Professional Photography
www.bipp.com

Royal Photographic Society
www.rps.org

Master Photographers Association
www.thempa.com

British Film Institute
www.bfi.org.uk

Film London
http://filmlondon.org.uk

Royal Television Society
www.rts.org.uk

Skill Set
www.skillset.org

Broadcast Entertainment Cinematograph and
Theatre Union
www.bectu.org.uk

Producers' Alliance for Cinema and Television
www.pact.co.uk

Production Guild
www.productionguild.com

Association of Professional Videomakers
www.apv.org.uk

Institute of Videography
www.iov.co.uk

The Guild of Professional Videography
www.gpv4u.co.uk

Applied arts and crafts

Contemporary Applied Arts
www.caa.org.uk

Contemporary Crafts – Scotland
www.craftsscotland.org

Guild of Master Craftsmen
www.guildmc.com

Society of Designer Craftsmen
www.societyofdesignercraftsmen.org.uk

Art Workers Guild
www.artworkersguild.org

Carpet Foundation
www.comebacktocarpet.com

Textile Society
www.textilesociety.org.uk

Textile Institute
www.texi.org

Worshipful Company of Cordwainers
www.cordwainers.org

Vintage Fashion Guild
www.vintagefashionguild.org

British Costume Association
www.incostume.co.uk

Worshipful Company of Pattenmakers
www.pattenmakers.co.uk

Association of Guilds of Weavers, Spinners
and Dyers , www.wsd.org.uk

Worshipful Company of Weavers
www.weavers.org.uk

UK Handknitting Association
www.bhkc.co.uk

Braid Society
www.braidsociety.com

Embroiderers' Guild
www.embroiderersguild.org.uk

Worshipful Company of Broderers
www.broderers.co.uk

British Hat Guild
www.britishhatguild.co.uk

Worshipful Company of Glovers
www.thegloverscompany.org

Worshipful Company of Fan Makers
www.fanmakers.com

International Feltmakers Association
www.feltmakers.com

Worshipful Company of Feltmakers
www.feltmakers.co.uk

Worshipful Company of Woolmen
www.woolmen.com

Lace Guild
www.laceguild.org

Worshipful Company of Drapers
www.thedrapers.co.uk

Worshipful Company of Haberdashers
www.haberdashers.co.uk

British Clothing Industry Association
Includes the following associations:
British Footwear Association
www.britfoot.com
British Menswear Guild
www.british-menswear-guild.co.uk
UK Fashion and Textile Association
www.ukft.org

Silk Association of Great Britain
www.silk.org.uk

Fashionweb
www.fashionwebuk.com

Worshipful Company of Basketmakers
www.basketmakersco.org

Association of British Wood Turners
www.britishwoodturners.co.uk

Worshipful Company of Turners
www.turnersco.com

British Woodworkers Federation
www.bwf.org.uk

British Woodcarvers Association
www.britishwoodcarversassociation.co.uk

British Furniture Manufacturers
www.bfm.org.uk

British Contract Furnishing Association
www.thebcfa.com

The Office Furniture Advisory Service
www.ofas.org.uk

Association of Master Upholsterers and Soft
Furnishings, www.upholsterers.co.uk

British Antique Furniture Restorers Association
www.bafra.org.uk

Furniture, Furnishings and Interior Trade
Organisation (FFINTO), www.ffinto.org

Institute of Carpenters
www.instituteofcarpenters.com

Worshipful Company of Carpenters
www.thecarpenterscompany.co.uk

Marquetry Association
www.marquetry.org

Guild of Rocking Horse Makers
www.rockinghorse.co.uk/guild

British Toymakers Guild
www.toymakersguild.co.uk

British Toy and Hobby Association
www.btha.co.uk

Worshipful Company of Glaziers and Painters
of Glass, www.worshipfulglaziers.com

British Society of Master Glass Painters
www.bsmgp.org.uk

British Society of Enamellers (glass-on-metal
artists), www.enamellers.org

British Glass Manufacturers Confederation
www.britglass.org.uk

Contemporary Glass Society
www.cgs.org.uk

Guild of Glass Engravers
www.gge.org.uk

Goldsmiths' Crafts and Design Council
www.craftanddesigncouncil.org.uk

Worshipful Company of Goldsmiths
www.thegoldsmiths.co.uk

Association for Contemporary Jewellery
www.acj.org.uk

British Jewellers Association
www.bja.org.uk

Designer Jewellers Association
www.designerjewellersgroup.co.uk

Association of British Designer Silversmiths
www.theabds.co.uk

British Jewellery, Giftware and Finishing Federation
www.bjgf.org.uk

The Jewellery Distributor's Association
www.jda.org.uk

Worshipful Company of Cutlers
www.cutlerslondon.co.uk

Worshipful Company of Pewterers
www.pewterers.org.uk

The Ironmongers' Company
www.ironhall.co.uk

Welding Institute
www.twi.co.uk

British Art Blacksmith Society
www.baba.org.uk

Craft Potters Association of Great Britain
www.cpaceramics.co.uk

International Association of Papermakers
and Artists, www.iapma.info

Society of Bookbinders
www.societyofbookbinders.com

Designer Bookbinders
www.designerbookbinders.org.uk

Calligraphy and Lettering Arts Society
www.clas.co.uk

Society of Scribes and Illuminators
www.calligraphyonline.org

Miscellaneous organisations

Institute for Conservation
www.icon.org.uk

British Association of Paintings Conservator-Restorers
www.bapcr.org.uk

Society of London Art Dealers
www.slad.org.uk

Visual Arts and Galleries Association
www.vaga.co.uk

Society of Artists' Agents
www.illustratorsagents.co.uk

Fine Art Trade Guild
www.fineart.co.uk

Greeting Card Association
www.greetingcardassociation.org.uk

Tattoo Club of Great Britain
www.tattoo.co.uk

British Travel Goods and Accessories Association
www.btaa.org.uk

Association of Suppliers to the British Clothing Industry, www.asbci.co.uk

National Childrenswear Association
www.ncwa.co.uk

Royal Society for the Encouragement of Arts, Manufactures & Commerce, www.rsa.org.uk

Institute of Materials, Minerals and Mining
www.iom3.org

Manufacturing Technologies Association
www.mta.org.uk

Federation of British Hand Tool Manufacturers
www.britishtools.co.uk

Manufacturing Advisory Service
www.mas.bis.gov.uk

Plastic Historical Society
www.plastiquarian.com

Hidden Art
www.hiddenart.com

Craft Central
www.craftcentral.org.uk

AUSTRALIA

Key organisations

Australia Council (Arts)
www.australiacouncil.gov.au

Craft Australia
www.craftaustralia.org.au

Australian Film Commission
www.afc.gov.au

Professional bodies and associations

Art and design

Australian Graphic Design Association
www.agda.com.au

Design Institute of Australia
www.dia.org.au

Australian Institute of Professional Photography
www.aipp.com.au

Australian Commercial and Media Photographers
http://acmp.com.au

Australian Film Institute
www.afi.org.au

CANADA

Key organisations

Canada Council for the Arts
www.canadacouncil.ca

Canadian Crafts Federation (formerly Canadian Crafts Council)
http://canadiancraftsfederation.ca

National Film Board of Canada
www.nfb.ca

Professional bodies and associations

Art and design

CARFAC Canadian Artists' Representation
www.carfac.ca

Society of Graphic Designers of Canada
www.gdc.net

Canadian Society of Children's Authors,
Illustrators, and Performers
www.canscaip.org

Canadian Association of Photographers and
Illustrators in Communications
www.capic.org

Canadian Association of Photographic Art
www.capacanada.ca

Professional Photographers of Canada
www.ppoc.ca

USA

Key organisations

National Assembly of State Arts Agencies
www.nasaa-arts.org

Americans for the Arts/Public Art Network
www.artsusa.org

American Crafts Council
www.craftcouncil.org

New York Foundation for the Arts
www.nyfa.org

Artist Help Network
www.artisthelpnetwork.com

National Endowment for the Arts
www.arts.gov

Professional bodies and associations

Art and design

Organisation of Independent Artists
www.oia-ny.org

Graphic Artists Guild
www.gag.org

American Institute of Graphic Arts
www.aiga.org

American Print Alliance
www.printalliance.org

National Sculpture Society
www.nationalsculpture.org

Society of Illustrators
http://societyillustrators.org

Society of Children's Book Writers and Illustrators
www.scbwi.org

National Cartoonist Society
www.reuben.org

American Institute of Architects
www.aia.org

American Institute of Interior Designers
www.asid.org

Surface Design Association
www.surfacedesign.org

Society of Publication Designers
www.spd.org

Society of Photographers and Artists
Representatives
www.spar.org

Professional Photographers of America
www.ppa.com

American Society of Media Photographers
http://asmp.org

Photographic Society of America
www.psa-photo.org

Association of Independent Video and Filmmakers
www.aivf.org

Art Directors Club
www.adcglobal.org

Applied arts and crafts

Jeweler's Resource Bureau
www.jewelersresource.com

Handweavers Guild of America
www.weavespindye.org

American Ceramic Society
www.ceramics.org

Further Reading

A&C Black, *Who's Who 2010* (162nd edn) (London: A&C Black, 2009).

Abbing, Hans, *Why are Artists Poor? The Exceptional Economy of the Arts* (Amsterdam: Amsterdam University Press, 2002).

Allen, Paul, *Your Ethical Business: How to Plan, Start and Succeed in a Company with a Conscience* (London: Ngo Media, 2007).

Arden, Paul, *It's Not How Good You Are, It's How Good You Want to Be* (London: Phaidon Press, 2003).

Arden, Paul, *Whatever You Think, Think the Opposite* (London: Penguin Books, 2006).

Austen, Pam and Bob, *Getting Free Publicity* (Oxford: How To Books, 2004).

Baile de Laperriere, Charles (ed.), *Who's Who in Art: Biographies of Leading Men and Women in the World of Art in Britain Today* (32nd edn) (Calne, Wiltshire: Hilmarton Manor Press, 2006).

Barbrook, Richard, *The Class of the New*, (London: Openmute, 2006). (Free download: www.theclassofthenew.net)

Barrow, Colin, *Starting a Business from Home: Choosing a Business, Getting Online, Reaching Your Market and Making a Profit* (London: Kogan Page, 2008).

Beckwith, Harry, *Selling the Invisible: A Field Guide to Modern Marketing* (New York: Texere, 2001).

Bently, Lionel, *Between a Rock and a Hard Place* (1st edn) (London: Institute of Employment Rights, 2002).

Benun, Ilise & Peleg, Top, *The Designer's Guide to Marketing and Pricing* (1st edn), (Cincinnati, Ohio: How Books, 2008).

Berry, Cicely, *Your Voice and How To Use It*, (London: Virgin, 2000).

Binks, Martin & Lumsdaine Edward, *Entrepreneurship from Creativity to Innovation*, (Oxford: Trafford, 2007).

Borkowski, Mark, *Improperganda: The Art of the Publicity Stunt* (London: Vision On, 2000).

Braddock Clark, Sarah E. & O'Mahony, Marie, *Techno Textiles 2: Revolutionary Fabrics for Fashion and Design Bk 2* (1st edn) (London: Thames and Hudson, 2007).

Branagan, Alison, *Making Sense of Business: A no-nonsense guide to business skills for managers and entrepreneurs* (1st edn) (London: Kogan Page, 2009).

Branagan, Alison, Taylor, Fig & et al. *The Illustrator's Guide to Success* (London: AOI, 2010). (Forthcoming)

Braungart, Michael & McDonough, William, Cradle to Cradle: *Remaking the Way We Make Things* (London: Vintage Books, 2009).

British Design 2007/08 (3rd edn) (Amsterdam: BIS Publishers, 2006).

Burke, Sandra, *Fashion Computing, Design Techniques and CAD* (1st edn) (Oxford: Burke Publishing, 2008).

Burke, Sandra, *Fashion Entrepreneur: Starting Your Own Fashion Business* (1st edn) (Oxford: Burke Publishing, 2008).

Butler, David, *Making Ways: The Visual Artists' Guide to Surviving and Thriving* (Sunderland: an Publications, 1989).

Buzan, Tony and Buzan, Barry, *The Mind Map Book* (2nd edn) (Essex: BBC Active, 2006).

Card, Nell, *The Guardian Guide to Making Video* (London: The Guardian, 2008).

Carnegie, Dale, *How to Develop Self-Confidence and Influence People by Public Speaking* (2nd edn) (London: Vermilion, 1998).

Carnegie, Dale, *How to Win Friends and Influence People* (2nd edn) (London: Vermilion, 1998).

Casewit, Curtis W., *Making a Living in the Fine Arts: Advice from the Pros* (1st edn) (New York: Collier Books, 1984).

Caves, Richard E., *Creative Industries: Contracts between Art and Commerce* (1st edn) (Cambridge, Mass.: Harvard University Press, 2000).

Chappell, David & Willis, Andrew, *The Architect in Practice* (9th edn) (Oxford: Blackwell Publishing, 2005).

Charvet, Shelle Rose, *Words That Change Minds* (2nd edn) (Iowa: Kendall/Hunt, 1997).

Clark, Ross, *How to Label a Goat* (1st edn) (Petersfield, Hampshire: Harriman House, 2006).

Coats, Caroline, *Designer Fact File: A Guide to Setting up a Designer Fashion Business* (London: British Fashion Council/DTI, 1997).

Covey, Stephen R., Merrill, A. R. & Merrill, R. R., *First Things First* (London: Pocket Books, 2002).

Covey, Stephen R., *The Seven Habits of Highly Effective People* (London: Simon & Schuster, 1999).

Cushway, Barry, *The Employer's Handbook: An Essential Guide to Employment Law, Personnel Policies and Procedures* (6th edn) (London: Kogan Page, 2008).

Davies, Gillian, *Copyright Law for Artists, Photographers and Designers* (London: A&C Black, 2011).

Deeks, Sarah, Murphy, Richard & Nolan, Sally, *Money Matters: The Artist's Financial Guide* (Sunderland: an Publications, 1996).

DiBiasio, Rick, *The Affluent Artist* (1st edn) (New York: Morgan James Publishing, 2009).

Dyson, James, *Against the Odds: An Autobiography* (New York: Texere, 2002).

Fleishman, Michael, *Starting Your Career as a Freelance Illustrator or Graphic Designer* (2nd edn) (New York: Allworth Press, 2001).

Florida, Richard, *The Rise of the Creative Class: And How It's Transforming Work, Leisure and Everyday Life* (1st edn) (New York: Basic, 2002).

Foster, John, *Effective Writing Skills for Public Relations* (4th edn) (London: Kogan Page, 2008).

Goldstein, Noah J., Martin, Steve J. and Cialdini, Robert B., *Yes! 50 Secrets From the Science of Persuasion* (London: Profile Books, 2007).

Goltz, Jay, *The Street-Smart Entrepreneur* (Nebraska: Addicus Books, 1998).

Gomez-Palacio, Bryony and Vit, Armin, *Flaunt: Designing effective, compelling and memorable portfolios of creative work* (Texas: Under Consideration LLC, 2010).

Goworek, Helen, *Careers in Fashion and Textiles* (Oxford: Blackwell Publishing, 2006).

Grant, Daniel, *The Business of Being an Artist* (3rd edn) (New York: Allworth Press, 2000).

Greenfield, Susan, *Tomorrow's People* (London: Penguin, 2004).

Hart, Tina, Fazzani, Linda & Clark, Simon, *Intellectual Property Law* (4th edn) (Hampshire: Palgrave Macmillan, 2006).

Hedges, Roy & Walkley, Roger, *Bookkeeping Made Easy* (3rd edn) (London: Lawpack Publishing, 2006).

Heller, Steven & Arisman, Marshall, *Inside the Business of Illustration* (1st edn) (New York: Allworth Press, 2004).

Herbert, Jo (ed.), *Writers' & Artists' Yearbook 2010* (103rd edn) (London: A&C Black, 2009).

Hill, Napoleon, *Master Key to Riches* (2nd edn) (London: Vermilion, 2007).

Ilasco, Meg Mateo, *Craft.inc* (1st edn) (San Francisco: Chronicle Books, 2007).

Intercity Design, *Art & Sole* (London: Laurence King, 2008).

Kao, John J., *Entrepreneurship, Creativity and Organization: Text, Cases and Readings* (New Jersey: Prentice Hall, 1989).

Keen, Andrew, *The Cult of the Amateur: How blogs, MySpace, YouTube and the rest of today's user-generated media are killing our culture and economy* (Boston and London: Nicholas Brealey Publishing, 2008).

Kennedy, Jamie, *Wannabe* (London: Aurum Press, 2004).

King, Stephen, Macklin, Jeff and West, Chris, *Finance on a Beermat* (2nd edn) (London: Random House, 2008).

Kulagowski, Yvonne, *The Earrings Book* (London: A&C Black, 2007).

Lefteri, Chris, *Making It* (1st edn) (London: Laurence King Publishing, 2007).

Levine, Feythe, *Handmade Nation* (1st edn) (New York: Princeton Architectural Press, 2008).

Love, Sara (ed.), *Handbook: Pricing and Ethical Guidelines* (11th edn) (New York: The Graphic Artists Guild, 2003).

MacDonald, Kyle, *One Red Paperclip: The story of how one man changed his life one swap at a time* (2nd edn) (London: Ebury Press, 2008).

Magnus, Sharon M., *Think Yourself Rich* (1st edn) (London: Vermilion, 2003).

Manser, Sally & Wilmot, Hannah, *Artists in Residence: A Handbook for Teachers and Artists* (2nd edn) (London: St Katherine and Shadwell Trust, 2007).

Marcan, Peter, *The Marcan Visual Arts Handbook* (6th edn) (London: Peter Marcan Publications, 2006).

Mariotti, Steve, *The Young Entrepreneur's Guide to Starting and Running a Business* (New York: Three Rivers Press, 2000).

Mason, Matt, *The Pirate's Dilemma* (1st edn) (London: Allen Lane, 2008).

McClean, Daniel and Schubert, Karsten, *Dear Images: Art, Copyright and Culture* (1st edn) (London: UCA and Ridinghouse, 2002).

McCormack, Lee, *Designers are Wankers* (1st edn) (London: About Face Publishing, 2005).

McKendrick, Ewan, *Contract Law* (8th edn) (Hampshire: Palgrave Macmillan, 2009).

Michels, Caroll, *How to Survive and Prosper as an Artist* (5th edn) (New York: Owl Books, 2001).

Micucci, Dana, *Artists in Residence* (1st edn) (New York: The Little Book Room, 2001).

Millard, Rosie, *The Tastemakers: UK Art Now* (2nd edn) (London: Scribner, 2002).

Miller, Harley & Miller, Cally, *A proper living from your art: how to make your painting pay* (1st edn) (Findhorn Bay, Moray: Posthouse Printing and Publishing, 2000). (Revised free edition available on download from www.harleymiller.com)

The Mind Gym, *The Mind Gym: Wake Your Mind Up* (London: Time Warner, 2005).

Mornement, Caroline, *Crafts Galleries* (9th edn) (Yeovil, Somerset: BCF Books, 2009).

Mornement, Caroline, *Galleries of Australia and New Zealand* (1st edn) (Yeovil, Somerset: BCF Books, 2009).

Mornement, Caroline, *Second Steps* (4th edn) (Yeovil, Somerset: BCF Books, 2006).

Moses, Rachel, *Business Start-up Guide for Designers and Makers 2008* (4th edn) (London: Design Nation, 2008).

Olisa, Elinor, *The Artists' Yearbook 2010/11* (London: Thames and Hudson, 2009).

Palmer, Judith, *Private Views: Artists Working Today* (1st edn) (London: Serpent's Tail Publishers, 2004).

Parrish, David, *T-Shirts and Suits: A Guide to the Business of Creativity* (1st edn) (Liverpool: Merseyside ACME, 2007). (Free download on www.t-shirtsandsuits.com)

Pease, Allan & Pease, Barbara, *The Definitive Book of Body Language* (London: Orion Books, 2004).

Poehner, Donna (ed.), *Photographer's Market* (33rd edn) (Cincinnati: Writer's Digest Books, 2010).

Portas, Mary, *How to Shop with Mary Queen of Shops* (1st edn) (London: BBC Books, 2007).

Portas, Mary, *Windows: The Art of Retail Display* (1st edn) (London: Thames and Hudson, 1999).

Presley, Hovis, *Poetic Off-Licence Holiday Annual* (1st edn) (Bolton: D2, 1997). (Ref. Quotation from Chapter 8, Funding and Sponsorship)

Price, Barclay, *Running a Workshop: Basic Business for Craftspeople* (3rd edn) (London: Crafts Council, 2000).

Rees, Darrel, *How to be an Illustrator* (1st edn) (London: Laurence King Publishing, 2008).

Rose, Walter, *The Village Carpenter* (2nd edn) (Ammanford, Carmarthenshire: Stobart Davies, 2009).

Ruston, Annabelle, *Starting Up A Gallery and Frame Shop* (London: Fine Art Trade Guild and A&C Black, 2007).

Ruston, Annabelle, *The Artist's Guide to Selling Work* (London: Fine Art Trade Guild and A&C Black, 2005).

Scratchmann, Max, *Illustration 101: Streetwise Tactics for Surviving as a Freelance Illustrator* (2nd edn) (Orkney: Poison Pixie Ltd, 2007).

Sennett, Richard, *The Craftsman* (2nd edn) (London: Penguin, 2008).

Shaughnessy, Adrian, *Graphic Design: A user's manual* (1st edn) (London: Laurence King Publishing, 2009).

Shaughnessy, Adrian, *How to be a Graphic Designer without Losing Your Soul* (1st edn) (London: Laurence King Publishing, 2005).

Shaughnessy, Adrian, *Studio Culture* (1st edn) (London: Unit Editions, 2009).

Simon, Francesca (ed.), *Children's, Writers' and Artists' Yearbook 2010* (6th edn) (London: A&C Black, 2009).

Smithson, Pete, *Installing Exhibitions: A practical guide* (London: A&C Black, 2009).

Southon, Mike & West, Chris, *The Beermat Entrepreneur* (Harlow: Pearson, 2002).

Stern, Simon, *The Illustrator's Guide to Law and Business Practice* (1st edn) (London: Association of Illustrators, 2008).

Stokes, Simon, *Arts and Copyright* (2nd edn) (Portland, Oregon: Hart Publishing, 2003).

Sturt, George *The Wheelwright's Shop* (Cambridge: Cambridge University Press, 2000).

Sudjic, Deyan, *Future Systems* (1st edn) (London: Phiadon, 2006).

Taylor, Fig, *How to Create a Portfolio and Get Hired: A guide for graphic designers and illustrators* (London: Laurence King, 2010). (Forthcoming)

Taylor, Karen, *The Internet for Artists* (1st edn) (England: Eyelevel Books, 2002).

Thackara, John, *In the Bubble: Designing in a Complex World* (1st edn) (Cambridge, Mass.: Mitt Press, 2006).

Thomas, Gwen & Ibbotson, Janet, *Beyond the Lens* (3rd edn) (London: Association of Photographers, 2003).

Thompson, Don, *The $12 Million Stuffed Shark: The Curious Economics of Contemporary Art and Auction Houses* (1st edn) (London: Aurum Press, 2008).

Thompson, Rob, *Manufacturing Processes for Design Professionals* (1st edn) (London: Thames and Hudson, 2007).

Thornton, Sarah, *Seven Days in the Art World* (1st edn) (New York: W. W. Norton, 2008).

Veksner, Simon, *How to Make It as an Advertising Creative* (London: Laurence King, 2010).

Vitali, Julius, *The Fine Artist's Guide to Marketing and Self-Promotion* (2nd edn) (New York: Allworth Press, 2003).

Wainwright, Martin, *The Guardian Book of April Fool's Day* (1st edn) (London: Aurum, 2007).

Walne, Toby, *101 Extraordinary Investments: Curious, unusual and bizarre ways to make money* (Hampshire: Harriman House, 2009).

Wedd, Kit, Peltz, Lucy & Ross, Cathy, *Artists' London: Holbein to Hirst* (1st edn) (London: Merrell Publishers, 2001).

Wells, Paul, *The Fundamentals of Animation* (1st edn) (Switzerland: AVA Publishing, 2006).

Wilkinson, Carl, *The Observer Book of Art* (1st edn) (London: Observer Books, 2008).

Williams H. M., *101 Ways to Pay Less Tax 2009–10* (5th edn) (London: Lawpack Publishing, 2009).

Williams H. M., *Tax Answers at a Glance 2007–08* (7th edn) (London: Lawpack Publishing, 2007).

Williams, Sarah, *The Financial Times Guide to Business Start-up* (Harlow: Prentice Hall, 2010).

Wind, Yoram Jerry, Crook, Colin & Gunther, Robert, *The Power of Impossible Thinking* (New Jersey: Wharton School Publishing, 2005).

Wiseman, Richard, *Did You Spot the Gorilla?* (London: Arrow Books, 2004).

Wiseman, Richard, *The Luck Factor* (London: Arrow Books, 2004).

Zeegan, Lawrence, *Secrets of Digital Illustration* (1st edn) (Hove: RotoVision, 2007).

Quotation Credits

Abbing, Hans, p.14: from p.122, Abbing, Hans, *Why are Artists Poor? The Exceptional Economy of the Arts* (Amsterdam: Amsterdam University Press, 2002).

Allen, Woody, p.92: from p.107, Rees, Nigel, *Cassell's Humorous Quotations* (London: Cassell & Co, 2003); sourced from *The New York Magazine*, 13 August 1989.

Allen, Woody, p.63: from p.4, Knowles, Elizabeth (Ed), *Oxford Concise Dictionary of Quotations*, 4th edn (Oxford: Oxford University Press, 2001); sourced from 'Sayings of the Week', the *Observer*, 10 March 1996.

Anonymous, p.187: from p.17, Rees, Nigel, Rees, Nigel, *Cassell's Humorous Quotations* (London: Cassell & Co, 2003); sourced from *Time* magazine, 19 April 1993.

Antonelli, Paola, p.220: in an interview with Evan Davis on the *Today Programme*, BBC Radio 4, 2009.

Baylis, Trevor, p.143: from p.60, 'Intellectual Property with Trevor Baylis' in *Start Your Business Magazine*, June 2007.

Beckwith, Harry, quoting Picasso, p.69: from p.137–8, Beckwith, Harry, *Selling the Invisible: A Field Guide to Modern Marketing* (Texere, New York: 2001).

Beuys, Joseph, p.30: from p.121, Lippard, Lucy, *Six Years: the dematerialisation of the art object from 1966 to 1972* (Berkley and Los Angeles: University of California Press, 1997); sourced from an interview with Willoughby Sharp, *Artforum*, November 1969.

Bonheur, Rosa, p.156: from Micucci, Dana, *Artists in Residence*, 1st edn (New York: The Little Book Room, 2001).

Boone, Mary, p.76: from p.29, Thompson, Don, *The $12 Million Stuffed Shark; The Curious Economics of Contemporary Art and Auction Houses*, 1st edn (London: Aurum Press, 2008).

Borkowski, Mark, p.107: from p.101, Borkowski, Mark, *Improperganda The Art of The Publicity Stunt* (London: Vision On, 2000).

Bourne, George, p.187: from p.87, Sturt, George, *The Wheelwright's Shop* (Cambridge: Cambridge University Press, 2000).

Brooks, Mel, p.200: from Rees, Nigel, *Cassell's Humorous Quotations* (London: Cassell & Co, 2003); sourced from the film *The Producers*, dir. Mel Brooks (Crossbow Productions, 1968).

Butler, Samuel, p.173: from p.61, Rees, Nigel, *Cassell's Humorous Quotations* (London: Cassell & Co, 2003); sourced from Bartholomew, A. T. (ed.), *Further Extracts from the Note-Books of Samuel Butler*, 1934.

Childish, Billy, p.93: from 'Divided they stand' by Sally Williams in *The Guardian*, 6/6/09.

Clark, Ross, p.192: from p.31, Clark, Ross, *How to Label a Goat*, 1st edn (Petersfield, Hampshire: Harriman House, 2006).

Covey, Stephen, p.22: a popular version of Covey's quotation: 'Live out of your imagination and conscience instead of only your memory', from p.304, Covey, Stephen, *The 7 Habits of Highly Effective People* (London: Simon and Schuster, 1999).

Edgar Degas, p.57: from Guerin, M., *Degas Letters* (Oxford: Cassirer, 1947).

Emin, Tracey, p.142: in an interview with John Humphrys on the *Today Programme*, BBC Radio 4, 2004.

Galliano, John, p.57: from report by Imogen Fox in *The Guardian*, 6/3/09.

Genn, Sara, p.39: from p.186, Briot, Alain, *Mastering landscape photography: the luminous-landscape essays* (Santa Barbara: Rocky Nook, 2007).

Griffin, Susan, p.102: from Griffin, Susan, *The Eros*

and Everyday Life, Essays on Ecology, Gender and Society, (New York: Knopf Doubleday Publishing, 1996).

Jackson, Alexander Young, p.48: from p.196, Briot, Alain, Mastering landscape photography: the luminous-landscape essays (Santa Barbara: Rocky Nook, 2007).

Johnson, Garth, p.213: from p.30, Levine, Feythe, Handmade Nation, 1st edn (New York: Princeton Architectural Press, 2008).

Kaye, Tony, p.171: quoted during a seminar to celebrate the life of Paul Arden at Central Hall, Westminster, London, 9/6/09.

Karp, Ivan C., p.175: from p.138, Casewit W. Curtis, (1984) Making A Living in the Fine Arts: Advice from the Pros, 1st edn (New York: Collier Books,1984).

MacDonald, Kyle, p.182: from p.286, MacDonald, Kyle, One Red Paperclip; The story of how one man changed his life one swap at a time, 2nd edn (London: Ebury Press, 2008).

Millard, Rosie, p.129: from p.167, Millard, Rosie, The Tastemakers: U.K. Art Now 2002, 2nd edn (London: Scribner, 2002).

Miller, Harley, p.41: from p.7, Miller, Harley, A proper Living from Your Art – how to make your painting pay,1st edn (Findhorn Bay, Moray: Posthouse Printing and Publishing, 2000).

Miller, Jonathan, p.39: from interview with Nicholas Wroe in The Guardian, 10/1/09.

Monet, Claude, p.211: from p.40, Micucci, Dana, Artists in Residence, 1st edn (New York: The Little Book Room, 2001).

Nafi, Gulnur Mustafa, p.39: from conversation with the author February 2009.

Neal, Gareth, p.211: Gareth Neal in his talk 'Selling Collectable Design' at the 2009 Hidden Art Forum.

Parker, Cornelia, p.27: from p.142, Palmer, Judith, Private Views: Artists Working Today, 1st edn (London: Serpent's Tail Publishers, 2004).

Pearson Wright, Stuart, p.33: from Palmer, Judith, (2004) Private Views: Artists Working Today, 1st edn, Serpent's Tail Publishers, London, page 198.

Price, Barclay, p.80: from p.14, Price, Barclay, Running a Workshop, Basic Business for Craftspeople, 3rd edn (London: Crafts Council, 2000).

Presley, Hovis, p.136. from, p.15, Presley, Hovis, Poetic Off License; Holiday Annual, 1st edn (Bolton: D2, 1997)

Rose, Walter, p.81: from p.14, Rose, Walter, The Village Carpenter, 2nd edn (Carmarthenshire: Stobart Davies, Ammanford, 2009).

Sennett, Richard, p.27: from p.22, Sennett, Richard, The Craftsman, 2nd edn (London: Penguin, 2008).

Shaughnessy, Adrian, p.76: from p.67, Shaughnessy, Adrian, How to be a Graphic Designer Without Losing Your Soul, 1st edn (London: Laurence King Publishing, 2005).

Sibelius, Jean, p.127: from p.94, Törne, Bengt de, Sibelius: A Close-Up (London: Faber and Faber, 1937).

Smith, Paul, p.211: from p.169, McCormak, Lee, Designers are Wankers, 1st edn (About Face Publishing, 2005).

Stern, Simon, p.154: from p.17, Stern, Simon, The Illustrators Guide to Law and Business Practice, 1st edn (London: Association of Illustrators, 2008).

Toos, Andrew, p.127: from p.3, DiBiasio, Rick, The Affluent Artist, 1st edn (New York: Morgan James Publishing, 2009).

Warhol, Andy, p.110: from p.328, Knowles, Elizabeth, Oxford Concise Dictionary of Quotations, 4th edn (Oxford: Oxford University Press, 2001); sourced from a volume released to mark Warhol's exhibition in Stockholm, February–March 1968.

Warhol, Andy, p.19: from p.92, Warhol, Andy, The Philosophy of Andy Warhol (From A to B and Back Again), (New York: Harcourt Brace Jovanovich, 1975).

Westwood, Vivienne, p.107: from interview by Iain R. Webb in Wonderland Magazine, April–May 2009.

Wilde, Oscar, p.14: from p.803, Hart-Davies, Rupert (ed.), The Letters of Oscar Wilde (London: Hart-Davies, 1962).

Wilde, Oscar, p.122: from p.62, Rees, Nigel, Cassell's Humorous Quotations, (London: Cassell & Co, 2003); sourced from Wilde, Oscar, 'Phrases and Philosophies for the Use of the Young', in the Chameleon, December 1894.

Index